M000289977

IN HER PURPOSE

40 Principles of Asian Women
Redefining Success on Their Own Terms

Rose Buado
Jennifer Redondo-Marquez

IN HER PURPOSE
PUBLISHING

ISBN: 978-1-7347320-1-6

In Her Purpose™ (IHP)
California, USA

🌐 www.inherpurpose.com
✉ hello@inherpurpose.com
📷 @inherpurpose
🐦 @inherpurpose
f @inherpurpose

To our moms, Juanita Redondo and Rosalinda Rosales.
Thank you for paving the way for us.

To my daughter, Olivia Buado. The path is clear; get it baby girl.

And to the future generation, keep dreaming.
Rise and achieve your dreams!

TABLE OF CONTENTS

* Chapters written entirely by the featured woman herself.

FOREWORD

I have seen a trend among women wanting more from their careers and their workplace. They want to make an impact in their organizations and the status quo is not enough. They want to be connected to a higher purpose. But how do you get there? What is the formula? Most importantly when you are connected to your purpose, what does it feel like? Finding meaning and purpose can be a constant battle between life's challenges, the outside world, and yourself. When it comes to becoming clear on and finding your purpose, one of the most impactful forms of influence that I have seen is having others who you can relate to and who you see reach their own success in each phase of life. *In Her Purpose* is a collection of women whose stories illustrate their constant pursuit of truth and purpose in their respective industries.

A prime example of someone who continues to pursue her purpose and gain clarity in that is my mentor, and co-author, Jennifer. One evening she and I were catching up during a mentoring session when she told me that she was co-authoring this book with her cousin, Rose Buado. I thought to myself, "While she's writing, she will probably also discover another layer in her purpose." Prior to this book, I remember Jennifer expressing how she was still rediscovering her calling. She was figuring out what new projects she could dip into, how she could better serve her community, and who she was in this season of her life. At some point in our lives, many of us find ourselves stagnant, settled, or unsatisfied. Like many of us, she was asking what was her "Why."

As a speaker, I always tell my audience that you will undergo many seasons in your life. Some are winning seasons when you feel invincible. Other seasons you will feel like you dyed your hair, looked in the mirror, and say, "What was I thinking!" One of the most inspiring experiences I have seen is when women have a change of focus in the middle of their careers. They ask themselves who they are, at this moment, and they take a risk in reinventing themselves. It is true that people, even your best friend and long-time lover, do change. It's better to embrace the changes inside and around you than to reject them when life is asking you to evolve. It is so empowering to see other women take leaps of faith despite historical, cultural, and familial barriers.

I thought Jennifer was crazy when she asked me to write the foreword for this book. I have never written a blog post, an essay I thought was worth sharing outside of academia, or even a Yelp review. I never envisioned myself being a writer or contributing to anything at this scale. That's because I didn't know what was possible for me. When I was younger, I didn't know what I would make from my life or what job I wanted simply because I didn't know what was available to me. Being able to see other women who look like you and share similar experiences opens up the possibility of all that could happen...all that you could be. I have come to realize that visualization is key. *In Her Purpose* was the childhood storybook I needed. I would have benefited from a book that included stories of visionary women across a multitude of industries and stories of women not limited by their upbringing, finances, bodies, past relationships, politics, and other adversities, but who were empowered by those circumstances and so much more. This book reveals how large the professional landscape really is for women. It gives you the opportunity to see how vast and fruitful life can really be when you begin living in your purpose.

Truly yours,

Bobbie Reyes
Entrepreneurial Leader and Speaker
Amplifying Future Leaders for Change

TO ACQUIRE
independence,
freedom & peace
—— IS TO BEGIN ——
making decisions
FOR
yourself
—Bobbie Reyes

ABOUT BOBBIE

Bobbie is a Bay Area native and a graduate from the University of California, Berkeley. She is a speaker, entrepreneur, and pitch coach who empowers others to take action and achieve goals. She began her entrepreneurship journey at the age of 15 and since then has competed in and won global business plan competitions. She has spoken at organizations and events such as Salesforce for Dreamforce (Future Executive Summit), the Bay Area Financial Education Foundation, and several K-12 schools in the Bay Area. Bobbie is also a founder of Investing in Inclusion, a conference bridging minority entrepreneurs to venture capitalism. Bobbie believes in fostering female leadership and empowerment by hosting International Women's Day events, the largest happening at the Federal Reserve Bank. Today, her work and initiatives are focused on building pipelines to success for underrepresented communities.

Introduction

"The most important thing is to try and inspire people so that they can be great in whatever they want to do." - Kobe Bryant

Visibility and accessibility are powerful tools to have in your everyday arsenal of life. However, not all of us are fortunate enough, nor do we have the privilege needed, to obtain them. Regardless, we are lucky to live in a time where women's voices, stories, and lives are being recognized and celebrated. We are able to define ourselves through stories, which helps us, and others, understand who we are, our world, and our capacity to maneuver through difficult challenges that life throws at us.

Amongst us are real, powerful stories of inspiring women who have experienced impactful and compelling successes. These are true stories that give us hope, courage, and motivation to persist. *In Her Purpose* creators, Rose Buado and Jennifer Redondo-Marquez, introduce you to 40 strong Asian women, through their personal stories, redefining success on their own terms. Like the women featured in this book, many of us struggle to find a career path or follow a life goal, and we face different challenges, ups, and downs. These women open up and share their personal journeys of how they got to where they are now. They all took different paths to different careers ranging from fashion, medicine, art, entertainment, education, and other industries. The women in this book have defied social and cultural conventions that have shaped our existence as we know it.

THE VISION

We certainly wished we had access to resources and networks while we were growing up. We, Rose Buado and Jennifer Redondo-Marquez, were born and raised in the United States (U.S.). Our parents were the first generation to leave the Philippines to start a better life for themselves and their families. Filipino culture is highly focused on stability. Many Filipinos pursue "proven paths" like nursing, engineering, and the military. Growing up in the U.S., we learn that America is the "land of the free!" – Freedom of thought and speech. This is in direct contrast to the Asian culture where parental expectations create conflict because our career goals and definitions of success are not aligned. We are just two examples of first-generation children learning what it means to be successful in the U.S. and how to navigate through that! Since we are the first generation born and raised in the U.S., there were a lot of firsts that we had to figure out: how to sign up for the SAT (a standardized test used for college admission), how to fill out college applications, what major to study, how to write a resume, and how important it is to build a network. This book aims to bridge the gap of knowledge, experience, and support that we felt coming of age and finding our true purpose.

JENNIFER:

In Her Purpose is a project born from my search for mentorship. After working in corporate America for over 15 years, I was pushing up against the "glass ceiling[1]" and "bamboo ceiling[2]." I saw many of my colleagues get promoted even though we were working alongside, doing long hours and producing quality work

---

[1] "Glass ceiling" is a metaphor used to represent an invisible barrier preventing a particular demographic (typically applied to women and minorities) from moving up the corporate ladder.
[2] "Bamboo ceiling" was coined by Jane Hyun in *Breaking the Bamboo Ceiling: Career Strategies for Asians*, where she addresses how individual, cultural, and organizational factors hinder Asian Americans' career growth and progress.

together! I felt like my hard work ethic and intelligence were not enough. Working in Silicon Valley's tech space, I am often the only woman or person of color (POC) in the room. As I "mature" in my career, the sighting of a woman or POC is still far too rare. When I do see a female POC executive, it's like I've come across a unicorn! Luckily, I do have one trusted source in my family who is not in a traditional field who I can turn to: my cousin, Rose!

ROSE:

At the age of 18, I started my own business, however, I was taught that the right path was working for a huge company. So I followed what I thought was right even though my heart pushed against it. After spending 12 years in the corporate world and three years as a vice president at an advertising agency, I decided to fully jump into entrepreneurship. During Jennifer's journey of rediscovery, she reached out to me for recommendations on anyone that could mentor her. That's when I connected her to Sheila Marcelo, the founder and former CEO of Care.com. At the same time, I was managing The Filharmonic, a Filipino-American a cappella band. As their manager, I was introduced to a whole new world that I never knew existed. I was meeting powerful decision-makers who looked like me! Immediately after meeting them, I was interested to learn more about them: who they were, where they came from, and how they got to where they are. Unfortunately, I wasn't able to find much about these individuals, but my research did lead me to a book about "how to date an Asian woman!" I found this disturbing, but it inspired me to change the problem. I wanted to solve the lack of information about these amazing people I'd met. So, I told Jennifer that we should write a book in the future and she encouraged me to do it NOW! She is truly the driving force behind our vision. So here we are, 40 women later! It's crazy to think that we more than doubled our original, lofty goal!

This was the beginning of *In Her Purpose*, a collection of stories about women who look like us, told by us! These women were identified to be part of this carefully curated project because they are all of Asian descent, living in the U.S., working in non-traditional roles (for Asian women), and they are succeeding in their respective field of work. The narratives of these women include references to their personal challenges and accomplishments while navigating and living in multiple, often clashing cultures. This is more than a book; it is a reminder to celebrate women, highlight our successes and struggles, and it is also a means to give back to our community and society. We want to present real-life examples of boss ladies who found their purpose and are living out their dreams. We hope that these women speak to you and that you are able to hear their voices, feel their power, and be inspired by the truth poured out in their stories.

THE FLOW AND METHODOLOGY

Beginning in November 2018, we conducted interviews with each of the women in this book. The questions we asked drew upon cultural, familial, and personal experiences, and based on those interviews, each woman has a dedicated chapter. The majority of the chapters were written by us, Rose Buado and Jennifer Redondo-Marquez, based on the interviews we had, and with the guidance of each featured woman. Through the writing process, we worked to make sure every chapter captured her story and was in the voice of the woman featured. Each chapter was titled based on the personal stories and theme of the content. A few women opted to write their chapter entirely on their own, as noted in the Table of Contents. Through this process, we found a common theme with all of the women's experiences: It all starts with you, your story, and understanding your vision and goals!

The Takeaway

We all have a purpose in life! Through the stories in this book, you'll see that in order to figure out their purpose these women often took time, made errors, and required learning and tenacity. When you are clear about what matters to you and are aligned by a purpose, it becomes a lens through which every experience gets processed. Clarity of purpose allows us to take a growth perspective on our lives and makes it easier to overcome challenges. Meaning and purpose are so important because they change the stories we tell and the narrative we create. One woman's purpose can inspire many others.

Our goal for this book is to advocate for women, to feed and fuel the future generation, and to spread the love! It is our deepest hope that these stories will guide you to find your purpose and motivate you to become confident enough to live that purpose. We hope that you are inspired to amplify your voice and share your true gifts with the world.

Lead in Love,

Rose and Jennifer
Founders of In Her Purpose
#inherpurpose

IT DOESN'T HAVE TO BE

perfect,

IT JUST HAS TO

start.

—Angelia Trinidad

BE FREE

Angelia Trinidad

Playing basketball has always been one of my most favorite pastimes. At just six-years-old, I wanted to play basketball with the boys but they didn't let me play because they didn't want a "girl" to beat them. So, I found another girl who was willing to play, and then the boys let us join, one girl on each team. Back then, it was important to have the confidence that I was going to bring something to the table and that I was worthy of playing with the big boys. Learning how to hold my own playing basketball on the streets taught me that I could find a way to do what I wanted, even if it meant going a different route than others. Every time I wanted to play, and even now, I am constantly challenged to define my place in this world. Today, I'm sitting at a table, where the majority of entrepreneurs are Caucasian males, but I'm holding my ground and showing that I can bring value to the table too. It took me a while to get here.

Growing up, I wanted to become a teacher. I've always thought teachers were the pinnacle of what a human should be. They use their skills to help others better themselves by providing the structure and tools needed to grow. Eventually, I would build a business based on those same principles. But before that happened, for seven years, I worked at my aunt's flower shop. I watched her build a successful business with passion, courage, and sheer determination. Over time, I saw the weaknesses in the analog way of conducting business and I convinced her to buy a computer so that I could help optimize her business. Technology and the internet enabled me to build her a website and digitize her finances, bringing her business to a new level. Through this process, I became very interested in business and started reading self-help books and learning about entrepreneurship. I became consumed with the idea of building my own reality and making my own rules. I didn't expect to end up on this path, but I did know that entrepreneurship would lead me to a fulfilled life.

After finishing my second year at the University of California, Los Angeles (UCLA), I hit a mid-college crisis. Growing up in a strict military, Asian household, I was expected to become a doctor, engineer, lawyer, professor, or nurse. I had no desire to be any of those professions. I wanted freedom! I wanted to pursue my passion so without telling my parents, I made the bold switch from pre-med to art. But the more classes I took, the more out of place I felt. Most art students came from wealthy families that found value in contemporary art, whereas, my parents didn't think art was a viable career and at best, a fun hobby. My parents continued to question how I was going to find a "real job" and why I went to college if I wanted to be an artist. I persisted. However, after learning more about the politics of the contemporary art scene, I knew I didn't want to become a contemporary artist. Earning my degree taught me patience, collaboration, direction, and focus – so I don't regret majoring in art. Most of all, it gave me confidence in my ability to have a crazy idea and make it into reality.

Upon graduating from UCLA, I didn't have a "real job," paid benefits, or a 401k. However, I did have big dreams, a giving and grateful heart, a driven soul, and an amazing support system of friends and family. I had a lot to be grateful for! There I was with an art degree, and I didn't love art! I realized, though, that I could substitute the word "art" with any other passion which led me to become a passionate chaser of learning. I believe success is having the freedom and resources to live life exactly the way you want, without worry. I created the Passion Planner to give people a tool to turn their passions into a priority. The Passion Planner is an all-in-one weekly appointment, journal, goal setting guide, and to-do list integrated into one notebook. It's like having a life coach that fits in your backpack. To get started, I ran a Kickstarter campaign. Within a month, I raised almost $50,000 from 1,000 people from over 40 countries. The Passion Planner peaked as the number two best-rated planner on Amazon. It was amazing to see a sketch in my notebook turn into an actual product that was helping people all over the world find clarity, balance, and gratitude in their lives.

I was inspired to create the Passion Planner because I wanted to help people walk that talk. My life is an example of trying every day to do this. I believe that it doesn't have to be perfect, it just has to start. People always want things to be perfect and they think they have to have it all figured out before they can start, but I'm a firm believer that you can start where you are and take baby steps to get to where you want to go. Fail fast. Fail smart. Fail small. Because failure means you are one step closer to figuring out what does work and that in itself is great. The hardest part is starting! I wanted to create a planner where people pursue their passions and no longer push them on the back burner and focus on what they can do today to make it a reality. I also wanted it to serve as a paper life coach where they could write their goals and have something to hold themselves accountable. And I did that. With the Passion Planner, I went from not having a job with benefits to being an employer that provides all employees with full health coverage, vision, and dental insurance. Health coverage was something that my mom was always afraid of me not having, so being able to give that to others really makes me proud.

Most of the mentoring I received throughout my life came from the books I read. A lot of times we are paralyzed by things that we can't control so we don't take action because there's too much uncertainty. I love the quote: "Action cures fear" because it says that if you act, your fear will be cured. When I'm afraid to do something, that fear helps me take the step to get through it. With many things in life, there might be someone out there already doing what you want to do. They may be more or less qualified than you but it makes you wonder if you can do it too. Action really does cure fear and can change reality.

I want to encourage you to define what makes you feel the most fulfilled and happy and build your life around that instead of allowing your dreams to fall through the cracks. And when I say encourage, I mean "in-courage": find the courage within yourself. Once you've defined what fulfills you, start anywhere. Every step towards fulfillment is a step in the right direction. Even if in the beginning it's an internship, get the experience so that you can eventually get hired to do what you love. From starting anywhere, you get closer to figuring out what you want to do and what you love. Know that every single experience is a learning lesson that you can take into the next chapter of your evolution. Failures are just lessons in disguise. And, when you find what you love, that *thing* that you are emotionally connected to and that you believe in, it will feel less like work.

Even though I had found my passion, learning how to work with people was one of the most difficult challenges I've faced. I'm a Virgo *and* raised by a perfectionist mom, so I'm a double-perfectionist. This proves difficult when working with other people because delegating tasks to others is very hard. I tend to be very hands-on with my work. I have learned to embrace the good that others are doing rather than focus on ways that they can improve. I have learned to communicate effectively and pick and choose my battles. Working with different people from different backgrounds can be challenging because everyone thinks and will handle situations differently. Diversity is important to me and it's good to get different perspectives despite any challenges that may occur. I've overcome those challenges by focusing on the values and morals of who I'm hiring, rather than ethnicity. As long as we are in alignment with what we want to achieve, our differences will only help us create better ideas.

It is important to surround yourself with good people that love and encourage you but who are also willing to tell you the truth. I'm blunt and honest and am most proud of these traits because it took me a long time to find my voice and truly be myself. In Asian culture, it's not really encouraged to be this way, but I've grown the most from people who were honest with me so I try to be that for other people.

However, for a long time, I wasn't being honest with myself, my friends, family, or customers. For ten years, I was silent about being queer. It was a sacrifice to fully embrace and acknowledge to the public who I really am because I didn't want it to negatively affect my family, the people close to me, and my business. It wasn't until I was financially successful and in a committed queer relationship that I felt it was the appropriate time to come out. I was finally free!

Thankfully, now, there isn't anything that keeps me up at night; I sleep really well. If I can't do anything about a situation, I just write it down. I shift my focus away from the things that are out of my control. I create a game plan for what I can control. Then take action to attack those things. I can always control acknowledging when I do a good job and recognizing that I need to take care of myself. I prefer to think of it as self-maintenance. I maintain myself every day by meditating, reading, writing, reflecting, writing in my planner, eating good food, exercising, hanging out with people I love, reading my oracle cards, and traveling.

My favorite place in the world actually can be anywhere, because it's in my planner. My planner is where I find clarity, peace, hope, and excitement. Sitting with my planner makes me feel at home, because wherever I am, I know I will never be lost. To be in nature with my planner is my favorite. That's when I feel the most connected to the Earth and my mind is most clear to listen to my heart. Knowing what I know now, I would have told myself to enjoy the process and the journey!

the most important
thing is to keep going!
You honestly never
Know when an
oppotunity
will be there.

– Alexandra Carson

BE FEARLESS

Alexandra Carson

Honey, *Save the Last Dance*, and *You Got Served* are dance movies I loved while growing up; I wanted to have a part in all of them! Ever since I could walk and talk, all I ever wanted to be was an entertainer! As a kid, if I wasn't dancing, I was watching others dance. I spent my weekends glued to the television watching music videos and imagining myself dancing in them. Growing up in Canberra, Australia, on the other side of the world, I dreamed of dancing in Los Angeles (LA) or New York. But being so far away from those places, it was hard to believe that I'd get there. But I dreamed of it and hoped for it, and now I still have to pinch myself and sometimes even ask myself how the hell am I even here?

The education system in Australia is different than in the United States (U.S.). College is year 11 to 12, followed by university. During my two years in college, I majored in dance and fashion. At 20-years-old, I told my parents that I was moving to Sydney for fashion school, but really, my intentions were to dance! As excited as I was, when I got to Sydney, I had a rough time. It was my first time moving away from home and I didn't know anyone. Life hit me in the face really quickly! When I was living at home, I had all the comforts I was used to: my car, I knew where to go, and I lived with my family. But in Sydney, I had none of that. On top of school, I had to find a job, which is tough in Australia. Compared to the U.S. there are not many opportunities, especially in the dance industry. The dance scene is very small and exclusive. It's extremely hard to break into the scene especially coming from a smaller town in Australia. I started out working in hospitality, which wasn't ideal because the pay was low and the hours were tough. Frankly, the pay I received for the number of hours I was working was insufficient for my expenses so I had to sell everything just so I could afford to pay rent. Meanwhile, I was studying something that I wasn't passionate about. Life wasn't really working out the way I imagined. All I wanted to do was dance!

While I was studying and working in Australia, I attended a hip hop dance workshop in New Zealand. The dance crew hosting the workshop invited me to audition to join their group. I decided to stay in New Zealand for a couple more days to try out. As luck would have it, I made it, but I was left with an ultimatum – either I drop everything to dance in New Zealand or I stay in Sydney to finish school and work. I was at a crossroads – Do I join the dance crew where I don't make any money, but I get to live my dream and dance? Or do I stick to the plan that I shared with my parents? I told myself: You're either going to grow some balls and make a difference in your life or you're going to be stuck here feeling sorry for yourself. I hated that feeling. That was enough for me to take a new direction.

I packed up all my stuff in Sydney and moved to New Zealand after a week. I didn't have the money saved to flip my life around like that, but I did it anyway. I quit school and never ended up with my degree. However, this bold decision snowballed to the next phase of my life. I became part of a dance crew called Request and had been dancing for a year and a half in New Zealand when one of the choreographers I worked with was approached to do choreography for Janet Jackson. She works with famous artists such as Jennifer Lopez, Rihanna, Kanye

15

West, Justin Bieber and plenty more. When opportunities come her way, she makes an effort to submit people from home to be part of these amazing gigs.

Request put together a video submission to dance for Janet but in order to move forward with the audition, we had to fly to LA. I didn't have the financial means to book a flight on a whim, nor am I the type of person to ask for help, especially for something of that magnitude. My parents were unable to help me, but they encouraged me to ask others for assistance. Luckily, my auntie from Indonesia graciously booked a flight for me with hours to spare; I was able to fly to LA with the rest of the girls! Immediately after we landed, we went straight to the audition. I couldn't believe that I was auditioning for Janet! There were hundreds of people: girls, boys, young, and old. I was terrified, but I told myself that I had to at least try! I auditioned at the first round and a few of us got called back for the second round that afternoon. Afterward, we flew back to New Zealand and we didn't hear back for seven weeks.

During the waiting period, not only was I in debt, but I felt that the trip to LA was a big waste of time and money. I was back on the road and touring with my dance crew around Europe. On our last stop in Dublin, Ireland, we finally heard back. Our leader and manager of the group pulled me aside to tell me that I got selected for the last round of Janet auditions! I was beyond excited, but in order to move forward, I had to go back to LA and I still didn't have any money. I was dancing for the love of dance, not the money. The only person who could help me again was my auntie. I tried to explain my situation to her, which was difficult because everything was confidential. We had no idea that Janet was coming out with new music or going on tour. The only thing I knew was that I was auditioning for Janet. My aunt graciously sent me back to the U.S. This time, I went alone.

On the day of the final audition, I don't know what possessed me; I became someone I didn't know. I wanted this job so badly! I no longer wanted to dance for free. I wanted to make something of myself and I didn't want to walk out the door without that job. There were over 1,000 people there, and auditions went on for many rounds. We danced for over ten hours and people were getting cut by the hour. Halfway through the auditions, Janet came to watch us. All of us were in awe! It came down to 15 girls. Each time my name was called out, I had to calm myself down! This was my first time ever auditioning for a professional dance gig. Everyone else I was competing against was crazy-professional. With just eight of us standing in a line, Gil Duldulao, Janet's creative director told us that we were going on tour with Janet! Oh my God! I couldn't believe it! I walked to the back of the room to gather myself. Tears started coming down my face. I didn't know what to do with myself – it was the most phenomenal feeling. That night, I was on the phone telling everyone. I flew home the next day.

The first hurdle of getting hired was behind me but then I had to deal with obtaining a visa to work in the U.S., and quickly! I had to convince the American government that I deserved a visa even though this was my first real job offer as a professional dancer. I had no idea what I was doing, so I needed legal help. I was put in touch with lawyers, which I couldn't afford because I was broke as ever. Still, I remained optimistic. One night, I went to dinner with two friends. We brainstormed my options: family support, a loan, or a GoFundMe account. At that point, I was working at TopShop, so what did I have to lose? I didn't want to ask anyone for help, but I gave in because I really wanted this job. When I saw the first $5 donation come through my GoFundMe campaign, I started crying. I was emotional that someone cared. Through the generosity of my friends and family, I raised $15,000 to get my visa. With all of the delays, I arrived in LA nearly a month late, which is a long time for a dancer. A lot can get done in that time, but luckily, Janet was so nice and patient with me. However, once I was there, I had so much to catch up on. I was determined to do well; I didn't want to let myself or my supporters down.

I started with Janet during her *Unbreakable* tour, and stayed with her through the *State of the World 1* and *2*, and *Metamorphosis*, dancing with Janet for nearly five years at the time of writing. And, now, I'm still here, living in LA, dancing ever since! When I am not working with Janet, I work with other artists including Cardi B, Jennifer Lopez, and Gwen Stefani, to name a few. That's the life of a working artist. It's a constant hustle: working, auditioning, or creating submissions to audition. If I'm not doing that, I am going to class or shooting a video. There is no time to chill, and this life is unpredictable! For example, when Janet got pregnant, I didn't have any work and had to start all over again. Surprisingly, it was a little difficult for me to find other jobs because when you work for Janet, people don't see you as anything else.

Growing up, my parents didn't put any pressure on me to be anything in particular. They were really supportive of everything that I wanted to do, but perhaps it's because I am the youngest of three children. I was brought up in a family with some incredibly strong women! They all encouraged me: my mom, aunties, and godparents. Each of them played their part in filling my life with this feminist energy; I was born to be a badass woman! My mom wasn't surprised when I told her at 18-years-old that I was going to Germany for a dance camp, or when I came home at age 19 with half my head shaved. Even when I moved to Sydney and New Zealand, my parents supported me. I don't remember many people telling me that I couldn't do anything. Everyone made me feel like my dreams were possible.

As a young kid, all I really wanted was to bring a smile to people's faces. I still do. I pray for that before every show. I know that life is hard, so if I can provide some joy in people's lives, especially through something that I love to do, even better. I know how much people's lives are impacted by Janet's music; she brings light into people's lives. I want to be remembered as a light. I want people to think of me and laugh, and I want people to smile. I want to inspire people to do something bold and if people are doubting themselves, I want them to be inspired to try. The most important thing is to keep going; I still have to remind myself and amp myself up at times! I yell at myself at the gym and on stage to help motivate myself. You just have to keep going. You can't stop! You honestly never know when an opportunity will be there. Do your research and know what you have to do to be ready and prepared for anything! As a dancer I have to keep up with my skills – I take classes, I workout to be fit and healthy, I stretch, and every once in a while I get massages. You have to be versatile if you want to have longevity in this industry. I have always been disciplined and focused on working hard. Literally this is the difference between a yes and a no.

During my career, I've had to overcome, and I am still battling with, lack of self-confidence, which is crazy because on stage I am fearless and I can do anything. There are some days where I wonder why and how I am here. I am surrounded by amazing and talented people – top-tier dancers who are professionally trained. I was picked out of the pond and dropped into the ocean. When you set a high standard for yourself, it's human to have self-doubt. I make sure I have good energy around me to help maintain my positivity.

Success to me is if you wake up, you are motivated, and you are happy with where you are at in life. At the end of the day, success is being surrounded by great people who support, love, and believe in you. If I have people who bring me joy, even at my lowest moments, I am still successful. Even though I am living out my dreams and passions, I have sacrificed time away from my home and family. Time is moving so fast. It's exciting, but I sometimes forget that my parents are aging. In my career, I've missed out on important personal milestones and celebrations such as my dad's 60th birthday. I am terrified when I see my mom not being able to do some of the things that she used to be able to do. Now, I am fortunate to be in a position where I can spend time, give back, and take my family on holiday!

We should constantly reevaluate our lives to tease out what's nonsense and what's really important. I have a daily routine that helps me do this: I make my bed, I clear bad energy by burning palo santo, and I jot down ten things that I am grateful for. Going back to my Indonesian roots, I have an altar in my room, which I picked up during one of my visits to Bali. I use it to manifest everything I want in my life. It helps me be clear on what I want for my life and what I want to achieve and attract. I need to check in on that daily so that I don't lose my focus. I set the tone for my day and I do so with positive thoughts. So far, things have been going well. I am enjoying the moment! I am so in awe of this stage so I focus only on the present. I am living fearlessly and trying to trust it all!

BE
positive
&
passionate,
you'll
light up
THE ROOM.

–Anh Duong

Be Positive

Anh Duong

Have you ever asked your parents why they left "home" and how they ended up where they are today? I never knew the answers to these questions for my family until I was in college. I remember being a kid and wanting to know, but my parents would brush me off because they didn't want to talk about it. I didn't really know why, but I knew it made them mad when I asked questions about the past. It wasn't until we went back to Vietnam as a family, 20+ years after my parents left their home country, that I had a chance to hear their story. I listened intently as our local relatives shared how my mom and dad both escaped the Vietnam War and ended up in Houston, Texas.

In 1975, my dad was 24-years-old and working for the United States (U.S.) Army fixing helicopters. The Vietnam War had already lasted 19 years by this point, nearly his entire life. He was working in Thailand when the shocking news broke over the radio – South Vietnam had surrendered. Shortly after, his bunker was attacked by bombs. My dad and his two best friends had no choice but to run without giving notice to their families; this became a common story in the last days of the war. They escaped by helicopter and eventually made it to safe harbors in Guam, a U.S. territory. My dad, with overwhelming pain, left behind his wife (who was 20-years-old at the time) and his 1-month-old son.

During that time, many American families were accepting refugees through the Catholic Church. That's how my dad made it to Florida, Illinois, Oklahoma, and then finally to Texas. For the next four years, he worked hard in the U.S., a foreign country to him, to save enough money to get his little family out of Vietnam. He had learned of a shrimper with a boat who had successfully helped others escape and who could help my mom, brother (four-years-old at the time), and uncle escape too. Finally, after years of hard work he was able to send money back to Vietnam to the man who could help them escape. He had to trust that this man was honest and wouldn't steal his money, while he waited patiently in Texas. How does one even do that without the internet?! When the time came, in the middle of the night, the three of them rode a bike quietly through the city to board the shrimper's boat. They laid in the cabin below deck and hid underneath a stockpile of shrimp. Imagine the smell! My mom got sick and kept throwing up until they arrived at international waters near Hong Kong. From there, they were greeted by allies and flew to Paris, France. For many years after the war ended, many families tried to escape unsuccessfully and were imprisoned or executed if caught. My family will be forever grateful that my mom, brother, and uncle made it out safely that dark night.

One day while digging through old family photos, I found a beautiful picture of my mom (in bell-bottoms!) and my brother in front of the Eiffel Tower. On the back, it said, *"nh ba"* ("we miss you Dad" in Vietnamese). I never understood the meaning and power of that photo until I learned about their journey. After only a few nights in Paris, my mom, brother, and uncle flew to Houston where they were reunited with my dad after four long years of tragedy, hardships, and hope. I was born in August 1981, and my younger brother was born two years later. We were both raised in Houston not knowing any of these stories until we were nearly 20-years-old.

We had an amazing childhood and I have fond memories of playing baseball with the neighborhood kids and playing tennis with my dad. We grew up middle-class and went to great schools. My parents could afford to let me join the tennis team, take piano lessons, karate lessons, go on school field trips, and eventually go on to college. My younger brother and I both went to the University of Texas, Austin, where I studied chemistry and sociology. Austin was only 2.5 hours away and we liked the idea of being close to home.

During my senior year of college, I learned that my older brother was in trouble with the law. After several acts of petty theft, he had broken his probation and was being sent to prison for two years. It was heartbreaking to see my parents' faces the night they told us. Things changed after that. My parents bought a bigger house to show that no one in our family needed to steal, and they purchased a dry cleaning business so that my brother would have a job once he got out. I graduated and was ready to leave Texas, to be on my own and to be an independent woman! But that would have to wait. Instead, I decided to move back home to help at the dry cleaners and to give my parents the emotional support they needed. I wanted to be a good daughter. I also wanted to continue my education so I enrolled at the University of Houston, where I graduated with a master's degree in sociology. I had no idea what I would do next but I was determined to figure it out.

By this point, I was 24-years-old and was expected to be on the search for a suitable husband. Many of my hometown friends were married with kids and my parents wanted me on the same path. Since both my brothers were back home, I felt like it was my turn to leave. I paid my dues so I packed one suitcase and moved to New York City (NYC)!

This did not happen without drama – there were many arguments in our house; many nights we went to bed angry. The night before

I left, I wrote my parents an overly dramatic letter about how their story of leaving Vietnam inspired me to leave too. They had taken care of me for 24 years and had given me the tools I needed to find myself and my purpose. Their sacrifices would not be wasted on the one and only daughter they had. I was ready to spread my wings and fly. Dramatic! In the end, I left and we only grew closer.

Moving to NYC was both easy and hard. It was easy because my best friend moved there just six months before me so I had a living room to crash in until I landed a job. The move was hard because what was I going to do with a B.A. in Chemistry and Sociology and an M.A. in Sociology? Surprisingly, people were excited about my degrees; they loved the people aspect of it, and how I could understand social dynamics and consumers. I had also worked as a marketing coordinator at the College of Business while in Houston so it made sense for me to apply and interview for marketing jobs.

So I did it! I kept applying until I landed an amazing job as the marketing coordinator at a start-up company. I was interviewed by the marketing director who was known to be a Korean "tiger mom." She came from a successful family where she and her three siblings all graduated from Harvard University. She was strong, smart, and she became my first up-close glimpse at a badass woman in the workplace. The first lesson she taught me: demand more. During my interview, I said I'd be willing to accept an annual salary of $30K, to live in the Big Apple! Who does that?! She followed me to the elevator and said I should have asked for $50K. I was shocked. I had been walking around for weeks shortchanging myself. When my offer letter came a few days later, it was for a starting salary of $50K. My boss was pivotal at the start of my career. She gave me constructive feedback and made me cry twice. But it was worth it! I kept learning, growing and getting promoted. I think about her any time I think about the young women I manage today. The next two years were filled with working long hours (7 a.m. - 11 p.m. was my regular schedule), complete dedication to my job, and lots of lessons. The two most important lessons I learned were to demand more and when you're early in your career, work harder than everyone else.

My plan was to live in New York for five years max so halfway through my stay I started exploring other job prospects. I had always been interested in skincare; I set my sights on working for a beauty company and landed my dream job at Elizabeth Arden. For the second time in a row, I had a strong and smart female boss who I could look up to. She cared about me as a person as well as my development in the workplace, and she always stuck up for me. The beauty industry can sometimes attract mean people, and when there were cliques, criticism, or blame, my boss didn't stand for any of that. She showed me it was OK to stand up for the unpopular idea and to not let anyone back you into a corner. I watched her be collaborative in meetings while also defending what she felt was right. From her, I learned to pick and choose my battles and to stand up for what's right. I couldn't fight with every department on the copy we wanted to use, the packaging we liked best, or the product names we wanted to trademark, but I could speak loudly when it mattered. She helped me find my voice and gave me the space to use it. I think about both of these managers/mentors often, and I always want to pay it forward, being the best manager I can possibly be and continuing to get better.

Five years had passed in New York and it was time to move home. I would be turning 30 soon and thought I should probably get married (or so I thought). My high school boyfriend was waiting in Houston for me, but when I returned, I realized that I had outgrown him and the city that raised me. I had grown accustomed to the diversity of New York, where people came from everywhere with all types of professions and hobbies. I wanted to see more.

That summer, in 2010, I went to San Francisco for a week to visit John, a friend who I met when we were living in NYC a few years before. He had just graduated from Stanford Business School and we had a wonderful time – the weather was amazing and warm (which it usually isn't in July), John took me to wine country in Napa, across the Golden Gate Bridge, to the beach, and on urban hikes around the city. His friends were wonderful people and they weren't married either! It felt like moving here could buy me more time before marriage, the stars seemed to be aligned. Spoiler alert – John and I got married three years later!

So I went back to Houston and packed my suitcase once again. This time my mom and dad were less shocked about my move. In San Francisco, I crashed on John's couch until I landed a job. I worked part-time at the Kiehl's retail store where I was supposed to be stocking the shelves but often helped customers find their ideal skincare products instead. That's what happens when you love something...people see that and ask for your advice! After three months of searching, I was hired as the marketing manager at Williams-Sonoma's corporate office. For two years I thought about brides and what they'd be doing at the start of their married lives, creating memories at home and in the kitchen. Ironic, since I was running away from marriage!

After two years, I was recruited back into the beauty industry, at bareMinerals. I was excited to join a company that I had been a customer for over ten years. I transitioned from marketing into sales and started managing a team of six people, which was the largest team I had managed to date. When I reflect on my time there, I had so many great memories – all the laughs with my team and the chance to try out different managerial styles. While there, I learned to always be kind and that you *will* make mistakes – having the chance to learn and try again has been critical to my growth.

I am currently the senior director of wholesale partnerships at Quay Australia. In less than four years, we have grown from five people in our San Francisco office to 65 people. This has been the most intense job I've ever had but also the most fun. I've had the chance to be an integral part of building our culture and for the first time, I have a group of best friends who I see every day. Being with this group has made our massive growth over the last four years fun and memorable. Our friendships make challenges so much easier to overcome. I've learned in this job to keep swimming (like Dory says in the movie *Finding Nemo*), and that work is so much better with friends.

It was also during my time at bareMinerals that John proposed. We were 31-years-old and had been dating for two years at that point. He took me on a weekend trip to Oregon. We were standing on the cliffs, overlooking the Pacific Ocean. Waves were crashing in, the moon was shining down, and it was just before Christmas so we were surrounded by holiday lights. When he dropped to his knee I was confused and shocked. I wasn't expecting it and I hadn't thought about what this moment would be like. My young, single life passed before my eyes! Was I ready? I wasn't sure. Would I ever sleep with anyone else? Probably not. Did I want to? No! So I said yes and marriage has been amazing ever since.

Early in my career, I was obsessed with work. This meant allocating my free time to working and missing out on major milestones. I missed the birth of my friend's first child because "I had to work." I missed visiting my best friend in Kenya because "I had to work." If I could do it again, I would have been there for them. Now, I make sure I'm there for the milestones. My friends and family will be the ones who are by my bedside at the end, not my co-workers. I am more intentional in my purpose to spend quality time with the people I love.

BE POSITIVE

Through my journey, I've learned the importance of being positive and passionate. When I'm passionate about what I'm doing, it gives me such great energy. I feel invigorated by the job, the goal, and the people. I am naturally positive so it helps me look on the bright side. But you can also train yourself to be more positive through gratitude. Focus on the little things. Every morning I wake up and thank someone (like God) that I have a bed, a home, my limbs, and food to eat. I try to remember that my positivity can help uplift others and it gives me the purpose to be a bright light every day.

The world is a big place and we are a small, microscopic part of it. During my time on this Earth, I want to be that person that makes others "laugh a little louder, smile a little bigger, and live just a little bit better."(anonymous). I want to add positivity to the lives of the people I meet and those I connect with along the way.

Vibe high,
lead in love,
AND
stay curious.

— Isis Arias

Be Mindful

Isis Arias

My whole life has been a series of huge risks and big leaps of faith! A big part of my life has been me riding the wave and figuring it out as I go. I did not have a straight and narrow career path – I kind of zig-zagged. During one of my spring breaks in college, I flew to Miami, Florida with some friends. We were underage so we couldn't get into any bars or clubs because our fake IDs didn't work. There were a ton of parties going on, but what caught my eye was this guy standing outside a kitted out tour bus: it was branded with a sneaker company's logo and when you opened the door, you saw a full display of the company's shoes. I saw people giving away free sneakers and throwing parties. They were getting paid. I wanted in! I confidently went up to him to ask what was going on and got an invite onto the bus. At the time, I didn't know what experiential marketing or influencers were. I wasn't aware of the jargon, but I knew I wanted to do what they were doing! It looked like fun and something that I could do.

After that visit to Miami, I returned back to reality as a communications student at Rutgers University. After graduation, I got a job in the music industry. After a few years of working in Public Relations (PR) at labels, I ended up losing my job and I was lost! I had spent my life wanting a career in music. I didn't know what else to do or what to do next, and I fell into talent management by joining a business partner's endeavor. My clients sometimes didn't show up to their appearances or interviews, would talk back, or do crazy things like trying to sneak a dog on a plane. I quickly learned that I would rather work with brands instead of personalities. I was feeling undervalued and talent management can be a thankless job. I was working for other people instead of working for myself. I started manifesting the lifestyle that I wanted. I wanted to do big stuff, but I wasn't sure if that was events or marketing? The biggest risk I made was going out on my own. I took an opportunity to partner with a friend on a talent management company, carving out my own space to manage their PR and event activations. It's very hard to trust yourself when you have a ton of expectations: of yourself, from your parents, and your cultural upbringing. You have to trust your ability, capability, and intuition. I also had to trust that there is a lesson. After a few years on my own, I finally was able to trust myself! This was my chance to try everything and anything.

I've always had an entrepreneurial spirit so I was always identifying where I could make an impact, have flexibility, and work on fun projects. Most of all, I wanted to learn! While working on the management business, I took on contract roles and started to carve out my own lane for my own company. As an event producer and marketer, I got to work on amazing events like Nike's World Basketball Festival, and with brands such as Airbnb, Reebok, and Google. In addition to event production, I was finally working on brand marketing campaigns and worked for Hennessy as a key account manager. For two years, I hosted tables and parties to build brand awareness and then moved to manage the program with a team across the nation. I was hustling and working to make some extra money so I also had a side gig. I worked nightlife as a door girl, which is the first touchpoint of any establishment. In New York, I hated how people who ran doors at the club often acted – I found they could be rude, brash, and even racist in their tone. Because I understood brand experience, I knew that the first impression is at the door and I wanted to create a different experience than what I'd seen in New York. I wanted to optimize the experience of going out to events, so my company created a service that hired and trained staff to be the front-facing people at the door for branded events. It worked very well, particularly for events targeting certain demographics – if an agency was all-white and didn't represent the audience, I was able to hire a crew of diverse faces to greet the guests that would be in attendance.

At the time, I was still in my twenties. Though things were on the up and up, they weren't always easy. I had to learn how to be comfortable being broke. There were ebbs and flows. I did the math and I knew that I could make enough money on nightlife alone. If I made $200 a night, I might not be eating well, but I knew that I could at least make rent! Thank goodness for rent control. Luckily, I had built a lot of trust with people. They knew that I could get things done. My network ended up recommending me and I was getting called for projects through referrals. I was being offered gigs even when I wasn't looking. Regardless of the situation, I was always confident that I could figure it out.

I was always hustling for the next thing. To be honest, I was learning as I went along. There is one project that I will never forget – I got an opportunity to work for a fancy French company. I felt like a diamond in the rough that had to be polished. At that point, I had only worked in very casual spaces. I needed to be groomed because I obviously wasn't there yet: I had to learn corporate-speak and how to code-switch. I was told that my emails were too casual. I couldn't say "hey," and I was reminded to write emails with proper greetings, full sentences, and proper punctuation. Most of all, I learned how to understand who my audience is.

Running my own business, I also learned some really difficult lessons, like how to pay taxes! Oh my God! When I was doing contract work, I didn't understand that I had to set aside 30% for taxes. I had money saved, but no one told me I should be saving for and paying quarterly taxes. On top of that, I had to learn how to save money for health insurance. There were times I had to pay out of pocket with cash because I didn't have insurance, like the time I got my wisdom teeth pulled out at New York University (NYU). I had NYU dental students to do the work for less than visiting a dentist, but that was still almost $1,000! The reality is, adulting is hard! I encourage women to understand financial management early on. You will be set up so much better if you start saving early. That money adds up!

In my mid-twenties, I had friends that were trippin' about turning 30. I decided I wouldn't live up to those standards that they were stressed about: be married and be a millionaire. I let go of the bar set by the age limit. When I turned 30, I had accomplished being self-employed for four years. I successfully ran my own business, made money, traveled, and met my husband. Since then, I've been able to mentor others, do speaking engagements, and connect people to put money in their pockets. Helping people on their journey is also a success for me. It all comes back – it's cyclical.

In 2013, an old friend that I met back on that spring break trip in Miami asked me to join him in his next venture at AKOO, a clothing brand for the artist, T.I. I had been building a business and slowly figuring out what I was going to do next, but this was another huge risk! I felt a bit behind in the full-time job market because I lacked corporate training. I didn't know how to negotiate my stocks or compensation package because I never had those opportunities. I ended up taking the job at AKOO as a senior brand manager. At the time, I was pregnant with my first child and it was important for me to secure a stable position and health insurance. AKOO's vice president and I put together a marketing plan and strategy. We executed a whole rebranding initiative as well as built the experiential activations and produced content campaigns, some which won awards. We were such a small team and we got to do everything. It was a lot of fun, but after a few years, I wanted to do something else at a larger company and to be in a diverse space. I wanted to be able to manage and lead, and to learn how brand work could be done in another industry, or at a higher level. After almost three years, I left to go to Complex Networks.

After looking at the job description, I almost didn't apply to Complex. Once I saw that it required 50% travel, I wrote it off as a real opportunity because I had my daughter. However, my friend submitted my resume. Because I was pushed to consider, I didn't take the job application seriously. I knew I wanted to do large scale event productions, but I wasn't even sure what that meant – festivals? Concerts? Though I didn't originally consider applying, I ended up working at Complex as the Executive Producer for ComplexCon, a large scale cultural event that includes concerts! My previous responsibilities had me leading productions for multiple brand partners on both video and event work. It turned out to be a more corporate job than where I was; I'd really built an understanding of the industry jargon including topics on headcount, budgeting, audience development, and networking. I've had to identify the challenges and figure out how to solve them, and I now know who to call if I need help to figure it out.

It took me a long time to realize the value that I bring to the table. When you're young, you might not always see the value you bring. You might have some doubt or insecurity. Your career is important, but your health and mental health are also important. Fulfillment is of equal importance; it's OK to have other outlets and passions. If you look at yourself holistically, you have to make sure you are filling up all of those spaces. You might not be happy at your job, but do you have other outlets and passions outside of work? We have these responsibilities and obligations, and sometimes we don't listen to the little voice in our heads. In addition to our own inner thoughts, there are aspects of ourselves that come from our cultural upbringing. How did you grow up in your house? My grandmother treated my younger brother and me differently. I had to stay home, do chores, and go to church. I wasn't allowed to go out. My brother, on the other hand, was allowed to do what he liked, and avoid what he didn't. I had to learn how to get past that. I had to become comfortable being uncomfortable. In my journey to become a leader, I'd learned the only place where you are constantly learning and growing is outside of that comfort zone.

There aren't many Asian women in my field. I feel like I have had to work twice as hard to make sure my voice is heard. It can be hard to get people to trust what you are saying, so it's important to know what you are talking about. Sometimes you end up being the worker bee instead of the leader. I had to figure out how to create opportunities and platforms to open the doors for myself and others. In the Asian culture, you are often taught to be respectful and a team player; it's very easy to be obedient and get things done. I found myself being too humble sometimes. Don't get me wrong, humility is wonderful. It is important, but moving around in the corporate space, you have to learn to take credit for your work. I had to learn to advocate for myself. I had to understand what my worth is and not to just take what I am given. I had to learn to negotiate – because I know what value I bring. Remember, you belong in the room! Don't sit in the back – You were invited, so sit at the table. Be present! When you speak, make sure what you're saying has some weight to it. You have to earn the respect of others. You can't just expect it! Do the work and highlight the wins. Don't be afraid to insert yourself and introduce yourself to others.

Being a diverse woman in a leadership position is challenging, but I am used to being different. I am half black and half Filipino. I never felt that I was black enough nor Filipino enough. I never fit in a box and no one ever understood what I was. I have become comfortable with not ever fitting in a box – I challenge everything. I diversify the room, and it's something that I constantly try to do and advocate for. I want to make room for other people's voices. If I am the only one in the room, I speak as loudly as possible to make sure everyone is represented. I always try to bring valuable insights to whatever room I am in.

I am most proud of my ambition. I don't know if it is always a good or bad thing because ambition creates pressure. Thankfully, I have learned to practice mindfulness – I can take my time, grow, and let whatever thought or question stay top of mind for a minute and see if I am still interested in it later. As much as I've learned to stay present and be appreciative of the moment, I am always thinking about what's next. I don't want to set a bar to cap my level of success; is it that once I become the CEO, then I've made it? I have a lot of growing to do and I've come so far, but I wonder – is there ever an end to what "success" is for me? Will I ever be satisfied? The question then becomes: How do I grow from here? While Complex is such an important place and I feel it added to my professional and personal growth, I was given an opportunity to try my hand at something else. Once you become really good at something, you're leading a great team, there is trust within the organization and you're proud of your work, you sometimes question what else you can do beyond it. Are you really that good if you go somewhere else? I'm excited to try a new venture in the arts and culture space, to continue to grow in my practice and really test myself in uncomfortable waters!

I am actively focused on a lot of personal growth. Along with that, I have more goals; I want to create a podcast, write a book, and do more speaking engagements. I want to continue to grow and understand my own voice and put out more positivity into the world. I try to stay present and mindful. Mindfulness is a key concept that I have to practice regularly and I encourage people to consider it.

As I start my new journey, I'll take with me the great experiences, lessons learned and countless friendships. I'm excited and ready for whatever comes my way!

— The —
golden rule says
we should treat
others as we wish to
be treated, but I disagree.
I always say let's treat
others as _they_ wish
to be treated, because
we're all different,
right?

–Jackie James

BE UNCOMFORTABLE

Jackie James

I grew up believing that being successful solely meant marrying well and having children. The women I looked up to followed that blueprint to a tee, and I didn't know anyone who had chosen a different path.

Although popular and seemingly confident, my insecurities ran deep. I struggled with my self-worth, often worrying that I wasn't "marriage material" because I didn't look like my peers. I remember praying that I would wake up one day with fair skin, blonde hair, and blue eyes because then I would be desirable and "wife material."

Even after serving as class president at Corona del Mar High School and then becoming the fourth female and first minority associated student body president in the school's history, I still didn't feel good enough or truly accepted. Growing up as a Korean-American in Newport Beach, a predominantly Caucasian neighborhood, it was difficult to find role models who I looked like and could relate to. It wasn't until the movie *Wayne's World* came out and Tia Carrere was globally embraced as an "exotic" and "hot" lead character that others started seeing me as attractive. What I didn't understand at the time was that it was never about what other people thought of me; it was always about what I thought of myself.

After high school, I did everything "the right way." I received a scholarship to the University of San Diego and graduated early to start working and climbing the esteemed corporate ladder. I still believed that the end goal was to get married and have kids so work was just something that I had to put up with until my Prince Charming came and rescued me. I never thought work was something that I could truly love and be passionate about.

I spent 14 years working at Nissan North America and the Irvine Company – two incredibly successful organizations and industry leaders in automotive and real estate, respectively. Those years taught me that there's a big difference between being good at what you do and doing what you love. I thrived off of making my parents proud and giving them bragging rights to my life that looked oh-so-good on paper. Towards the end of my corporate career, I unknowingly began to settle in my personal life. I dated men who were also great on paper and even thought I was in love but in hindsight, I was subconsciously putting my romantic relationships on a pedestal so that I could hurry up and get married. I was unfilled, exhausted, and ready to "retire." Looking back, I can't believe I didn't realize my own potential and all that life truly has to offer.

When I thought I finally found "the one," the universe gave me the best gift I never knew I needed. Our relationship ended abruptly and I was forced to reevaluate my priorities and purpose, both personally and professionally. In the corporate world, I found that my identity and value were often tied to my title and how much money I made. There were so many unspoken rules about who I could and couldn't talk to based on my position. Being someone who was raised to respect both the janitor and the CEO, I often struggled with the politics of it all. Later, I realized that so much of this was due to insecurity, new managers, and others' fear of being replaced. The end of my relationship caused me to realize

I wanted more in work and my personal life. For the first time, I believed I deserved more and knew I was capable of doing and being more. It was time to not only start a new chapter but to write a whole new damn book! I was more scared of living a life of mediocrity, of playing it safe and pleasing others than I was of taking risks and betting on myself despite what anyone else thought. I knew it was time to take a leap of faith and that I'd build my wings on the way down.

It was time! It was time to find my passion, my purpose, my people, and most importantly, it was time to find myself. By deciding to leave my job and end my relationship, I also left behind the benchmarks and expectations of what others thought my life should look like and what they define as success.

By creating room for more, I was quickly rewarded with incredible opportunities to work with extraordinary athletes and media as a content creator and on-camera host. Knowing almost nothing about the sports world, I was fascinated with how warm and welcoming the community was and how much they valued me and my opinions even though I didn't have the title or salary that I was so accustomed to being defined by. Like many sports outsiders, I only knew about domestic violence, DUIs and performance-enhancing drugs and yet in my own personal first-hand experience, what I saw 99% of the time was exceptional discipline, teamwork, humility, and an insatiable thirst for excellence. I needed to share my perspective to allow more people to experience and see what I was fortunate enough to. I learned and appreciated so much that I was inspired to create Girly Locker Room – a platform focused on the social side of sports and the relatable, human side of athletes. I wanted to build a bridge for people like me who weren't familiar with sports to help us to better connect with and understand professional athletes who until this point, I'd only heard negative stories about. Girly Locker Room taught me the importance of trying new things, appreciating alternative views, being brave and defeating stereotypes.

Getting out of my comfort zone, and out of my own way, I challenged myself to question and re-assess practically everything that I thought I knew. I switched cell phone carriers, tried different ways of eating, went to a Buddhism class, and changed my usual drink order...that last one, changed my life.

When you think of a whiskey drinker, who do you picture? Probably not me, and understandably so. Personally, I imagine a John Wayne, tough guy, type of man. A Caucasian cowboy who smells like leather and kills spiders with his bare, rough hands. That's clearly not me, but I loved my first taste of whiskey – and not just the taste, the whole experience. I loved the confidence I felt, the conversations I had, and the different kinds of people I met that if it weren't for whiskey, I'd never have the opportunity to. It was truly love at first taste but I felt uncomfortable ordering a bourbon neat, as my comfort zone screamed vodka soda or sauvignon blanc from New Zealand... I mean, that's what people like me are supposed to prefer, right?

It was that moment that I remember thinking, "I really love this brown juice – someone should really step up and make it more relatable and appealing for people like me." Then I realized, I AM SOMEONE! Suddenly, my purpose was clear and passion took over. It was no longer just about me – it was about all the other people who felt like me and needed someone to lead the way. It was about the misunderstood, stereotypes, and finding and celebrating commonalities with those who are seemingly different.

Just as I never thought of myself as "exotic" or "attractive" until *Wayne's World* came out, just as I never thought I'd have any interest in sports or have anything in common with athletes until

I started Girly Locker Room, I knew in my gut that sharing my whiskey story was about so much more than just whiskey – It was about relationships, confidence, and inclusiveness...and whiskey was how we would get there.

I decided to put my money where my palate is and became a certified, then executive, bourbon steward. Obsessed with learning more, I made several trips to Kentucky and continued to learn, taste, and study all things whiskey. Shortly after, I became the first global ambassador for *Bourbon Plus Magazine* and the 2019 host of the Whiskey Women panel at Bourbon & Beyond in Louisville, Kentucky. Now, I know what you're thinking because I was thinking about it too – how would people in the whiskey community respond to me? I didn't look like any of them and I was nervous about how I would be received. Well, just as the sports community blew my stereotypes and expectations out of the water, so did the whiskey community. I've never been so warmly welcomed and greeted with such kindness and love. I learn something new every day from the people I have met, and not just about mastering my craft – similar to my sports family, my whiskey family teaches me about the person I want to be and continues to encourage and challenge me to push myself harder than I ever thought possible.

I truly believe that this ever-expanding whiskey family is a gift from my step-dad in heaven. His unexpected passing left a huge hole in my heart and I'm grateful every day for the reminders he sends through this chosen family. My step-dad was the best dad a person could ever ask for, and because our last names didn't match, I always said I would name my first child James to recognize and appreciate him – but again, I was planning on a blueprint that wasn't meant to be. That being said, I took control of what I could and legally changed my own last name to James so that I could honor him.

Success means different things to different people and growing up, like many of us, I thought there was some kind of external checklist and required timeframes for success. For some, that is the case but for me, my success checklist is internal, flexible, and timeless. To me, success means believing in myself, choosing positivity, being kind (to others and to myself), adding value by sharing my passion and vision, and taking deliberate and thoughtful action to reach my goals. It's not something that can be achieved overnight and it's not something that is done once it's done. I wake up every morning and continue to pursue the same purpose. Having empathy for ourselves and for one another, putting ourselves in other peoples' shoes, thinking differently and taking action with a clear goal in mind, and being happy and truly enjoying the process of becoming and improving with a higher purpose of serving others – that's what success means to me.

Be you, boo!

-Jennifer Boyd Desai

BE BRAVE

Jennifer Boyd Desai

Have you ever felt that you had everything you've ever dreamed of in your life? A successful man, a lucrative career, a big house, a healthy child, and all the material things money could buy? Despite having it all, did you still somehow feel unsatisfied and unhappy? No matter what your dreams are, there are times when you reach them, and still...something is missing.

My older brother is an engineer and my twin sister is a nurse practitioner. Both of them received good grades, and I probably should have taken school more seriously. I am the black sheep of the family. Instead of following the stereotypical career path that most Filipino families steer their children towards, I created my own. Early on, I knew that I wanted to be a Chief Executive Officer (CEO); I was exposed to entrepreneurship by my dad. As a Certified Public Accountant (CPA), he started his own business and was a founding father of a nonprofit helping children in the Philippines. I saw him use his business skills to help others and I picked up some of his skills and traits (which I know he loves). I didn't realize that I would end up following in his footsteps.

In 2001, I felt like I had it all! As a junior at California State University, Fullerton, I had a lucrative full-time job waiting for me in corporate America with a Fortune 100 pharmaceutical company when I graduated. I had also met my future husband.

We were both members of the business club and after graduation, we started our careers together in the pharmaceutical industry. We were that power, #goals couple. By the age of 23, we were financially stable, bought our own houses, and had plenty of money to spend on traveling and investing in real estate. At one point, we were worth close to $2.3 million, spending a lot, but never giving anything back to charity! Unfortunately, a few years into our marriage, when our son was barely six-months-old, we ended up getting divorced. Overnight, my lifestyle was taken away, and I went from riches to rags when my husband told me to get out! With only $4,000 pulled from my retirement account and my son in tow, I had to figure out how to be a single mother. To make matters worse, shortly after our divorce, I was laid off from my job where I was earning a six-figure income. This was an extremely difficult time for me. I was dealing with severe clinical depression; my body and mind were shutting down. I couldn't work or drive; I could barely function.

After the divorce, I moved out and found myself a modest place in Huntington Beach. One day while I was out on the balcony, I looked up into the sky and told God I was going to just "let go" and give it all to Him. It was hard for me to conceptualize letting go of something that I couldn't see, but I felt something was spiritually and emotionally holding me down. From the moment I gave it to God, I felt lighter and emotionally liberated. By letting go, God started to create a new, purposeful path for me. I slowly started to get better and I was able to come out of severe, major depression. It has taken time, but I know I am meant to be here today. I have learned that when you let go, you'll be surprised with what amazingly manifests.

I turned my unfortunate circumstances into a positive opportunity. I used it as my chance to get out of the corporate world. I wanted to feel good about what I was doing instead of being focused on money. I wanted to be fulfilled and live a purposeful life. Even though I was the poorest that I've ever been, I wanted to help people. I learned to feel empathy, something I didn't know about when I had riches. After going through these difficult situations, and climbing back up after hitting rock bottom, I found myself in a very happy place, emotionally and spiritually. Everything I had gone through made me a stronger person.

During this time, my good friend, Desiree, was diagnosed with breast cancer. I saw her struggle with battling cancer while taking care of her toddler. It reminded me of my personal experiences with my mother who had a stroke at the age of 49. When my mom became ill, my siblings were away for college. I was living at home so I took care of my mother who was in a quadriplegic state. My parents and Desiree inspired me to start my own 501(c)(3) charity. I wanted to live a purposeful life helping mothers battling cancer while raising minor children. In 2013, the Mommy and Me Cancer Foundation (MAMCF) was born. MAMCF was founded on the premise that "no family fights alone." To date, MAMCF has been able to help hundreds of families in crisis across the nation.

Ironically, in 2017, I was diagnosed with cervical cancer. I was shocked because cancer does not run in my family. Through my involvement with MAMCF, I had the resources to guide me through my own battle. Luckily, the cancer was discovered at an early stage. I underwent elective surgery to become cancer-free, but that also left me unable to have children. Fortunately, I have been blessed with two healthy and amazing sons, Gavin and William. At the time of publishing, my youngest son William just started kindergarten. My eldest son, Gavin, is a star soccer player in our region. He has won many championships and is a true testament of my commitment to my children's success. Aside from my sons, my greatest success is MAMCF and helping hundreds of families in crisis. I didn't realize that it would bloom as much as it did. Originally, I knew I wanted to help people, but in return, I got so much more. I was able to bring more awareness about the difficulty of raising young children while battling cancer. I am proud that MAMCF was able to make a dent in the cancer care community. As a result, I have been honored with awards and featured on CBS News, KCAL-TV, KTLA, KIIS FM, *The Ellen DeGeneres Show, OC Register*, and numerous blogs. It has also afforded me the opportunity to become a guest professor at my alma mater.

For me, success means to be happy despite status or reputation. No matter where I'm at or what my title is, I am happy with everything and I don't care about what anyone else thinks. Everyone's definition of success is different. There's always going to be someone out there who has done more or better. I don't live a conventional life; I live a very colorful life and I embrace it to the highest degree!

I have two personal mottos. The first is "Be you, Boo." We are so focused on what society and others want us to do, but these things slow us down. You have to choose what you let infiltrate your mind. People need to figure out how to speak with empathy and grace. Instead of letting someone affect you, gracefully listen, but at the end of the day, be yourself. The second motto is "Just be brave." You have to be willing to take leaps forward without knowing what the outcome will be. Even though you can't necessarily see what's ahead, you have to be brave enough to take that first step.

It's important for you to, "Just Be Brave," and try to find your purpose in life. Find something that will be meaningful to you over time, not just now. I've always had a natural drive to build and do bigger things in life and I've seen that true leaders naturally emerge when they don't chase prestige or money. I am now the founder and CEO of two companies: MAMCF and Prosperity

MD. Prosperity MD, LLC is a for-profit business that focuses on cloud-based revenue cycle management. I help specialists and surgeons realize their full earning potential in this Affordable Care Act-era. Prosperity MD, LLC has been listed as one of the top ten revenue cycle companies in the nation and was recently listed as one of the top 20 consulting companies in *Mirror Review*. My success has not come easily. I have made sacrifices and difficult decisions in my life to mold my future and fix my past. With no regrets, I can look back knowing that I took major steps to make this world a better place, one mother at a time, one doctor at a time.

Hustle
FOR A
cause.

—Gina Mariko Rosales

Be a Leader

Gina Mariko Rosales

When I was in fourth grade, my teacher shook every student's hand as they walked out of the door on the last day of school. When it was my turn, she told me, "Gina, call me when you're the president in the White House." Thinking back, I always remember the people in my life who set high expectations for me: my parents, teachers, family, friends, and peers. It really mattered because I strived hard to not only live up to those expectations but surpass them. I guess I was an overachiever from the start (that's the Capricorn in me).

I grew up in a little California skater/surfer town called Pacifica where I attended a Catholic school from pre-school until eighth grade. I was one of the handful of Filipino people in my class of 30. Friends would refer to me as "Gina, the short Filipino girl" and people knew exactly who they were talking about. Everyone labeled me "the smartest in class": I always won the spelling bee and was valedictorian of my eighth grade class. This was a blessing and a curse. I remember on one report card my best friend got better grades than me by one A (I got a B in that section). Everyone in class made fun of me, and I cried. The school made me go see a therapist after that because they thought it was unhealthy that I got so upset over a grade, but it was the teasing and not the grades that was so upsetting to me.

I was also that *weird* girl with four names – Gina Mariko Alinea Rosales. Big name, little girl. "Just call me Gina," I'd say, since no one could pronounce Mariko correctly (Pro Tip: Accent the 'Ma'; roll the R). It wasn't until I attended high school in San Francisco that I had my first group of *Pinay* friends. Then I attended the University of California, Berkeley (Cal) where I really started exploring my identity as a Filipino-Japanese American through Filipino organizations like PAA (Pilipino American Alliance), PCN (Pilipino Cultural Night), and Japanese language classes. I started experimenting by signing my emails as 'Gina Mariko.'

During high school and college, dance was a huge part of my life. I danced with multiple companies but was mostly involved with Funkanometry SF, a professional dance company and 501(c)(3) nonprofit performing arts organization. In my junior year at Cal, the co-founder of Funkanometry SF (who was a close friend) sat me down and told me he was stepping down. "You're the only one who can take over, Gina," he said. The company meant so much to me and the community, so I accepted the responsibility and became the executive director of an award-winning nonprofit at the age of 20. I had no idea how to run a nonprofit! I remember going to Barnes & Noble to buy a book called *How to Run a Nonprofit for Dummies* and taking free classes at the Foundation Center to figure it out.

Leading Funkanometry SF aged me really fast and gave me my first case of imposter syndrome. I was running the company, leading people who were older than me, while I was in school, and with a side job at a restaurant. But, I took it on – we had big dreams and big goals as a small nonprofit. In two years, we expanded from two to five dance companies, created two new dance classes, started afterschool programs, and tripled our membership from 50 to 150. We were invited to international performances in the UK, Philippines, and Colombia, and were awarded a *Bay Guardian*

GOLDIE award. I taught myself how to use QuickBooks, got our first office, and applied for grants. There was so much growth and outward success, but at my peak, I was only making $600 a month. So I worked at a restaurant as a hostess, got a job at another nonprofit so I could learn, and sent emails for Funkanometry SF during my lunch break and at night. My parents supported me financially through college, so I didn't have to take on any student debt – for that, I'm forever grateful and know I am very privileged in that sense.

After floating around doing lots of nonprofit work and completing the AmeriCorps VISTA program, I eventually landed a contract job at Google as a recruiting coordinator. I almost didn't go to the interview since I thought leaving the nonprofit world would make me a sellout. My mom convinced me to go and I got the job. The work was easy and I excelled at it but was bored. I got promoted to a full-time employee and continued running my nonprofit during lunch breaks and on the Google shuttle (4 hours a day). I created my own side projects with engineers at Google to improve efficiency and build team culture through events and hosted many student visits to the Google campus for my friends' nonprofits and schools. It was my way to stay engaged and feel purposeful at work. I was able to give back to my friends in San Francisco while I worked in the Silicon Valley bubble.

Around this same time, I experienced a huge life change – my cousin Jonathan, only three months younger than me, died by suicide. It was unexpected, extremely tragic and traumatic, and it shook our entire family to the core. Jonathan had attempted suicide back in high school, and our family instructed us, cousins, to never talk about it so as not to embarrass him. Ten years later, we learned that he was suffering from depression for years when he took his own life. From this day forward, everything in my life changed. Tomorrow was NOT a guarantee. We had to live our lives more fully because Jonathan wasn't able to. I looked at every situation moving forward through a new lens: "If I were to die tomorrow, would I feel proud of my life?" This was the question I asked myself daily.

Over time my family began to heal. Eventually, my work got recognized, and I landed a job in Google X as the first administrative business partner for the self-driving car team (now known as Waymo). I also became the executive assistant to Megan Smith, an amazing lesbian in tech who had founded hella companies and was known for her bold ideas and vision. When Megan transitioned to the White House to become the Chief Technology Officer under Barack Obama, I helped her with the job transition out of X. I learned so much from Megan. She taught me how to think BIG and to focus on connecting the right people to make shit happen. There were no barriers for her. I remember the time she told me to just email Richard Branson, CEO of Virgin Galactic, and to ask him to feature a women-focused video on the Virgin planes. He never replied, but that wasn't the point; she taught me to go for big things without looking at the barriers that could get in the way.

Throughout my life, I've had many jobs: gymnastics teacher, restaurant hostess, dance teacher, nonprofit outreach manager, recruiting coordinator, administrative business partner, program manager, and most recently head of marketing events. Each company and role was a different adventure, but I always approached every job with the same mentality – be myself, unapologetically, have hella fun, build relationships, and go above and beyond in the work.

And trust me, being my unapologetic self – a short, smart, loud-ass Filipina woman – in a predominantly white tech company where I was once again one of a handful of Filipinos on the team, was tough. I had imposter syndrome often, and lived by the phrase "fake it til you make it." But, I had this confidence in me, a sort of boldness where I gave myself permission to be myself. I ate crab and rice with vinegar at the Google Cafe *kamayan* style (aka with my hands), I played pranks on my vice president on his birthday, and I planned roller disco parties in our self-driving car garage. All of this contributed to building the company culture.

Despite having one of the coolest jobs I could imagine, I was still uneasy. My tech guilt was growing by the day, and Jonathan's memory was constantly on my mind. In 2015, I decided to start my own company, which of course was met with uncertainty by my parents. But I did it – I became the founder and owner of my own company, Make it Mariko, an all women-of-color event planning team based in San Francisco, dedicated to curating magical, meaningful moments for the community. My company is inspired by Jonathan's memory and is rooted in my desire to celebrate all the magical moments that make our lives meaningful. I somehow convinced my boss at X to let me go part-time and work from home, which I did for the first two years of running my business.

In 2016, I went to a meeting that my friend Desi Danganan had planned for Filipino entrepreneurs. He did a PowerPoint presentation on his vision for SOMA Pilipinas Cultural Heritage District (which I didn't know anything about) and building a commercial corridor. I was sold. I immediately volunteered to throw a "Launch Party" for SOMA Pilipinas as a means to get a lot of media and press attention so that more people would know about the cultural district. I applied for a $5K grant and won it. Then Desi got more grant funding from the City of San Francisco and it turned into a monthly event that we now know today as UNDISCOVERED SF Creative Night Market. We planned six back-to-back UNDISCOVERED events in that first year of 2017! It was insane, emotionally challenging, and physically exhausting.

But we did it and we welcomed over 35,000 Filipinos from all over the country that first year to the cultural district.

The following year in 2018, I finally quit Google X to go full time with Make it Mariko, and the company took off at an insane pace! I was getting referrals from everywhere without doing any marketing. I planned 30 events that year, started building multiple teams, all while planning UNDISCOVERED Season Two at a new and bigger location. Inspired by the success of UNDISCOVERED and having met so many more *Pinay* entrepreneurs through our night market, I launched the first daylong summit for *Pinay* entrepreneurs with the mission to "build sisterhood in the hustle." After the summit launched, I was so moved by the entire day and felt like I had fallen into my life's work. It was truly transformative being in a space with 130 other *Pinays* with similar goals of running businesses, being independent, and taking up space. We followed up by launching an online community and support system, and it was beautiful to see so many connections being made.

I somehow stumbled into being a leader again without knowing it. It was really challenging work and I often wanted to quit. But as stressful as being a leader was (and believe me, it was stressful AF), I felt deep in my gut that I was working on something bigger than me, something important, and meaningful. I felt called to the work and knew I had to keep going. The more I do this work, the more it's clear to me that being a good leader is not about being smart, efficient, or connected. Anyone can learn stuff, work faster, and meet people. I realize that good leadership IS about having a vision, communicating that vision, inspiring people, and learning how to constantly grow and evolve as a person. That's the hardest part for me.

My immigrant parents taught me from a young age that I should learn to be perfect. Straight A's, perfectly made bed, folded clothes, clean room. I learned to hate myself when I was wrong, punish myself for making mistakes, and to speak indirectly so as not to bother anyone. I've had to actively unlearn ALL of that colonization to be a good leader. I've learned (and am constantly learning) how to admit when I'm wrong, to forgive myself for being human, and to communicate directly. It feels good to shed that shame. *Walang hiya* (shameless in Tagalog). Because we truly are "our ancestors wildest dreams" – we just need to step into our power and claim it.

Ponytail up
— AND —
PUT IN THE WORK.
You've got this
girl!

— Rose Buado

BE GRATEFUL

Rose Buado

"It is only with gratitude that life becomes rich."
- Dietrich Bonhoeffer

This quote hangs on my dining room wall, to remind me to be grateful for everything I am and that I have – past, present, and future. I come from a loving and humble home. My parents have been strong influences in my life. My dad is a hard-working and strict man who served in the United States (U.S.) Navy for 21 years. His discipline is carried out through my brothers and I. My mom was a respected and admired school teacher in the Philippines. When she arrived in the U.S. with my dad, she wasn't able to teach since her college degree and credentials didn't meet the American educational standards. So she ended up taking a basic materials manufacturing job. Even though I may not have had extreme struggles in my past, we experienced growing pains and hardships. For instance, when my mom got laid off and had to start all over again. Fortunately, my mom loved us and cared for us unconditionally. She taught us about God and made sure my brothers and I were able to pursue any profession we wanted even if it wasn't a traditional known path, like nursing or engineering.

When the doors opened for me to pick any path, the challenge was immense. I wanted to be so many things; I wanted to try

61

everything! I wanted to be a teacher like my mom, but then I realized, I'm not that patient. Then I pursued acting; I once made my dad drive me all the way to Hollywood to meet with an agent. My dad and I drove an hour to do a five-minute audition then drove two hours back in Los Angeles traffic. Oh, he was pissed! During my senior year in high school, my teacher asked us to write down what we wanted to be after graduation. I wrote that I would work in marketing for a huge corporate company like Nike. Then, at one point in my life, I really wanted to be a radio host so I co-hosted college radio while at California State University, Long Beach (CSULB). That was fun but I quickly figured out that I'm not as savvy with music pop-culture as one should be when pursuing this field. Next, I walked into the school's fashion department. However, my college counselor didn't sell me on the idea of pursuing a fashion degree. I wasn't convinced that I should study fashion, but I did end up being in the school's fashion show that semester! Most of all, deep down inside I knew that I really wanted to be in entertainment! Yeah, I was definitely all over the place.

During college, I needed to find a way to make extra money so I started my first business in event planning, creating perfect debuts (18th birthday coming-out parties for Filipinas) and weddings. I enjoyed it but, quite frankly, I had no idea that being an entrepreneur was even a thing, and I didn't take it very seriously! I thought to start a real business and being an entrepreneur was only for rich people. I'm definitely grateful for the journey of all of my studies, starting a business, and taking the time to explore because it all gave me such great experience. At the end of all of that, I obtained a Bachelor of Arts in Communications Studies from CSULB. I was excited and happy about what my future held.

Looking back, I'm not surprised that I finally accepted being an entrepreneur. Nearly 20 years after graduating from college,

I now own and run several businesses in different industries. I am an artist manager, cafe owner, business success coach, and most recently, a co-author. All my businesses have one thing in common: being able to serve people to live their best selves.

The journey to get to this point has been the biggest challenge in my life. After college, I went straight into corporate America. Climbing the ladder was easy for me since I had my dad's work ethic and my mom's faith. But after a few years into it, I couldn't help but feel stuck and incomplete. I knew I was missing something but I just didn't know what.

I prayed every night giving thanks to God, but I also asked Him for answers and signs. I had everything I wanted. It felt wrong and I felt like I was being selfish. I regularly complained to my husband about what I hated. It had nothing to do with the people I worked with or the projects I worked on. I was good at what I did. But I questioned what I was doing it for? To make more profit for companies that already made billions of dollars? I didn't feel good about it.

Fast forward to 2011, I wanted to be with my six-week-old daughter and watch her grow instead of waiting for a photo of her from my parents or husband. I was sad that I couldn't be with her most of the day because I was at work. I remember pumping milk in my office and sometimes my car, just so people wouldn't hear the loud sound of the breast pump. It was very time consuming and being one of the only females at the agency made it even more uncomfortable. I wore breastfeeding pads because I was afraid of milk leakage at work. That certainly would have been embarrassing while pitching clients' annual media budgets.

As hard as that was and as much as I disliked it, I did it all over again in 2013 when my son was born. I had stayed in corporate work because it was stable but the tradeoff is that I was miserable. I told myself that I would quit after the birth of my second child, but I actually stayed for four more years! Even though I hated being there, I was comfortable and loyal to my CEO. I didn't fully let go until 2017. I was drained, stuck, and unhappy. However, I was still very grateful. I took every chance I had to learn and picked up knowledge about business procedures and policies because I knew they would come in handy in the future.

To balance it out, I still enjoyed creating events and making a bride and groom's vision come to life on their big day. I loved the sound of beautiful music playing, watching people mingling, and running around making sure the day was going perfect. That natural high made me happy for a short second until Monday came when I had to drag myself back into the office. Why couldn't I just do events every day? I asked myself, "Is event planning what I was meant to do instead of being in an office all day?" The answer was: no. As much as I loved planning events, that is not my purpose in life. It is part of my life but it did not make me whole. I have a gift of knowing what I don't want, but I never focused on what I do want. Maybe if I put more energy into the places that felt right earlier on, I would have found the right path much quicker.

One night, my prayers were finally answered! My youngest brother, Vj Rosales, told me he was going to audition for NBC's singing competition show, *The Voice*, for the third time. I was excited because I've supported him throughout his musical journey. I've always been his #1 fan next to our mom. Unfortunately, he couldn't get past the interview portion of the audition. I did what came easy for me. I put questions together and gave him a format on how to effectively answer them during the interview. By sharing my business skills and marketing tactics, I was able to help my brother land a spot on national TV! That's when everything started to trickle in. All of a sudden, he needed a manager! That's how a business was born. Shortly after *The Voice*, my brother joined an a cappella band, The Filharmonic. We started to live that popstar life: attending red carpets, flying around the world, and meeting A-listers left and right. We were definitely living the dream. God truly answered my prayers by giving me something to be passionate about, and I finally found something that felt purposeful.

I did all that while still working in my corporate job. I was making ends meet and keeping happy. However, I lacked sleep and spent a lot of time away from my family, which was a major concern to me. There's always something, right? However, the true underlying feeling was that I was scared! I had been in advertising for over 15 years and became the vice president (VP) of my agency. If I quit my career, I wouldn't be able to pay our bills, my family wouldn't be able to eat, and we would end up homeless. In my mind, we were doomed! There was no way I could quit my job as a VP even if I was unhappy. I felt that no full-time job meant no money and no home. What I realized was that the biggest problem wasn't me being unhappy in my career but it was the limiting beliefs I had within myself. I lived in fear of never reaching my full potential because I was living my "plan B." What I believed was that I could not survive and make a sustainable living on my own because I was not good enough and the only way to live was to work for someone else, so that's what I did.

In 2016, my kids were only four and two-years-old when my mom passed away. That moment was a real turning point for me. I received a call at 5:15 a.m. while I was working on The Filharmonic's tour plan. I had to stop what I was doing because I felt my heart sink to the ground. I woke up my husband and we rushed to the hospital. When we got there, she was still warm; she looked peaceful. It was a hard time and it was sudden. I was depressed that I wasn't there with her. I had to keep it together – The Filharmonic business ran solely through me. On top of all of this, I was still at my corporate job! I had to plan the funeral and everything else that comes along with losing a parent. I'm known to be strong and resilient, but not this time. I lost it! My whole life went out of control and lost all structure. My mother's death broke me. But when I think about it now, it truly defined me. With the help of friends and family, we got through it. I knew that I was capable and I gave myself permission to breakdown. Not everything is business. Philippians 4:13: "I can do all things through Christ who strengthens me." This is a verse that gave me strength and courage! Shortly after this, I left my day job. I decided that something was missing, and I couldn't give into my limiting beliefs. I had to venture out to see what I was really made of. I made the biggest sacrifice and leap of faith to finally leaving my full-time VP level position.

Now, three years later, I've been able to travel the world as an artist manager and business coach. I can volunteer at my children's school and attend amazing conferences where I've met people from all over the world! I am so fortunate for the opportunity to co-write and bring this book to life. I've also opened a cafe that serves over 800 guests a week. Not only that, I've been able to connect with empowering women who are living in their purpose and making a big difference on this Earth. My heart is open to new possibilities and opportunities to create an impact within our community.

My advice to any woman who is ready to go down their career path or change it, don't live within your limited beliefs. Don't wait for something major to happen to finally decide that you can do what you love. Go out and travel, meet new like-minded people and always be grateful for everything you had, have, and will have. It really will make you richer because you'll focus on your blessings instead of problems. You will be rich in hope and perseverance. I truly believe that everything you want was put in your heart by God so that means He wants exactly that for you! If you don't pursue it, you're not fulfilling God's purpose, your purpose. So if you managed to come up with a great idea and you didn't do anything about it, don't be mad if someone else did. Ponytail up and put in the work. You've got this girl!

I'm excited about my future. I plan to help bring passion and purpose to goal-oriented, career-minded and professional entrepreneurs. I want to help and support others to do what they love while they go through their business journey. I plan to put a stamp in the music and entertainment industry helping Asian-American talent break through the glass ceiling. Last but not least, I plan to organize and develop charitable events raising money for children of the Philippines and America. Moreover, I plan to do this with my husband and children by my side. Nathaniel and I are teaching our kids, Olive and Niko, to grow up loving God, being kind and respectful to others, becoming leaders in our community, having fun and most of all, being grateful for everything that comes their way. With that, I'd like to send you good energy, light, and love. I pray and hope this book inspires you to live fully and gives you the confidence to take action to do what you love. We need you to, it's what you're made for.

—Joanne Encarnacion

Be Relentless

Joanne Encarnacion

**Trigger warning: Mention of depression and suicide.

I am a modern-day mother-hustler sharing my fitness journey towards a happier and healthier life. I am a mother of two daughters, a wife, and a health and wellness blogger and coach who empowers women to redefine health and wellness on their own terms. But that hasn't always been the case. At the young age of 15, I suffered from depression, and I attempted suicide. I had always struggled with my self-image, which didn't match the beauty standards that we are taught by society, culture, and our upbringing. Due to my suicide attempt, California's state law mandated that I attend therapy throughout my teenage years. During therapy, I tackled my own pain and experienced healing. In hopes of sharing this gift with the world, I flirted with the idea of becoming a psychologist. However, my first job, I ended up being a hairdresser, which was far from what I aspired to be. I've always viewed hair to be a form of self-expression and as a hairstylist, I found great joy in helping others bring out their beauty. Unfortunately, my career was cut short at only 20-years-old when I found out I was 24 weeks pregnant! Becoming a mother at 21 was difficult because I sacrificed my twenties and I had to grow up much quicker than I anticipated. However, my daughter was (and still is) my biggest blessing. She helped fuel the motivation for me to do better for myself and our family. It wasn't just me anymore. I was now a wife and a mother!

Pregnancy drastically changed my body. Slowly, I began to hate myself and my body. In 2013, I was 29-years-old with two daughters. I didn't want to go into my thirties feeling overwhelmed, stressed, and tired. On paper, I had it all! I had a beautiful, healthy family and a career as the director of community and curation at VSCO. Despite it all, I still felt that something was lacking. I distinctly remember a time when I was getting ready with my eldest daughter, Airis. She told me, "OMG Mom! You're so beautiful." I looked at myself in the mirror and responded with "NO, I'm ugly and fat." I will never forget the look on her face. I was filled with so much hate and self-loathing, and I lacked self-confidence. How was I supposed to encourage my daughters to be the woman that they should be when I wasn't leading by example?

I did not realize the downward spiral of negative thoughts. It was only until I had a healthy relationship with myself that I understood how the power of thoughts impacted my relationships with people, things, and activities around me. While at VSCO, I was managing teams of employees; I took pride in building up self-sufficient individuals who were motivated to excel in their roles and projects. The combination of people management and wanting to empower others is what drew me into becoming a health and wellness coach. My health and wellness journey stems from my own depression and anxiety along with my desire to be a better example to my girls.

After I got laid off in 2016, I could have easily stayed in my comfort zone by going back into tech to help corporations like Facebook or Instagram, but I decided to see what I could do that would be more meaningful and intentional. I find that our greatest transformations happen within ourselves. Even though I was scared, I decided to pursue my passions because I didn't want to regret missed opportunities to try something new. Sometimes you have to put up the blinders to block out the peripheral noise so that you can work towards your goals, even if you don't have a plan. During the time I started my fitness career, both my husband and I worked as freelancers. There were some months where we couldn't figure out how to pay rent nor did we have a future forecast. When I became open to opportunities and the possibility of abundance instead of holding on to scarcity, the world truly opened up like I never imagined.

I started GoFitJo to help share my wellness journey. In the beginning, it was partly a weight loss journey, but over time it evolved into a platform for me to share how I find harmony in my life as a busy woman. I want to be remembered as a woman who gave people the space to live out their most authentic and genuine selves. When I meet with people, they tell me things that they've never even told their closest friends. I create a space that holds no judgment. When a woman opens up to me, I want her to feel that I love her in the darkest and brightest moments. I encourage women to find and do things that make them feel alive. This not only applies to your career, but also to how you show up in life.

My advice to other women is to embrace failure because it is going to happen. Once you do, you no longer give it this power of shame, vulnerability or weakness. You start to look at your failures as stepping stones to success. We put so much pressure on ourselves to be perfect, but sometimes trying to aim for perfection leads to paralysis. If we can start learning how to embrace our failures and imperfections, then we might be able to switch our mindset. Instead, we should view our imperfections as roadmaps to success. By no means do I have a traditional background that led me to where I am today. It was my own struggle and journey with my self-image that allowed growth and evolution.

Traditionally, the business of health and wellness is associated with food (what we put in our body) and exercise (how we move our body). I always believed that health embodies food, exercise, and all other areas of life. Ultimately, it impacts how we thrive in our careers, relationships, spirituality, and our connectivity to our most authentic selves. When one of those things is not in play, we can't have forward movement in other areas of our lives. When these things aren't in a place and we aren't surviving or thriving, our world crumbles.

Growing up Filipino, I felt that I could never make my parents proud; they pushed so hard and only knew how to give tough love. Basically, if I had a dream that wasn't theirs then *bahala na* (whatever will be, will be in Tagalog) and whatever the outcome, I would never dare to come home crying! The best advice I've been given, surprisingly, came from my mom, who despite the tough love, always used to tell me to "keep going." She would say this even though she had no idea what "keep going" looked like for me. Until this day, I still keep going even if it's not perfect or doesn't turn out as planned. I fell in love with the word relentless because it embodies who I am as a person. I am relentless as fuck. I'm going to go for something I want – It might take me forever, but I am going for it! Relentless describes someone who doesn't give up, but it also sounds very graceful. When you say it, there is a softness to it. When I go through adversity, people view me as a person that does it with grace. Relentless embodies strength and grace at the same time.

I am a true believer in manifestation and putting things out into the universe. One of my goals was to have a partnership with Adidas, which came into fruition in June 2018. Before that, I gave myself permission to say the biggest, scariest goals because you never know what can happen! You have to let love in and let life surprise you! I am also proud of my partnership with Gap. When

Gap reached out to me, I was not the fittest or in the best shape of my life. I was scared, but I also didn't want to go on a crash diet for the campaign. That's not who I am. Although I am not the skinniest and have stretch marks and a loose midsection, Gap was willing to embrace all of me. They wanted to proudly put me out there for the world to see! I was chosen as an example of what the human body and self-acceptance look like. I didn't accept this opportunity simply to see myself on billboards or in-store advertisements, but once I did, I was able to get outside of my head and accept why I was chosen to be a part of this campaign. I needed to step into that light and be proud of the fact that there is something beautiful about me that they see, and I needed to see it too. Over the years, I have worked on getting past my body dysmorphia and these opportunities have helped me do that. Beauty comes in different shapes, colors, and sizes. I thought it was beautiful that the Gap didn't want to cover my tattoos. I was also very proud to represent my Filipino-American community! Finally, women around the world can see a true representation of what a real, raw woman looks like. If women are constantly exposed to body types that don't look like them, how can they fall in love with themselves? Personally, I admit that I had a hard time loving myself when I saw advertisements of women who didn't look like me.

Through my experience over the last few years, I found that there is not enough representation of Asian-American women in the health and wellness industry. It's been a bit of a struggle, but also empowering, to have the opportunity to have that role in our community. Much of the Asian-American upbringing is based on a scarcity belief system. Finding camaraderie with other Asian women has been a challenge because some get stuck in a mindset of, "Why can't I do that? Why not me?" Sometimes I find that there is a sentiment of fear when an Asian-American woman is rising. Instead of viewing other women as competition, we need to learn to lift each other up and understand why we need to compare ourselves to others. I want to empower other women, but how do we do that when our moms tell us that we are never enough? I have hope that Asian-American women will start looking within themselves to find that courage. We don't have to hide behind these family belief systems and we don't have to be afraid of stepping outside what our family wants us to do. We want to make our parents proud, but at the end of the day if we aren't making ourselves proud then what does that truly mean for our parents? For me, success is thriving and living my most authentic life. It also means enjoying life! It's hard to do, but I am working on it and I am a work in progress. My biggest fear is that I will not be able to provide a future that my girls are looking for. I have to keep reminding myself that my daughters will have a future that they design. I am only here to help guide and mold them. I make a conscious effort to be a good role model for them and others.

There are a lot of women thinking about starting a family or trying to be a career mom trying to create work-life balance. Modern-day women want to see a role model who doesn't quite have it all figured out but is still thriving at home. Often times, my followers see that I am constantly working and traveling; they send me messages challenging me on how I live my life. I know they're judging my family and trying to wrap their heads around how it's possible for my family to be nourished when I am always hustling. But my family vibrates on a higher frequency and how we live works for us. Once we get rid of that guilt and assuming we need to have our lives function like others we see then we can build our family lives the way we want to define them. In modern-day society, family structures don't look like they used to. How do we shape that, give light to, and have conversations around these topics? The conversations I have with my kids about sex, marriage, and drugs are much different from what I had with my parents. My kids don't know any other life, other than the one they are living now. As long as I can give them the best, then that's all that matters. We need to remove the shame from these topics. I want to put it out there and I want people to embrace their own messiness. I recently launched a new podcast, @HellaMarried, where my partner and I help folx get comfortable with conversations around sex, love, and relationships. In addition to that, I'm starting a new online platform called WOMXN IN PROGRESS, a space for all womxn who want to celebrate their identity freely and unabashedly.

I truly believe that you are allowed to be beautiful and messy all at the same time. I have this written on my wall because it keeps me grounded and serves as a reminder that everything is going to work out, in the end, the way it's supposed to. We tend to go through life scrambling to figure out what we are going to do next, and this quote inspires and motivates me to remember that I don't need to be put together all the time, nor do I have to have it all together. I am allowed to be that messy person. There's beauty within that. There's beauty within me. I'm both of these things combined. It's a message that I want to share and remind you of! We are all women in progress! Own it, celebrate, and live your life even if others don't understand it. Whether you are trying to start a new career, business, relationship, or parenthood, you have to remember that life is messy but beautiful at the same time. Choose to show up for yourself, take up space in this world, and create a life that brings joy, pleasure, and all the variety of emotions that come with the journey.

Relationships
MOTIVATED ME TO
build MY business
AND IT'S THOSE
relationships
THAT HELP US
grow;
IT'S WHY I DO THIS WORK.
—Jhoanna Alba

Be Humble

Jhoanna Alba

I was born in Manila, Philippines and came to the United States when I was only a year old. At six-years-old, I was already sewing and making my own clothes. On the weekends, my mom and I would go to Joann's Fabrics and buy the supplies we needed for our projects. Our sewing machine would often break so she also taught me how to sew by hand. I would sit on the floor in front of the TV, watching the Lakers and Dodgers while sewing blankets, pillows, and clothes.

Growing up, I wanted to be a teacher. I took summer school so I could finish high school early and I was only 16-years-old when I attended West Valley Occupational Center where I obtained my degree in child development. I taught pre-school every day and because the minimum wage was only $8 an hour, after school, I worked at Gary's Tuxedo Shop. I worked seven days a week!

While working at the tuxedo shop, I kept getting promoted and ended up transferring to the Beverly Hills store. At 19-years-old, I quit my teaching job to run the highest volume store in the country. Then, in 1995, I did a wedding for actress, Holly Robinson, who was on several TV shows including *21 Jump Street* and *Hangin'* *with Mr. Cooper*. Holly was engaged to Rodney Peete, a National Football League (NFL) quarterback. The Los Angeles Lakers' point guard, Earvin "Magic" Johnson was a good friend of the Peete family and his son, EJ, was the ring bearer. Meeting Magic Johnson helped change the course of my life. The company that was making Magic's custom clothes recruited me to do women's clothing. I ended up doing clothing for athletes' wives, mothers, and girlfriends for a few years, but I found that it wasn't my niche.

At the age of 20, I started my own company with the support of Magic Johnson. He saw that I was making money for everyone else so he pushed me to be my own boss. He was my first client who asked me to deliver ten suits, and this was the start of my own bespoke clothing business. Bespoke clothing is custom-made to fit a person's exact specifications. Because of my hard work and talent, he referred me to his network, and it was a complete domino effect. It's funny how everything came full circle; members of the teams I watched on TV when I was little, became my clients. I made custom clothes not only for long-time Laker, Magic Johnson, but also Tommy Lasorda from the Dodgers.

Traditionally, bespoke clothing is designed and made by men. Even now, you don't see a lot of female custom clothiers. It's not easy being in a male-dominated industry, but over time, I've been able to get men to respect me, my product, and my business. I have been making custom clothing for over 25 years and I have grown a lot in that time. Early in my career, I was so quick to please people but I was trying to please people who were taking from me. As I've gotten older and wiser, I now make different choices about who I want to work with. I've become more willing to make my personal life a priority rather than continuing to make sacrifices as an entrepreneur. I dressed Lebron James for four years when he came into the league, but when I became pregnant, I chose to stay home with my daughter. I lost him as a client but I didn't want to sacrifice my family for my work. Every day I make sacrifices so that my employees are taken care of, but no matter what, it is important to stay true to yourself and to always be honest.

When I started ALBA Legacy, I wanted it to have a purpose and I didn't want it to be all about me. ALBA is named after my dad and grandfather but also stands for "A Light Beyond Your Appearance." We're not just dressing you – we want to get to know our clients, build relationships, and get involved with our community. Relationships motivated me to build this business and it's those relationships that help us grow; it's why I do this work. With ALBA Legacy, we don't just create clothes; we go to our client's houses, play with their kids, dress them for their weddings, and when amazing things happen like getting inducted into the Hall of Fame, we're there. It's amazing to be a part of all that!

Even now, Magic Johnson motivates and challenges me. I learned humility from Magic's actions. He is the most humble guy I know! He's never too good to sit down and eat with his employees. Having an ego is your worst enemy; we are all here on the planet to do good. I once asked him how I could ever repay him and he said, "by your success." Magic believes that "You can't take that knowledge with you. You gotta pass it on! That's what I've been put on this Earth to do. I have been blessed to be successful but it wouldn't be nothing without helping others become successful." I try to pass this same message on to my mentees because I want the same for them and it's rewarding to see them grow.

To date, I have over 1,200 clients in sports and entertainment including Russell Westbrook, Terrell Owens, Klay Thompson, Anthony Davis, Dwayne "The Rock" Johnson, Lisa Leslie, Sheryl Swoopes, Laila Ali and more. Despite this roster of clients, I remain humble and faithful. God has definitely blessed me and I want to be able to share with others. In addition to ALBA Legacy, I have another company called Mi Armore, a versatile fashion accessory brand. I created this company to empower other women through fashion. I want women to be confident, stylish and free.

Prior to starting ALBA and Mi Armore, I had another company for 13 years. During that time, I took a trip to the Philippines, which really helped put things into perspective. I saw my family in the Philippines who were happy with nothing. They took baths with a bucket of cold water and they didn't go to the bathroom until after three in the afternoon to conserve water and power. Here I was, working so hard and I didn't understand why. I had to go back to my roots to realize that something was wrong. I realized that I don't really need a big house and nice cars. My goal now is to have peace and happiness. Because of that shift in my perspective, one of the core values at ALBA is giving back. Before, I couldn't do that! But now that I can, I have made it a priority to partner with our clients and the charities they support. In addition, my daughter and I also do an annual project. In 2013, there was a typhoon in the Philippines. My daughter and her friend drew pictures and painted ornaments that they sold around the neighborhood and to my clients. They ended up raising $2,800 in three weeks, which we used to buy canned foods, supplies, a stove, printer, and surveillance cameras for my great grandfather's school in the Philippines. We are currently helping with the housing projects that are being built across the street from the school. ALBA Legacy's motto is: "Our family is a circle of strength, founded on faith, joined in love, kept by God." I faced it all, I stood tall and did it God's way. I now know I'm on the right path. I am beyond blessed and grateful to live the life I've always imagined. My team and I are passionate visionaries dedicated to designing #thelookofyourlegacy.

IF —
you could
be one thing
IN THIS
world,
CHOOSE TO
be kind.

— Ginger Lim-Dimapasok

Be Kind

Ginger Lim-Dimapasok

My love for food has always been a big part of me. Growing up in the Philippines, I watched my parents run their insurance business. One thing that really struck me was how my mom always walked into meetings carrying food for her clients. I eventually grew to love baking and I was constantly in the kitchen making goodies for my family and my mom's clients. I respected that and carry on these values of connection and nurturing with me to this day. I'm always the one making sure everyone is fed and that they have had enough to eat; food is a part of my culture and who I am. Even when I was headed down the path to becoming a lawyer, I was drawn to the kitchen. I realized I wasn't too keen on academics, and my parents both said yes when I asked to go to culinary school in the United States, which meant moving away from my whole family. While I was enrolled, I met my future husband, James. A year and a half later, in 2001, we got married and had Jayden in 2007 and Lia in 2009. Being a mom was the one thing I always wanted to become. When our kids were born, I decided to be a stay-at-home mom, but I never gave up my love for baking.

In 2014, James was stuck in a dead-end computer job where he didn't really see the future he envisioned. He wanted to start something that we could call our own. Rather than spending time and effort on someone else's business, he thought it would be more worthwhile to put in 100% of our time and energy into doing our own thing! We live in Chino Hills which is a suburb an hour away from Los Angeles. We had to travel more than 25 minutes just to get boba (Taiwanese bubble tea) or something good to eat. During one of our food trips, James joked about opening a Tapioca Express in our hometown so we wouldn't have to drive that far out for boba.

I've always been the fearful and conscientious type. Even though we were aware that it would be difficult to break into the foodservice industry, we stepped out of our comfort zones to pursue our own business venture. At that time, the franchise model wasn't an option so we decided to start our own and create something unique! We weren't satisfied with opening an ordinary boba shop or coffee house. I wanted to create a space that would highlight our Filipino culture. Growing up in the Philippines, *ube* (a purple yam often used to make Filipino desserts) was my vanilla! Just as Americans like the combination of peanut butter and jam, I partnered *ube* with just about anything and everything. When we developed our drink menu for the new café, we kept *ube* in mind. We also incorporated *calamansi* (Philippine lime) in our teas instead of the typical lemonade you would find in an Arnold Palmer. We really wanted to highlight the flavors we remember from home. With the drinks planned, a week before our soft opening, we still didn't have a food menu. At the last minute, James asked me to bake anything I could come up with! I got creative and started baking Thai tea brownies, *ube* truffles, *ube* cinnamon rolls, and cookies with potato chips. I baked at home, alongside my niece, Angel, in an oven that only fit two cookie trays. To our disbelief, at the opening, the response to our products was truly astounding and the outcome was far beyond our expectations. I thought I baked to complement our drink menu, which was really the focus of our business. However, people were more focused on our pastry case at Café 86.

The name of the café was inspired by James' beloved car, his Toyota AE86. In 2014, Café 86 was born in Chino, California, where James is part of a local car community of AE86 drivers. The following year, we opened the Pasadena store. At that point, my oven at home could not accommodate all of the desserts I had to bake for both locations so we opened a commissary kitchen to keep up with our pastry demand. In 2016, we opened our third café in Artesia. We took a break in 2017 to figure out our next move, which led to the opening of our first location outside of California. In 2018, we opened a café in Las Vegas, Nevada. In 2019, we opened our fifth location in San Diego, California. In 2020, we opened our sixth location in Mira Mesa, California.

Through God's grace, it is amazing to see how far we have come, considering neither James nor I were business savvy. We had to take everything day-by-day, making a lot of mistakes along the way, which we learned from. One of our main challenges was tackling human resources. For us, we value family. No matter how large our company gets, we try our best to maintain a family-oriented atmosphere. I believe in humanity and that life happens; we have to be able to adjust. We have to be able to take care of the company, our staff, and our customers.

There is one customer who will forever stick out in my mind. Four weeks after opening the Pasadena location, we no longer had lines out the door. Business slowed down and I started to worry about whether we were going to make it. Since business was slow, I had time to calculate the numbers we needed to hit in order to make rent. While I was running the numbers, a guy walked into the shop; he was very distraught, and he ordered a coffee. I asked him to take a seat. He put his head down and cried. The second hour he was there, I gave him a sandwich, but he didn't eat it. He would look up briefly, but he would put his head back down and continued to cry. For the next six hours, all he did was cry; All I could see were tears dripping from his face, down onto the table. The entire time, he didn't speak a word except to order. When he was done, he packed up and said, "Thank you!" Despite business being slow, I didn't ask him to pay for anything. After that day, I always wondered what had happened to him.

In 2018, my staff from the Pasadena café called me. That same guy who came into the café three years earlier came in looking for me. He wanted to thank me for feeding him that day. It turns out his partner of eight years passed away that day and he didn't know what to do or where to go – he just wanted to cry. He was appreciative and told me, "You let me cry and you even tried to feed me. I wanted to thank you for that day. I am happy now." He also wanted to introduce me to his new boyfriend. Situations like this make me realize that the café is much more than a business. Customers come back to see us and tell us how much just being in the store means to them. So many things that happen are beyond our control, but one thing I believe we *can* control is how we treat people. I believe God put me on this Earth to nurture. It's a trait I know I have inherited from my mom. We need to be a good example and be a shining light.

Establishing this business is important for my family's future. Everything we do is for our children. During this process, we sacrificed time with the kids. There is never enough time, especially since we want to be able to give so much to them. My kids have grown up alongside the café. I admit that I hold a lot of guilt because the last few years have revolved around the business. Because of this, we missed out on a lot of family trips and holidays. My kids had to grow up prematurely because of the business. They learned to understand things that your normal child doesn't have to. Thankfully, they understand that we are doing this for them and for their future. At the same time, we are paving the way for them to be able to watch their Filipino culture flourish in ways we never got to experience back in the day. On the other hand, learning to achieve work-life balance is something we are working on, as we have come to realize that each day is a gift and that we need to make the most out of it.

My advice to others who want to start their own business is to always maintain integrity and make God the center of all that you do. Be prepared to work harder than everyone else. As Filipinos, we were built for that! We were built to do everything, but we must not forget to do it with integrity. That's how you will grow. For me, success isn't measured by our bank account. I gauge our success based on the fact that I am able to shine a light on our culture by using our business as a platform. In 2020, I competed on Food Network's spinoff of the ultimate culinary competition, *Chopped*. I am the proud winner of *Chopped Sweets!* I competed against three other skilled bakers and won through my experience with unique ingredients (like *ube*), skill, concentration, and imagination. I feel successful, especially on those days when our kids say they are proud of us and proud of Café 86. We are honored to have this opportunity to bring *ube* into the limelight. I love that we can leave this legacy with our children and that someday, they can proudly tell their kids about how mom and dad helped share *ube* with the world.

Above all else, I hope our kids will remember that everything we did was for them, that they remember the lessons we all learned through all of this, and that at the end of the day, family matters most.

"you should be able
to admire someone
else's beauty, intelligence,
and success without
questioning your own."
— Ami Desai

Be Tenacious

Ami Desai

When I was a teenager at Ayala High School in Chino Hills, California, I wrote a paper about having my own studio where I would get women ready: dress them, do their hair, makeup, and nails. That's Glamsquad and the Drybar all in one! If I had pursued that, who knows where I would be right now?! Even though that wasn't my path, ever since I was a young child, I always knew that I wanted to do something creative and be involved in the arts. Looking back, I wish I was able to stick to my passion without being told that I couldn't do that because it wasn't a commendable job. I grew up in an Indian household where I was brought up to believe that I had to do something in law, engineering, or the medical field. My parents were both engineers and my older brother is a cardiologist, but I wanted to figure out how to do something creative in one of those fields; I decided I wanted to be a veterinarian.

However, my career choice kept changing. When I began college, I decided to pursue broadcasting journalism. After graduating from the University of California, Berkeley with a mass communications degree in 2003, I started in the entertainment industry working for E! and then CNN for a couple of years before going to grad school. After graduating from Boston University, I didn't stay in a small market to do journalism. Instead, I chose to be behind the scenes so I could stay in Los Angeles for my family. I went straight into producing for *Inside Edition*, a syndicated television newsmagazine. Over the next four years, I covered a lot of red carpets and did some investigative pieces. Through this work and planning my own wedding at the same time, I rediscovered my passion for hair and makeup. Through the process of planning our wedding, I realized there was a lack of hair and makeup options. That's when I created my own business! In 2010, I left producing to start my own business: Makeup by Ami. Having my own business has given me the flexibility to focus on building my family while still having a career, and I've been able to get back to my passion to be creative.

After a year-long audition process, in March 2014, I officially became a host for The Oprah Winfrey Network (OWN)'s *#OWNshow*, which is a digital exclusive web-show. I was riding high from the *#OWNshow* experience when I received a call from the OWN producers. I was pregnant with my second child, Mila, when they asked me to go on Oprah's "The Life You Want" tour. The tour kicked off in August 2014, just six weeks after I gave birth. It was not a decision I made lightly, but I accepted the opportunity and found myself traveling up to four days each week, up until Mila was six-months- old. This experience helped me realize that it takes a village to raise children and that I shouldn't be afraid to ask for help so that I can reach my own dreams. Though I was initially scared to have kids, they really lit a fire under my ass. I am willing to sacrifice being home so that my kids can look up to me and know that they can do whatever they dream! I worked for OWN for another four years. I went on a lot of casting calls but things weren't working out; fate, hard work, and networking weren't working in my favor. I was trying to pitch the mom category, which wasn't popular at the time. I guess I was ahead of the game because back then, the mom space was starting to have a buzz around it and now, it's exploded: there are digital creators, web series, and endless blogs written by moms for moms. At the time, no one was giving me the time of day or paying attention to me because I didn't have the social media following to back me up. As a result, I had to promote myself and create my own work!

When I was in grad school, I was a one-woman show: I shot, edited, and produced my own content. Now, I am able to use these skills to do what I am doing now as a content creator! I started mixing all of my passions into one thing: recreating celebrity looks, getting ready with me, looks for less, and product reviews. It's a culmination of what I was doing in the early 2000s except for this time, I get to authentically generate my own content. About one year into blogging full-time, brands started to notice I had a voice and a following. That's when they started to reach out and finally wanted to work with me! A year prior, I was dabbling in social media but not really committing, whereas in 2017, I went in full force and the brands noticed!

As a freelancer, I am able to pitch to brands about bringing their product to life for the demographic that follows me. As fun as my work is, being a content creator is not easy! There is so much behind it, including understanding the analytics, like what time and days to post, what your demographic wants to see from you, and the type of content you need to be creating. To sell yourself to a company, you have to show conversion levels. I spent a lot of time doing this in 2017 and my work and following have evolved from there. For some creators, it's a fast incline to the top and for others like me, it's a slow and steady climb. I've built my following up to 90K in two years and have had brand partnerships I could only dream of. I've learned not to compare myself or my path to anyone else. We all measure success differently so stay laser-focused on what that means to you. For me, it's about creating a career where I can have a flexible schedule while incorporating aspects of my life that I love to share – family, kids, beauty – and doing so with meaningful partnerships that I organically fit with.

I'd rather have five quality campaigns throughout a year than fifty small ones that I'm not truly into.

In my role as a content creator, I am trying to lead my business and empower other women who are similar to me to do what they want to do. I have so many people reaching out to me, especially South Asian mothers, many of whom worked on an MBA or went to law school, and are now staying at home. They want to go back to work and contribute to the family, but they aren't sure how to do that in a way that's socially acceptable. A lot of stay-at-home moms ask me if they should do network marketing, like Stella and Dot or start a blog. These are examples of unconventional work that are not known or respected by our community, but I encourage them to go for it.

When I was younger, I wish I had the voices and platforms that are out there today. I had such self-doubt. I encourage others to just do it! Don't doubt yourself! When you doubt yourself, it will prevent you from doing what you want to do. You are going to fail; It's going to happen. But focusing on the fear of failure isn't going to help you get where you want to be with your goals. Instead, get to work! There are so many tools readily available to create content on your own terms like YouTube, iPhones, and digital cameras! It's amazing to see others making a legit earning doing what they love through their side hustles. Remember, as you build a new business, don't ever think you're too good to do the most menial tasks. Everyone has their turn to roll up their sleeves to put in some work. The non-glamorous stuff is not always shown, but it needs to be learned. Even now, I do all my shooting, lighting, and editing. You have to work at it just like everyone else!

I want to challenge you to also remember the small things that can make a huge difference. Try your best to remember every single person's name. You never know who you are working with or if you will ever run into them again. You never know who's connected to who, who that person is, or who they are going to be. No matter what, be kind! It's just good karma! In the movie *Wonder*, I love the quote, "If you have the choice of being right or being kind, always choose kindness." Kindness takes you further than being right. More than ever, there's a lot of judgment being passed without knowing someone. Everyone does it! You don't really know the person even though you see them on social media. You should be able to admire someone else's beauty, intelligence, and success without questioning your own. You can replace the word beauty with whatever word you want it to be. With social media, it's hard not to compare yourself to another person. Even at 38, I have to remind myself not to do that.

Success is something I have to define for myself. For me, success is being able to contribute to my family: monetarily and socially. I don't think there is such a thing as work-life balance. When I am working, I am fully working. When I am home, I am fully present and not worrying about work. There is a give and take in my personal and professional life. I am really happy about what I am giving and still putting out the content that I want, without excuses. I sacrifice a lot on the daily. For example, there is so much more networking I could be doing, but I choose to do things related to my kids. I don't go to evening events because I am at home with my kids and holding it down when my husband is traveling. However, I want to figure out how to prioritize and work with my husband so that I can attend these events.

My husband has helped me recognize the importance of goal setting and having a business plan. I am realizing that you have to have a clear focus on what you are trying to accomplish. It helps you identify what your objective is. If you know what your mission is, and have a clear sense of how to get there, you will have a clear understanding of what you're doing versus trying to figure it out. If you don't have a clear focus, you are wasting time. He sent me this quote that I love: "Attract what you expect. Reflect what you desire. Become what you respect. Mirror what you admire." (anonymous). I try to live by that personally and professionally.

Aside from being a wife and mommy to my two kids, I am continuing to grow my business as a content creator, but I want to evolve into something else. I don't think I want to be in front of the camera in five years, but more so be back behind the scenes. It's a bit scary doing this work while raising my little kids. I am putting all of us out there, and it's a bit daunting having my kids in the limelight. I want to make sure I am doing it for the right reasons. This world can be self-absorbed. I don't want my kids to get the wrong idea of what they need to do to succeed in this world. I want them to do what they really love. I don't want them to do something because other people are doing it. I want them to be authentic and not have self-doubt. As I shift into this next phase of my career, I am expecting my third child and I am in the process of creating a beauty/skincare line with my dear friend who is a dermatologist and also a mom of three. I am combining my passion for beauty and skincare in one! Though, we aren't rushing into it because family comes first!

One thing I will leave you with is: Could you have done more personally and professionally? When you get older, it always comes down to "I could have or I should have." I don't know about you, but I don't want to go through that! Go after what you want, take your ideas and bring them into existence!

humble yourself in the sight of the Lord and He will lift you up.

— Christine Gambito

Be Happy

Christine Gambito

Growing up, every day before leaving the house, my Filipino mom would remind me to wear a half-slip under my skirt. However, the way she would pronounce the phrase was misleading. In her Filipino accent, she would say, "Christine, don't forget your hap e-slip. Be sure to wear your hap e-slip!" Naturally, I thought a half-slip was called a "happy slip." Who would have thought her little reminder would one day become the name of my entertainment company? "Happy Slip" has a dual meaning; Not only does it serve as a funny memory from the past, but it reflects my want for people to slip into happiness while they watch my videos and see me perform.

As young as seven-years-old, I was entertaining my family: during our gatherings, they would ask me to entertain bored guests. I would get in front of everyone and imitate my mom and other relatives at their request. It was imitation on demand! At that time, I didn't know that I was doing standup comedy, but I knew I enjoyed it. I also knew I wanted to become an actress. When I was 13-years-old, I forced my dad to take headshots of me. During that phase of life, my mom mandated that I wear the large, thick, plastic bifocal glasses the eye doctor had prescribed, instead of allowing me to wear contacts. Although I was totally awkward in my appearance, I was hopeful in my aspirations. I excitedly submitted those headshots to a local agency hoping I would get a call! To my dismay, I didn't get any calls or auditions. Eventually, thanks to a miracle from God, my mom allowed me to get contacts and braces. These physical changes helped me land some cool acting gigs, but I needed to go beyond my local market to keep finding work. I continued to act, but as an adult, I still had to please my family by getting a "real job." Like most obedient Filipino daughters, I studied nursing and became an LPN (Licensed Practical Nurse). I didn't pursue any more education because I wanted nursing to be a backup profession to the main thing I wanted to pursue – acting.

At age 24, after getting referred to a manager, I made the big move to the Big Apple. I thought that being in New York would give me more opportunities to audition. Although I was ahead of the game by belonging to SAG and AFTRA (the film and TV unions for acting), as well as being represented by a reputable commercial agent, opportunities were very limited. Jobs would mainly be for the "token Asian woman" and they were very creatively dissatisfying. To make ends meet, I worked as a nurse while I waited for auditions.

Trying the mainstream acting route had required me to try and fit into specific boxes according to how others saw me or how they defined their own projects; this left me lacking creatively, in a severe sense. With the acting jobs I'd go out for, I felt like I couldn't truly showcase myself and everything I could do. It wasn't until I started my YouTube channel a few years later that I felt the creative freedom I had always wanted. With YouTube's slogan of "Broadcast Yourself," I truly felt a sky of opportunity open up. I could act however I wanted, writing my own skits, and directing and editing them all on my own. Anything was possible and left up to my imagination. After creating and uploading my first video, I was able to watch the video count grow to 55 views within five minutes and I was flabbergasted! Who around the world was watching this? That first upload had a thrill to it that surmounted any of the thrills of landing acting jobs previously because this had my name all over it. It was completely and thoroughly my own project and reflected more of my talent than any of the token Asian roles that I had before. I got to wear all the hats and control every part of the process of creation.

The whole journey of acting is too complex to summarize it into a few paragraphs and I definitely don't define my life just from these career developments. There have been times of sacrificing or "giving up" the dream in order to prioritize what matters most in life. In wanting to first and foremost honor God in my life, and to build a family, I walked away from my acting dream thinking I had to give it up permanently. If I had pursued it in my own way and in my own timing, I probably would not be married with four kids right now. Of all of my roles, the most rewarding roles are that of being a wife and mother. And little did I know that God would give me back the dream in much better and more far-reaching ways, not in order to give me glory or set myself on a pedestal but to be really humbled and point to Him, who should get all the glory. I want to build in eternal things and for me, that means building into people's lives. Building into a career that will fade away eventually is not where I want to place all my efforts. Investing myself into others is where eternity lies, and there is a defining moment of this that sticks out in my memory.

In 2009, three years into making YouTube videos, I received an email from a lady named Leti. She had two sons, just like I had two sons at the time. She was dying from cancer and was given a diagnosis of only a few days to live. In her email, she said, "Your videos have given me joy during the most difficult and painful points of my treatments." She had watched so many of my videos, and one, in particular, contained an original song that was about wishing someone well as they entered heaven. She asked for my permission to have that song sung by a local artist during her celebration of life ceremony. When I read her email, I cried and showed my husband because I couldn't believe she was planning her own service and wanting my song to be part of it. Immediately, I responded to her email to let her know that I was coming to Hawaii so I could meet her and sing the song for her. Unfortunately, she never saw my email. A week later, her husband emailed to inform me of her passing. He asked for permission to use my song. I called him right away, and I ended up flying to Hawaii to meet her family and attend her celebration of life. During that week, different family members and friends came to their house just to visit and pay respects. The grief was so intense and lasted for such a long time that eventually her parents asked me to tell humorous stories about my family. They needed some lighter moments and some comic relief. At that moment, I realized this is why I do comedy.

I used to think my skits were silly or dumb at times. I didn't think they would have a significant impact, as in Leti's life, but through that experience, I saw the practical help that comedy provided for her family. They wanted to enjoy the laughter that Leti enjoyed even amongst the pain and hardship. Somehow the humor made the time bearable and everyone could enjoy it together. I felt I was able to help these people who lost their daughter, mother, sister, and friend. Since then, I have formed a lifelong relationship with her family and they treat me as one of their own. I believe that's why God invented comedy – to bring people together to enjoy moments of laughter and even healing. That to me is where the treasure is. Not in the number of subscribers or likes you have on social media, but the quality of impact you have on even one person's life.

Currently, my performing has gone back to my roots of stand up comedy. No video beats the experience of live performance and honing the skills to be able to improvise on the spot with different audiences. In 2018, I did my first tour, performing in 20 cities, with plans of more cities to come. What is most wonderful about touring is connecting with people face-to-face and seeing their reactions live. It's just another phase that I always dreamed of but never thought I would get the chance!

I have learned through my own journey that if you put blinders up, and insist that things have to happen the exact way you plan, then you can miss out or shortchange yourself of the better way things can unfold. I think that life is like that, not just a career. You make your plans, but you also need to stay open to changes and the exact way God will have things play out. Success is in learning through a journey of supposed failures. Through those failures, you find the treasure along the way: perseverance, true friendship, loyalty, and things that actually matter and last. It's not an end goal. It's not about the praise of man or the golden "Oscar" that I dreamed of as a kid. It's about the people you touch along the journey of many failures. It's living a life that would honor God and bringing joy to people. I do what I do to give glory to God and to bring joy and happiness to others.

Be a leader even when no one is watching.

—Raquel Cutchon-Quinet

Be Driven

Raquel Cutchon-Quinet

Ask either of my sons to describe me, and without a doubt, they will say, "She is very driven!" My drive is fueled by my life experiences which are deeply rooted in family. I come from a family of immigrants and our home was the gateway for all the family members that my mom petitioned to come over to the United States (U.S.). We were poor, lived off food stamps, and received government rations of bread and butter. I was raised by a household of strong women who worked extremely hard to get out of poverty. My mom started her nursing career in the U.S. making just $3 an hour. Even though she had two jobs, it was still not enough. Despite the language barrier, both of my grandmothers figured out a way to make money using their skills of sewing and catering. My dad, a retired Bechtel engineer, had his own video rental business. Back then, no one had internet or other streaming options so customers came to my dad's shop to rent VHS tapes. I was working for the family business long before I received my official worker's permit at 15-years-old.

My dad had a big impact on my personal development. He pushed me to the limits in school, sports, and life. When I was in sixth grade, my brothers and I came home on report card day. I was always a straight-A student, but that day, I came home with one B. My dad told me, "I can't believe you would actually bring this home." From that day forward, I had a chip on my shoulder. I wanted to prove him wrong and after that, I always came home with straight A's. Junior year in high school, I had three jobs, got straight A's, and I even graduated early. I convinced my school to let me work instead of going to school. I had many jobs: Karts N' Golf, Kid's Castle, Forever 21, Ross, and eventually, I got into cellular phone sales at the age of 16. In cellular phone sales, I was a triple minority: a woman, young, and Filipino. I had to learn how to drink coffee, understand stocks, and how to carry on intelligent conversations with older, white males who were often the decision-makers for the business and family. When I was younger, I overcompensated in my career so that I could fit in. Today, I would advise others to be who you are, but with caution. There is a time and place for everything. For example, some of the jokes I would say around my friends wouldn't be received well by some of my colleagues. I had to learn these lessons to be successful in the workplace at a young age.

My parents' relationship was also a major driving force behind my motivation. My dad and I did not always have the best relationship due to his infidelity. Early on, I learned how to be independent. I studied business because I wanted to be able to provide for our family. I didn't want to see my mom struggle, even though she was the breadwinner of the family. They divorced when I was in my second year in college, a month later, my dad got remarried. However, my parents are now, somehow, back together. I used to think my mom was weak because she stayed with my dad. Only now that I have my own family, I realize how strong my mom was for our family. I have so much respect for her and how she embodies unconditional love. She takes on challenges with grace and I wish I had that quality. This experience motivated me to strive hard so that I could build a life where I would not struggle if anyone were to come to me for help.

As far back as high school, I knew that I was different. I was already reading *Success* magazine and interviewing CEOs including the CEO of American Express while most of my circle of friends were looking for what they were going to do on the weekends. When I graduated from high school, the rebellious side of me told my parents that I didn't want to go to college. To prove my point that college does not guarantee you success, I handed them a list of successful people who didn't finish college. I had been a good student so my high school counselor took it upon himself to fill out my college application to California State University, Hayward (now East Bay) – he felt like college would be a good place for me and that I would regret it later in life. Of course, I got accepted and my counselor's words of wisdom haunted me. I realized I had my whole life to work and knowledge is something people can't take away from you. I didn't want to miss out on what my friends were experiencing when they were talking about their college stories. I started taking as many classes as I could even though I really didn't want to be there.

In addition to college, I got my real estate license and started building my business. As my clientele grew, I eventually dropped out of school to pursue real estate. I worked at a local real estate agency with my classmates' parents, but they didn't take me seriously because to them, I was just a kid. They didn't think I would make it in this business so I moved to another real estate brokerage in the next city over, thinking it would be different. Instead, it was worse! I had an Asian female realtor tell me that "Looking young in this business is a handicap. No one is going to trust you to sell their home because you don't even own a home." Little did she know, I already owned two properties outside of California. However, her comments drove me to become more knowledgeable. She lit up the drive I already knew I had in me. That year, I was awarded the top salesperson of the year in my brokerage! There's not a better feeling in the world when a person that doubted you, asks you how did you succeed? When she asked me how I was able to help so many clients buy or sell a home, I told her, "It's because I look young."

I was doing well for myself in real estate. I got a taste of what success felt like and I still felt I wanted more. I thought about how I would tell my story to my future kids. There was something inside of me that didn't want to ever tell them I didn't finish college. It was at that moment when I started planning for school and thinking about how I was going to manage my business. I began hiring a team of people to help me so I could make time for school. The research began on how I could go to school and continue to build a business. I discovered the University of Phoenix, which allowed me to work and go to school at the same time. Unfortunately, they did not accept students younger than 23-years-old. I wrote an appeal letter asking them to consider me for their program. Through my efforts, I was the youngest person to be accepted to their school. Despite the brief hiatus and an overload of classes, I was able to graduate from college on time.

I always knew I wanted to be two things: a CEO and a mom! I wanted the freedom to own something and the ability to provide opportunities for people. When I was younger, after a bike accident, a doctor told me that I would never have kids. I told myself, if I was given the opportunity to be a mom, I would never allow work to take over my kids. I've given up huge deals, salaries, and partnerships because they did not align with my family values. I know God will take care of us someway, somehow. Remembering this has allowed me to take important leaps of faith! In 2007, after building my real estate business in California for eight years, we decided to move to Arizona. I had never led anyone, but I took on a role as CEO of Keller Williams Realty Professional Partners. Many agents told me that I was too young to have this role, but I said, "Let's see how we do." Three years later, we were ranked the

number one office in the Southwest Valley. By the time I moved
on from this role, I had 300 agents working for me.

I thought leaving the Bay Area was a sacrifice, but I wish I would
have taken risks earlier so that I could have failed faster. I always
tell my sons that they should never fail due to the lack of effort
because effort requires no skills. Fail at everything else, but don't
fail at giving it your best. If you have a dream, just go for it and
take action even if it scares the crap out of you. You will learn so
much more through fear than preparing for the unknown. There
is no substitution for experience. It's so much easier to succeed
today with access to information, networks, and mentors. Take
a chance on yourself because no one else will! What else do you
have to lose?

Life will always bring challenges. It's a matter of how you react to
them. Success is not about the money you make, but it equates
to happiness and what defines your happiness. Live on your own
terms; don't ever compare yourself to others. You can model
yourself after others, but you're on your own journey. I can proudly
say that I am successful because, despite life's challenges, I kept
going. I'm blessed to serve others and impact my communities. I
am an investor in real estate and different businesses, coach to top
real estate agents across the country, have a property management
business and created a community for female entrepreneurs to
thrive. I also serve as the Chief Revenue Officer at a start-up in the
real estate industry. Despite the titles and accolades, my greatest
success is my family.

Growing up, my parents were always working. My grandparents
really had a hand in raising me, picking me up from school
every day. I never want my kids to see me working all the time. I
purposely made my sons learn how to play golf so we can spend
four hours of quality time together. When we're on the green,

there are no cell phones allowed! The most beautiful thing in life is when you can truly be connected to others. There's a reason why you meet people and why they came across your path. No matter what, always be kind! Take the time to listen and be a leader even when no one is watching!

— Not — everyone looks like THEIR story.

—Evelyn Obamos

BE REFLECTIVE

Evelyn Obamos

As social creatures, humans interact with the world by relating experiences with each other. Struggles beget community. Victories beget comparison. For better or worse, children of immigrant parents in America get expert-mode at having to navigate a blended reality. Most of us even have an identity crisis at some point — just ask the ones who come from religious families and get tattoos in rebellion.

As I age and further reflect, I recognize my adolescent resentment continues to evolve. Because of this, I started evaluating relationships with each of my immediate family members, specifically with my mom — appropriately so, since she brought me into this world. Like any dysfunctional family, it hasn't always been pleasant. But thankfully every moment is a blessing, a lesson, or somewhere in between.

Age: 8
Location: Checkout counter at Bunny Market, Dededo, Guam

Mom: *Tara na. Bilisan mo, anak. (Let's go. Hurry up, child.)*
Me: Mom, we're in America. We speak English here.

BE REFLECTIVE

It didn't hit me until college that my youth had *colonial mentality* written all over it. It infected my speech, my skin, and how I showed up in the world. I grew up around a predominantly brown community among Filipinos, Chamorus, and Micronesians on Guam. Despite this, many of us grappled with valuing Western standards of existing: lighter skin was more beautiful, English indicated affluence, and we were inundated with many other self-sabotaging realities. At one point, I even told people I was Spanish because we learned how Spain colonized Guam and the Philippines for 300 years. Silly me, I wanted so hard to be anything other than Filipino that I identified as our colonizer.

Age: 12
Location: Taxi ride from Ninoy Aquino Airport, Manila, Philippines

Mom: *Tingnan mo yan. Pinabayaan ng mga magulang itong mga bata na ito. Magpasalamat kayo na hindi ganyan kayo lumaki. Mas mabuti sa America.*

(Look at that. These kids are just neglected by their parents here on the streets. Be grateful this isn't how you were raised. It's better in America.)

Me: But we live in a shipping container that leaks because dad built it with his bare hands. At least these kids on the street look happy.

Mom: *pinches my thigh, quietly*

I never understood how we regularly visited the Philippines just to buy our family three (yes, three) shopping carts full of groceries. We lived on Guam where home-cooked meals were a byproduct of government-sanctioned food stamps and food banks for low-

109

income families. Yet here we were, on a family reunion trip to the Philippines, splurging. Money was still a foreign concept to me, but any kid could easily recognize the power it made you feel — especially when other people were watching. I remember our relatives following us around the store, beaming with pride when they asked us about living in America. Their eyes followed me around, searching for similarities in our features. I could also tell they looked at mom differently. They still knew who she was, but she wasn't the same.

As she paid for all the food, a long receipt and VISA in hand, I saw her pride in bringing our whole family to buy whatever they needed. In their eyes, she made it. They didn't see how she had to sacrifice her law degree. They didn't know she worked random jobs to make ends meet. They would probably never even see the rusted shipping container we called a home. But it didn't matter, because there was an unspoken, universal rule in the value of American dollars.

Age: 17
Location: Apartment W-3, Kulana Village, Ewa Beach, Hawaii

Me: *running through the house, yelling* Mom! I got the Bill Gates Scholarship. I got it!
Mom: *grabs me, already sobbing* Thank you, Lord! *Magpasalamat ka.* (Let's pray.)

When you've lived your life in scarcity, abundance can be overwhelming. Being awarded the Gates Millennium Scholarship felt like my golden ticket. *Ate* (older sister in Tagalog) Edilen had gotten into the Naval Academy the year before, and we already commiserated on how we wanted to get out from "the ghetto" as soon as we got into college. It didn't take long to decide on attending the University of San Francisco. I often joke that I easily picked the most expensive school (and city) I was accepted into since a white man was paying for my tuition, housing, and personal expenses. Little did I know how academic capital played a role in climbing the ladder, so ultimately I'm glad I made that choice. Mom even tried bribing me to stay on the island to go to a cheaper school. Understandably so. She found comfort in the familiar, especially after dad and *lolo* (grandpa in Tagalog) passed away while we were in high school.

Dad's absence loomed over us, even when we tried to find refuge in moving to Hawaii. Three months we lived in a tiny motel. Three years we lived with the pastor's family. Finally, I couldn't wait to get out of our section 8 housing. We both didn't want to be alone, yet a creeping sensation of loneliness flooded me when I knew I couldn't ask mom for help anymore. I held on to the manila envelope with my name written in gold beneath the text that said, congratulations! I knew I wouldn't miss our apartment's paper-thin walls that seemed to amplify the sounds of our neighbors having sex or beating their kids.

For the first time in my life, I told mom how I understood why she wanted to move to America. What I wasn't prepared for was shifting from being a big fish in a little pond to being a little fish in a big pond.

Age: 25
Location: Pinterest HQ, San Francisco, CA

Mom: Ano ba ang "Pin-test"? (What is "Pin-test"?)
Me: It's a tech company mommy! I just got an offer to get converted to full-time from being a contractor for the last year. They're giving me a really good salary and RSUs!
Mom: *Ano ba yan?* RSUs? (What is that? RSUs?)

111

Me: I don't know either, but maybe it's something to
do with 401k?
Mom: *Baka nga*. (Maybe).

When I first brought my family to visit me at work, they couldn't believe we could eat three buffet-style meals a day — for free! They were impressed with our hip headquarters and inspired by all my colleagues they met. I could see mom light up at the opportunity to mention that she was an attorney in the Philippines, and blush with every mention to her of how well she raised us. She would reply in her best American-English, over-enunciating as if to hide her Filipino accent. After my colleagues walked away, my mom joked about how *"nag dudugo ang ilong niya"* (Her "nose was bleeding" from trying to speak English for so long). We laughed. I was touched to hear how proud she was, even if she didn't even know what my job entailed.

I also laughed because I couldn't help but smile at the fact that mom's resilience was the reason I was there. As I watched mom and *Ate* grab another plate of duck bao buns with a side of oyster sauce, I reflected on how mom felt buying our family in the Philippines three carts of groceries. Even if the environment I'm in now occasionally feels foreign to me, it's always comforting to share special moments with my family.

As I age, I recognize the natural distance I felt as a Filipino-American torn between two cultures was slowly, but surely, closing. In herstorian and academia *babaylan* (Filipina community "miracle worker") Leny Strobel's *Coming Full Circle*, she says, "A Filipino who comes to be centered within his identity and self, will want to know more and DO more for his or herself and for others." Instead of seeing the cultural, generational, and philosophical gaps between mom and my experiences, I saw the parallels in our perseverance, sacrifice, and care for building on our legacies.

LIVE WITH Integrity.

—Nancy Choi

Be Patient

Nancy Choi

I've had numerous jobs in my life; some that worked really well for me and others weren't the right fit. In these jobs, I have been promoted and fired. Some positions weren't the easiest, nor was I naturally talented or skilled for them. I've been told, "You can't do it" plenty of times, but when I have the desire to succeed, I keep at it.

When I was younger, my parents didn't always support or approve of everything I wanted to be. I dreamt of being a ballerina, but my parents said I couldn't make a living as a dancer. I wanted to be a businesswoman, but my parents told me that Asian women don't go to business school. Rather, women should have stable jobs and become a doctor, a lawyer, or a pharmacist, like my mom. When my parents came to the United States, they lost everything. I think that's why they put a lot of pressure on me and discouraged me from following my dreams. They wanted me to stick with what they believed was the safe route to success.

Ultimately, I needed to leave home and fly on my own. Despite my parents' opposition, I went into business. I studied economics at the University of California, Berkeley (Cal). It was my heart's desire that brought me to where I am today. Coming out of college, I became an actuary, which involves math, statistics, and financial theory. It is also a career path that requires several years of arduous exams to become a Fellow of the Society of Actuaries (FSA). I decided it wasn't for me.

At that time, a friend told me that I couldn't become an investment banker – that I wasn't smart enough. Funny thing is, we both attended Cal. In spite of that comment, I submitted my resume and landed a job at a premier boutique investment bank. As I furthered in my career, I spun off and started a consulting company where I helped early-stage companies by packaging deals, creating pitch decks, drafting private placements and more. That led to endeavors in various industries and eventually, I met my business partner, Ricky Miller, and we began working on developing a vodka brand, House of Carbonadi. We worked intensely for several years together to create the product, the brand, and the vision. I poured my heart and soul into this business, and found my passion! I am proud to say that I am the co-founder of the House of Carbonadi.

Similar to other start-up companies, we took an existing product and disrupted the industry. It was a creative endeavor for us to develop a new methodology that would impact the spirits and wine space moving forward. We took vodka from an almost century-old, fourth-generation distillery and elevated the liquid to perfection. After five years of iterations, we created a custom filtration process through carbonados: "black diamonds." Carbonadi was born.

Once the product was developed, one of our mentors, David Baker, shared a critical marketing strategy that worked well for him when he was first starting out in business. He shared how he identified key individuals and potential business partners, and mailed each one a personalized, handwritten letter with a small hand-picked gift that would resonate with them. The personal touch allowed him to connect with people deeply, and he advised us to do the same. We started out with a long list but decided to focus on three to four key people. The first person we reached out to was Isadore "Issy" Sharp, founder of the Four Seasons Resort. Prior to reaching out, we read his book, *Four Seasons: The Story of a Business Philosophy*, as well as his wife, Rosalie Wise Sharp's book, *Rifke an Improbable Life*. The letter we wrote to him displayed our gratitude toward the lessons we learned from their books and our admiration of his life's journey that will ultimately be his legacy. He responded with a couple of signed books and an invitation to meet with him at his house in Toronto! It was surreal and questions ran through my head: Was this for real? Who invites strangers to their house? Did our letter really work? As skeptical as I was, everything panned out nicely. We booked our stay in Toronto at the Four Seasons (of course!), not too far from his house, and even the day of our arrival, we still couldn't believe it was real.

Mr. Sharp was extremely nice and gracious. He spent a great amount of time getting to know us, listening to our story and our vision. He then shared his path to success. He strongly believes in encouraging his staff and promoting from within. He had recently promoted the presidents for their properties and they were all invited to a celebratory dinner at his house that same evening. He explained to us that he would present Carbonadi for a tasting during that dinner, and if they agreed it was to the standard of excellence for the Four Seasons, we would be hearing from them shortly. On the following Monday, the emails and phone calls began flooding in, and it changed our trajectory. I am proud to say, Carbonadi is available in many prestigious properties, including the Four Seasons Resorts, Montage Resorts, Rosewood Resorts, Soho House, Cecconi's, Eataly, Bellagio, Wynn, Encore, and Aria. We wouldn't be where we are if we didn't take the advice about reaching out to key people with heartfelt, handwritten letters.

Despite all of this "success," my parents still don't fully understand how I'm wired and the life that I've chosen. Regardless, I am glad I found the courage to spread my wings and live the life I want. I am doing more than I ever imagined. Seeing where I am now, I sometimes pinch myself. As I reflect on the ebbs and flows, I realize that I've spent a good amount of my life going against the grain, standing up for myself, and fighting with others. There are scary moments where I failed and moments of elation when I succeeded. There were exorbitant amounts of emotional and financial ups and downs, which affected not only myself, but also my husband and daughter as well. The growing pains were extremely difficult for our family, but eventually, we managed to get through them and we've learned that our love, respect, and sacrifices for each other truly endured the test of time.

The more challenges I overcome, the more I realize my life's journey is unique and taking me down the path I was meant to be on. Although Carbonadi continues to grow and has micro-successes every day, the greatest success is my family. With all the trials and tribulations we have gone through, I realize the vital importance of having patience and understanding. Those have been the key to happiness. I look back and realize that sometimes I fought unnecessary battles. Patience, understanding, and faith in God have given me the greatest joy and peace. I'm able to be who I am because of the peace I now feel.

Living
THE
magical life
IS NOT BEING IN A
fantasy
— OR —
fairy tale,
BUT THE CHOICE TO
live life
AT YOUR HIGHEST LEVEL
— OF —
cosmic Beingness.

—Lyn Pacificar

BE MAGICAL

Lyn Pacificar

I grew up in East Hollywood, California, during the 1990s. I loved all kinds of music, did lots of drawings and paintings, played the piano, danced, and practiced martial arts. I had mostly Latina friends and enjoyed hanging out when I had permission to do so (my father was very strict about where I went and who I was with). I wasn't popular with the *Pinays* (Filipino girls), as I was "different": I could sense spirits, communicate with dead people, see auras, and foresee future events. I used to make potions on an antique wooden chest that had mother-of-pearl inlay, recalling ceremonies of lifetimes past. Imagine, a 5-year-old Filipina child telling her mom at the library, "I used to live there," pointing out a picture of Alexandria in a book on ancient Egypt. I got my first tarot deck at 15-years-old, gifted to me by my mother, a devout Catholic woman with an open mind to folkways of fortune-telling and healing. These talents and skills actually run in her lineage. I have a number of aunties who admit to being able to foresee and sense impending dangers. It's nice to know I'm not the only one, but I am definitely the only one in my family who is open to the public about my "gifts from God," as my mother calls them.

At a young age, I was the designated family masseuse and healer. Growing up, I used to observe and learn from my dad who practiced ancient methods of healing that were passed down to

119

him. He was referred to as a *manghihilot*, a traditional healer who uses different methods of prayer, massage, special oils, and energy work. He practiced the old ways of folk Catholicism, which is still utilized in the Philippines. I was exposed to magic, medicine, and *lana* (oils). At a young age, my dad mentored me as a *hilot* (Filipino term for healer) and in creating the different types of oils used in his healing practice. These bottles were prepared in ritual and with specific intentions and became the foundation for my future business, Herbalaria. I began to practice plant medicine and healing abilities as a child. During my teen years, I earnestly pursued my studies in creating intention-infused potions for friends and loved ones.

As a child of Filipino immigrants, it's unusual to have someone like me "come out" to the public as a *katuuran*, a Visayan shaman, under the guidance and tutelage of my ancestral sponsor *Katuuran Apong Mansanat*. Actually, it's pretty much unheard of since I was raised as a Filipina-American in a very Catholic family. I am also an *albularya (or arbolaryo)*, a traditional folk herbalist and spiritual healer who uses a combination of modalities including prayers, ritual, diagnostic readings, smudging, ancestral communication, and mediumship to achieve a certain goal for the recipient. In essence, a child of the diaspora carrying these ancient traditions is like being a bridge between the motherland, the ancestors, and the descendants who live on new lands. I've even been given an unofficial name, *"Tulay,"* meaning "bridge."

Through the influence of my family, I became a full-force healer. My dad expressed to me that I would receive full energetic transference upon his death. Little did I know it would happen three days after that conversation. When my dad passed away in September 2015, I received ancestral blessings and abilities. The moment of transference occurred at Tinuy-an Waterfalls, in Bislig, Surigao del Sur, on the island of Mindanao, Philippines. I distinctly remember swimming in a waterfall where I felt connected with the spirits of the land and waded in the deep and pristine blue waters of the Hinatuan Enchanted River. When I felt my father leaving this Earth, I had a deep pain in my chest, as if something was ripping my heart out and I couldn't breathe. While in the water, I felt overwhelmed with love from ancestors and the land. I was ready. I breathed in the air and allowed it to permeate my being with ancient knowledge and blessings. This was my initiation as a healer.

Even as a healer, challenges are present. One in particular that cycles through my life every so often is trusting in the process and in people. I faced adversity with past business partnerships that were not in alignment with the original vision of the company, and ultimately caused the downfall of it. In 2012, things took a very wrong turn and it was then that my former company, Allied Acres LLC, began to crumble and fall. The company was originally founded to provide organic, hydroponically-grown food fed through an aquaponics system of fish ponds. That vision was never seen through. Many wrong decisions were made in attempts to "get rich quick." The former partner turned the business plan into canned hunting of Berkshire pigs, influenced by the next-door neighbor who was a hunter. The company would make a profit from Chinese tourists who were bussed in to kill these animals on our 408 enclosed acres of land in Central California. I didn't agree to it, but the former partner was insistent. In an attempt to stop these people, we locked up the land. We drove three hours to Cuyama Valley only to find all the gate locks cut, and our land was broken into. The partner and neighbor were in cahoots, freely using the land according to their will. Bullet casings were lying all over the grounds where they would practice shooting their AK-47 rifles into the distance. Without meaning to, we shifted far from growing food, to something that was horribly dishonorable, deleterious, and seriously offensive to the Spirits of the land and to our own core values. It was a great test of my marriage, and of my relationship with my mother, who was the main investor in it all. I fell into deep darkness to find and face my truth. It took so much time to heal. Although it was tremendously painful to go through this, I am grateful for the invaluable experience now. There's a quote by Dr. A.P.J. Abdul Kalam, "If you fail, never give up because F.A.I.L. means 'First Attempt In Learning.'" The Universe served up a lesson: trusting in the process of learning what it means to be true to oneself and mission. It also made me realize the importance of checking my ego, and the egos of those I work with. After, I questioned myself and my intuition. I didn't know who to trust, much less if I could trust myself. After the betrayal, failure, and great financial loss, I finally heard what my ancestors and Higher Self had been telling me all along. I wasn't living in authenticity and I need to. I conceded to the disillusionment of making money in ways that were not good for the Earth or its creatures. You can't learn about these processes in business school – only the school of life teaches you the hardest lessons. I found my North Star, and would no longer allow myself to be led down a path that is incongruent to my values and personal mission of healing people, environmental rehabilitation, and cultural preservation.

To complement my healing practice, I birthed Herbalaria, an ancestral roots movement company, connecting community to indigenous traditions through the art of Filipino herbalism. Herbalaria is the ancestral message to reclaim ancient plant and energy medicine. It's time for people to recognize and value our culture more deeply than just awesome food and entertainment. Herbalaria is medicine for the people. Our products are culturally rooted and contemporized for modern-day self-care. We are trailblazing the way for Filipino plant-based herbal remedies and wellness to be at the forefront of mainstream industries. At the time of this publication, my company is just two people: me and my husband, Gilbert. I guess you can say we are a "mom and pop" corporation. I want to be able to meet the market's demands and at the same time maintain my vocation as a healer. Being in the right mind and the right energy to create, in ritual, a valuable product that will make a real impact in others is an essential part of our mission.

When I started Herbalaria, I sacrificed security (and I still do on many levels). There was no investor money, no bank loans, and no financial backing. All I had was passion, drive, commitment, and $10 to make this company work. In 2013, before Herbalaria's inception, it was initially called Healing Room Apothecary, named after the place in my home where I do healing sessions and where historically my dad would see his *hilot* clients. After my dad passed away, I got the ancestral download to rename the company Herbalaria. My past experience with Allied Acres made me determined to bootstrap it and prove that I can grow this company organically. But to survive at first, I had to work at a retail job to get things rolling. I always hated working a 9 to 5 and being on someone else's schedule, but I did it. I was employed at Aaron Brothers, getting paid $8 an hour. Highly undervalued and underpaid, I brought in so much business and product knowledge, especially in the art department. But I accepted the pay because I didn't believe strongly in my own purpose or value. Eventually, I discerned that it wasn't a good use of my time. To really be sold on something, you have to be willing to sacrifice that security because your freedom is more important than anything. Freedom is one of my top values! You're not free if you allow others to dictate your worth. Make your own decisions instead of letting someone else make them for you! My piece of advice for everyone reading this book is to "do you," be yourself and live with purpose. It will all work out.

My favorite quote is from Deepak Chopra: "Success is the continued expansion of happiness." I live a happy and magical life with my husband, amazing kids, my mom, and have a home to practice and garden! We've been able to surmount some of the greatest challenges we've faced as a family and celebrate our victories in overcoming them. This is how I stay grounded and in my power as a wife, mother, healer, and culture bearer.

I want to be remembered by descendants seven generations down as someone who made a positive contribution to the world. We should all take the time to learn about our ancestors and what they did for us in order to be where we are now. What impact did they make on the family and their community? It is thanks to them that you are here to find your truth and live your best life. This is your greatest contribution in *kapwa* (Tagalog for shared identity, equality, and being with others) to other fellow human beings, the creatures of this land, and to Mother Earth. It begins with knowing who you are, where you come from, and the strength to stand in your truth. Our ancestors believed in the seen and unseen worlds, and that there is magic everywhere. Believe in yourself and harness the magic that is all around you. Explore as much as you possibly can, and always maintain gratitude for all the blessings you have. On your journey, take what you need. Leave what you don't need. Keep it simple. Keep it magical.

IF YOU *let go* —OF— CONTROL, YOU BECOME *free.*

—Danette Vives

Be Resilient

Danette Vives

Life has been an amazing journey! I never imagined all the turns and detours that would take me to where I am today. As a young girl, I was very involved in school – I was part of the student council, serving as secretary for one year and later I became the student body president. I am a people person and always ready to engage. In high school, I received many accolades including "Most Popular" and "Best Dressed." However, my whole life changed in the 10th grade. I was involved in a car accident that landed me in the Intensive Care Unit for almost a month. I was not even able to walk and was forced to miss a lot of class. I attempted to go back to school but because I missed so much, I was advised to go to continuation school. I was so unmotivated to even go! At the time, my parents' only concern was my health and recovery and they didn't quite understand how to guide me in school. My parents immigrated from the Philippines to the United States (U.S.). They started out in Hawaii, where I was born, and eventually, we settled in Los Angeles, California. In the U.S., everything was new to them and they just wanted to make sure our family was taken care of. My dad was a hard worker striving to achieve the "American Dream" and was focused on being a provider, but we were lower than the middle-class. My mom was a stay-at-home-mom of four kids: I am the eldest and only girl. My parents didn't have the wherewithal to support me to continue my high school education nor could they provide me with the direction I needed beyond that. It was such a struggle for me – I never finished high school.

When I was a kid, life was simple and I thought I would become a teacher because I loved being in front of people and talking. I didn't have the direction and was still figuring out what I wanted to do in life. I had so many interests and wanted to explore them all. That's when I decided to go straight into the workforce at just 18-years-old. Back then, I looked through the *PennySaver* magazine's classified ads to find a job. One day, I saw a job posting for a preschool teacher and I went for it. I don't know what I was thinking since I didn't have training or credentials, but things ended up working out in my favor. The administrator loved me and hired me on the account that I would bring in my credentials. Time passed and she forgot about it, at least, that's what I thought! A year later she asked for my paperwork again and even though I enjoyed being there, I didn't have the right certifications and it was time for me to move on. I immediately gave her my two weeks' notice and ended up enrolling at Valley College to obtain my teacher's certification in child development.

During my time at the preschool, I made some amazing connections. That's when I learned the power of networking, being open, and taking chances. I babysat for the parents I met, which ultimately led me into the entertainment industry. I didn't have the education or experience, but I did have a network to help me get my foot in the door. From there, I was able to move up! Thanks to the help of one of the parents, I landed an interview for a receptionist job at MS Distribution, which handled distribution for over 400 independent music labels. After working there for a year, I was promoted to be the West Coast sales representative where I serviced some of the biggest record stores: Virgin Records, Tower Records, and The Wherehouse. At 21-years-old, I was finally old enough to go to the club. So I also started an all-female promotion company called Jet Set Promotions, which promoted artists' albums at radio stations and clubs. A year later, I was hired at Spoiled Brat Entertainment (one of the independent record labels distributed through MS Distribution) as the vice president (VP) of marketing and sales. During my five years there, I learned all the ins and outs of the business: how to produce a record, marketing, and distribution. Unfortunately, Spoiled Brat went out of business and my life took a different turn. At 25-years-old, I was pregnant with my first child so it was critical for me to find a job that provided health insurance so that I could have the right care for my baby. Luckily, I landed a job at Red Ant Entertainment as the executive assistant to the VP of business affairs and the VP of finance and human resources. I worked there until they filed for bankruptcy. The president, Randy Phillips, requested that I stay on as his executive assistant for his new venture, Music One. During my time there, we co-managed Puff Daddy, Rod Stewart, and Toni Braxton to name a few artists. By this time, my daughter Leylah was three-years-old. I was burnt out! The music industry was such a man's world and I found myself dealing with a lot of egos. After spending 16 years in the industry, I chose to take a step back because it was too much, and it hardened me. In order for me to be the mom I wanted to be for my daughter, I decided it would be best for me to leave music. I needed to raise a little girl who deserved my full attention.

From music, I transitioned into the fashion industry through the help of my former boss. I worked for the Kathy Walker Showroom doing sales. After three years, I took a chance and started my own showroom at the Gerry Building in Los Angeles. I traveled to different cities to find independent designers to represent the West Coast. We had accounts with Macy's, Nordstrom, and various high-end boutiques. Eventually, I opened my own retail store, Asia Blonde, in Redondo Beach. Unfortunately, I was in over my head, trying to run a business while raising my young daughter as a single mother. It was logistically difficult because the boutique was far away from where I lived. I decided to sell my business and start over. I needed to figure out what I could do to support my daughter and be independent.

I had to take control and be the master of my fate, not a slave of my problems; I wouldn't make decisions out of fear. I had to dig deep to really reflect on and identify what I loved doing. I had to find something that brought out the best in me. As the eldest girl in my family, I was always the cousin who did everyone's hair and makeup for all occasions. It was something I was passionate about and enjoyed doing. I finally realized that my best asset was actually seeing the beauty in everybody. I am at my best when I'm helping other women! I finally knew what I needed to do. I decided to go back to school to become a licensed esthetician.

As soon as I obtained my license, I needed to quickly find a job that offered health insurance! My daughter was 7-years-old when she was diagnosed with Crohn's disease so I needed medical benefits for her. Thankfully, I landed a job at Equinox as an esthetician. As hard as it was to go back to the corporate world, I did it for my daughter's sake. Eventually, I got promoted to the spa manager, but I still wasn't making the money I needed. I knew that the best way to predict the future is to create it. I decided to start my own business by using the extra room in my house as a space to service clients. But shortly after that, while I was seven months pregnant with my second child, we learned our home was going through foreclosure. We needed to find a new place to live and I needed to find a new space for my clients. I found a workspace to rent, but as commission-based only. After maternity leave, I worked there for two more years, but I no longer wanted to work on commission. The company boldly told me, "If you want to leave, you can leave tomorrow morning." I didn't know what to feel. I kept calm and continued with my work. I knew I couldn't make rash decisions or quick moves because I needed to provide stability for my two children that I was raising and supporting on my own. I continued to work and one day, I had a client come in for a facial. I noticed she had pretty eyelash extensions so she passed on the salon's information where she had them done. I made an appointment to get my lash extensions and during my visit, I was fortunate enough to meet the owner who mentioned that she had a room for rent and not one that was commission-based. When this opportunity presented itself, I jumped right on it, securing the space by giving her two months' rent upfront. I immediately left the other space and haven't looked back since. The first week working independently in that salon, I made the most money I've ever made! And six years later, I'm still here!

I never imagined that I would start and run multiple businesses! It's definitely no easy task, especially as a single mother, but I did it! I had to take control, make my own decisions, and choose my own path. Ever since I was a young child, I have strived for more than I thought I could ever do. My advice to women aspiring to start their own business is to let go of control! If you let go of control, you become free, which then brings you to a positive state-of-mind. Also, be patient. Thinking back, I feel I rushed through life. Now that I am older (and wiser), I finally understand that everything has its own timing! If I were to go back, I would take my time. Stress makes you feel like everything has to happen right now. Faith reassures you that everything will happen in God's time. Success will come as long as you have faith, focus, and passion.

I am proud of how far I have come! My resilience is what's gotten me to where I am today. Over the years I have had to work on being in love with the person in the mirror; the person who has been through so much and is still standing! If you're looking for that one person to change your life, look in the mirror! A meaningful life is not about being rich, popular, highly educated, or perfect. It's about being real, humble, strong, and able to share ourselves and touch the lives of others. I've finally reached a point in my life where I can acknowledge my success. I am making money sharing my talents and doing something that I love, that I am good at, and that validates me! I am privileged to be able to work on my passion for 15 years and I'm still going strong! I'm in the process of expanding my business. In October 2019, I launched my own skincare line, Vives Experience, formulated with all-natural and organic ingredients. I always tell each client to invest in your skin. It's going to represent you for a very long time. Beautiful skin requires commitment, not a miracle. I am also working on a new technique called "HydroSmooth for men." I want men to be open to facials. I also want them to understand the importance of taking care of their skin.

Despite what I've accomplished, I've outgrown where I am and I'm ready to make bigger moves! I'm proud of the progress I've made with my business, but overall, my biggest success is my children: Leylah and Maxxon. At the time of writing, my son is in the fourth grade and my daughter is attending the University of California, Los Angeles on a full-ride scholarship! I am so proud of them. I always encourage them, and even myself, to just do it! Live your life and take that chance. You only live once!

find your purpose.

HOW DO YOU *love?*
HOW DO YOU *share love?*
— HOW DO YOU —
inspire AND *interact?*
WITH THOSE THAT ARE NOT
the same as you?

—Jennifer Oliveros Manilay

Be Curious

Jennifer Oliveros Manilay

I am a first-generation Filipino-American and the first American-born in my entire family. My mother was a nurse and my father was a computer engineer, exposing me to science at an early age. My first scientific "presentation" was in grade school, derived from my curiosity about the pine trees outside of my bedroom window. Reflecting back, I realize this was a super "nerdy" topic compared to my classmates, who were doing presentations on their pets, sports, or crafts. I think it was my destiny to gravitate towards a career in science. I was a very curious kid who had a lot of questions about biology.

Over time, I grew an even greater curiosity about more complex things, which included biological systems. When I entered the University of California, Berkeley (Cal), I intended to major in immunology. I started college in the late 1980s, which was the era that HIV and AIDS emerged. At the time, the scientific understanding of the virus was very unclear. Like most biology majors, I planned to pursue medicine (because that was the typical career plan). I was following my peers and going through the motions by preparing for medical school applications. I also joined the Pilipino American Health Careers (PAHC) organization, where I paired up with a medical doctor who was an allergist and immunologist. He invited me to shadow him over the summer between my junior and senior years. Through this experience, I realized that I didn't like the hospital environment. I didn't feel comfortable – something about the smell and the environment – It just wasn't a place I was excited to be in. During my internship, I listened to how the doctor was diagnosing patients. To my surprise, he was prescribing the same medication to patients who had different immune diseases. When I asked him why, he said he knew that the new medicine was working for various patients and their diseases, but he didn't quite understand how it was working at the cellular or biochemical level. I was really stunned, and I realized that medical doctors weren't focused on these types of questions. This may have been my first time understanding the value of an individual's "gifts" and purposes. My mentor's gift and purpose were to help patients alleviate their symptoms and to improve their health. I had not yet realized that curiosity was my individual gift and talent, and the purpose that it could serve.

After my summer internship, I was lost! Though I had plans to attend medical school, I absolutely had no desire to go. I turned to my immunology professor, who was a medical doctor and also a Ph.D., to talk about my career options. By asking me thought-provoking questions, she was able to help me narrow down to a couple of career interests: medical sciences or public health. These were two alternative careers that I had been unaware of. She helped me realize that I was already gaining experience in research via my work-study job and teaching, and she then helped me gain a summer research internship at the University of California, San Diego. Upon graduation, I worked at the University of California, Los Angeles as a lab research technician. Eventually, I pursued my graduate degree at Harvard. It was equally exciting and difficult.

My goal was to obtain a Ph.D. so I could become a scientist and a university professor. Along the way, my parents' emphasis on education and academics helped motivate me, but I couldn't help but think that they were disappointed I was not following my original plan for a career in medicine. During my education, identifying as a minority-woman scientist was sometimes confusing. Some people didn't understand why I identified as a minority because "Asian scientists don't have any problems." On the other hand, it was also liberating to identify as Filipino, because there were not many Filipina scientists that I could access as mentors. I found myself constantly trying to adjust to fit in and be accepted in different situations (with family, with my classmates, with my mentors). I think I learned this skill from my immigrant parents and by moving to New York, California, and Massachusetts and interacting with different communities. I believe the current term is "code-switching": adjusting to fit into the group one is interacting with, in order to be accepted. This can be exhausting, especially when I feel that I am unable to express my true self. Now that I am in a position of potential influence, I try not to be afraid to be vulnerable. I want people who interact with me to see that authenticity.

A career as a scientist is labor-intensive and mentally challenging. The main sacrifice I've made is dedicating my time to learning the craft and trying to explain to my family and friends what exactly a scientist does every day: that my job is not a 9 to 5, Monday through Friday. I am thinking all of the time. That is the nature of discovery and the gift of curiosity. Additionally, a lot of my female, scientific, mentors postponed having children before obtaining their tenure (which usually happens after the age of 35). For many of them, there were not a lot of benefits or accommodations for graduate students with children. Despite these issues, my husband and I decided to start trying to grow our family, and my daughter was born at the beginning of my dissertation year – I completed writing my thesis after she was born. I credit my husband for co-sacrificing during this time. He was working full-time and working on his master's degree at the same time while supporting our new family. We were living in Boston where we didn't have a lot of family to help with childcare. Still, I completed my Ph.D. in Immunology and we were fortunate to extend our stay in Boston for one additional year, thanks to a teaching fellowship I was awarded at Wellesley College. To help with all of this, we brought my sister-in-law to live with us to help with childcare while my husband finished his master's degree. Within two years of having our first child, we moved back to California when I was seven months pregnant with our son, where I had a postdoctoral position waiting for me at Cal. I personally didn't have a lot of downtime or formal maternity leave. Luckily, now there is more support in academia for parental leave and for graduate students who want to have children, but it is still a huge sacrifice and labor of love to raise a family and pursue a career in academia.

I am currently a professor at the University of California, Merced, which is the newest University of California (UC) campus, and I was one of the founding faculty members in 2005. My current research is focused on how our blood stem cells decide to develop into all the different blood types we have in our bodies. I am interested in the decisions that those blood cells make and how they are maintained throughout the lifespan. My research is interdisciplinary as it crosses the fields of immunology, stem cell biology, and developmental biology. In addition to my scientific research, I am also an instructor and administrator. With my colleagues, I make decisions that will have long-lasting implications on the lives of students and the viability of the academic program. Through this work, I find myself constantly telling my story to my students who also come from immigrant parents. Every year there is a new class of students that start at the university. In my interactions with the students, I want them to remember me as someone who encouraged them to ask questions, inspired them to pursue what they are curious about, and helped them find their passions. All the efforts that you put into your daily work should be for something because work without passion is useless. I want to be remembered for my impact on science, student learning, my local community and hopefully, the global community. If the people I interact with feel that I care, that is more than enough for me. I am working hard to leave a legacy. I am fortunate to have more than what I need, so I plan to create an endowment or scholarship for future generations who will attend the UC schools. My kids currently attend UC Irvine and UC San Diego and I have plenty of relatives who are UC alumni; I look forward to giving back to the students in the UC system.

Young women should know that persistence through difficult challenges is important! However, if I were to do it again, I might have slowed down a little bit to enjoy those special moments. My advice is to work toward your goals and consistently reassess your original plan to check that it's still relevant and that you're passionate about it. Be OK with a little bit of uncertainty. Life is a balance of persistence, perseverance, and risk-taking.

life happens
BUT BE
authentic;
BURN INTO YOUR
passion,
DIVE INTO YOUR
fears,
SOAR ON YOUR
confidence.

—Sunita Sharma

Be Focused

Sunita Sharma

I was born and raised in Chandigarh, the capital of Punjab, India. Growing up, I played basketball and toured around India through intercollegiate tournaments. I was also very much into the arts – my innate ability to sing and dance led me to pursue my master's degree in Indian classical vocal music. In the 1980s, I was selected by the Punjab Cultural Society to present songs, dramas, and dances in local arenas as well as abroad in England and Russia. I moved to the United States with my husband shortly after we got married in 1990 and shifted to another type of art: the beauty industry. I earned my esthetician license from the Fremont Beauty College and after running my own salon for a number of years, I acquired the Fremont Beauty College. Today, I continue to train a new generation of hairstylists, estheticians, and nail technicians. That's my journey in a nutshell, but the path to arriving here was not smooth sailing. It was very rocky – literally and figuratively.

After getting my license, I opened an eyebrow threading business, which began in a small rented booth, and grew by leaps and bounds from there. In 2001, I opened Skin Adore, a 600 square foot beauty salon. The small facility was a true fixer-upper. The property manager repeatedly asked me if I was sure that I wanted to lease the shop because the space did not have running water and she worried that the work and cost to dig the trench and

139

run the pipes could be astronomical. Sitting in the leasing office, looking over at my brother-in-law who is a general contractor, then over at my husband who is handy with home improvement projects, I knew I had a team on my side that would support any decision that I would make. I simply said, "Yes, I am sure," grabbed the pen, and signed the leasing agreement. The quick decision had an astronomical cost associated with it. The monetary cost was reasonable, but the test of my faith and ability to remain steadfast throughout the process had a huge price tag that I could not predict while sitting in the manager's office.

Like clockwork, my brother-in-law drew up the blueprints for the shop and my husband began assembling the metal-frames, then the sheetrock, and then the doors. My husband felt the urgency to complete the work but felt weighed down with the conviction that he needed to stop and pray. Day after day, the urgency to work won over the need for prayer. He felt that prayer could be done by listening to worship songs while he diligently screwed the sheetrock on to the aluminum frames. However, one afternoon, my husband felt like each screw was as heavy as a brick. The conviction that he needed to stop and pray felt like a ten-ton truck parked on his heart. He climbed down the ladder, laid on the cold cement floor, and closed his eyes in prayer. He told me that God kept reminding him to build, not with inanimate objects, but to build with faith which would require endurance. After four hours of prayer, he woke up with great confidence and a strong sense of purpose. However, he had no idea these feelings would be shattered when he ran into a roadblock while digging up the trench to connect the pipes to the underground sewage line.

We reached out to several contractors to help remove this blockage so that we could get water to the salon, which was needed to get state approval, and that approval was needed to open and operate the business. One company came out to mark up the area that needed to be dug in order to connect the sewage line. Another company came out with a sledgehammer to break open the cement so that digging could begin. My husband showed up with his shovel and began tearing up the concrete underneath, making a pathway that ran the length of 50 feet from the shop out to the sewage line. After several days of grueling work, the trench seemed to be almost done, so I scheduled the plumber to come and lay down the pipes. My husband's continuous digging revealed a five-foot boulder that was blocking the connection to the main sewage line. He feverishly used the pick and sledgehammer, but the boulder would not chip away even in the slightest. More importantly, the cement boulder was in place to hold down the large support column of the building, and any attempt to shatter the boulder would result in an unstable building structure. My husband cried out to me as he crawled out of the trench. In dismay, he stood trembling as though he had unearthed the remains of a monster. A sense of defeat came over his face, as he pointed to the situation. He did not say anything, nor did he need to. It was plain to see that there was no way to connect the pipes to the sewage system, and no running water could be arranged for the shop. All of our finances and effort that I invested appeared to be a waste!

I stood at the edge of the trench looking down at the boulder and remembered the words of my college basketball coach, whom we called, "Coach-Ma'am." She incessantly reminded her players to, "Step into every game ready to pour out your blood, sweat, and tears, such that when you exit the court, there is no looking back in remorse wondering if you could have done better or given more of yourself." I knew that I had to have a face-off with this boulder. My husband had poured out his sweat to dig this trench, now I had to step in and spill my blood and tears.

I knew that blood represented passion, sweat represented genuine effort and dedication, and tears defined an individual's own perspective on the significance and purpose of life. Coach-Ma'am's significance and purpose of life were not to elevate herself in the community. She was never married. She lived in a simple room that was located in the sports wing of the women's college hostel. Almost every evening, the team gathered around her as she discussed the details of her ongoing battle with the state government to have women's sports be recognized and well-funded. While additional funds began to trickle in, Coach-Ma'am used her personal savings to bring in a daily ration of fresh fruits and vegetables for her team. Our daily blood, sweat, and tears, which we poured out into practice, allowed our women's basketball team to compete in the 1982 Asian Games in New Delhi, India.

On the six-hour train ride to New Delhi, I had time to reflect on my life's journey so far. In basketball, there is a stance called "pivot foot" in which one foot stays firmly planted while the player's body shifts back and forth to scan the court and player positions. By moving about the "pivot foot," the player is able to evaluate and create new game dynamics. The train journey was my time to conduct a "pivot foot" evaluation. I reflected on how I became a part of this significant event in Indian history and where my life would go from here. Staring at the fields and grasslands racing by my train window, I also thought about my family, especially my brothers, who were my best friends. They were the ones who mentored me and protected me. My eldest brother suffered from polio, which left him with a limp. To cope with his disability, he turned to alcohol as a crutch to handle his difficulties. My middle brother was gifted with the mechanical ability to fix anything! However, he became addicted to crack cocaine, which he was unable to shake or fix. As their little sister, I had so much love, care, and concern for them. Dealing with all of this left my emotions twisted as I wondered if I was supposed to compensate for my family's distress with my own achievements.

I often wish I could go back in time and sit across from myself on that train ride, and tell myself, "Take a chill pill! It's not your responsibility. Don't put the world on your shoulders. They will all live out the ultimate purpose for their lives, regardless of the insurmountable boulders they face along the way."

That train ride, the game, and my time as a basketball player taught me so much. There are so many life lessons that stick with me from Coach-Ma'am. She taught me how to lighten my heart from distractions and how to apply these key principles to the game-of-life. If Coach-Ma'am ever raised her voice, it was to amplify the life principle: "It's neither great talent nor great physical abilities, instead it's always a clear focus which wins out in every challenge that comes about in a game." One morning, she asked me to bring some thread to clean up her neglected eyebrows. She did not fancy any high-end salon but appreciated the simple work that even an inexperienced girl could do. What I can do in minutes today, took me four hours of trembling and reworking the eyebrow shapes. Each time that I retouched her eyebrows, Coach-Ma'am would say, "Don't be distracted with self-doubt and fear of how it will all turn out. Just stay focused on the task before you, hair line-by-line." It was that very focus that helped us get through that obstacle when my husband and I stood over the huge boulder dashing our hopes of running water into the salon.

My heart was thumping out of my chest, but I mustered all my strength to not let my heart surrender to the boulder. I reminded myself of Coach-Ma'am's principle of focus winning out. "But, what am I supposed to focus on?" I wondered. To gain a better perspective, I climbed down into the trench and began to focus on where the PVC pipes would be running had this boulder not been there. In that precise place on the boulder, I saw an indentation of about eight inches in diameter, filled with dirt. Disregarding my fresh manicure, I began digging through the dirt with my bare hands. My fingers kept moving as my arm began extending further through the boulder. My husband was standing on the opposite side of the boulder unaware of the progress I was making. Suddenly his jaw dropped and he let out a big whimpering sigh as he saw my arm come through on the opposite side. The next day, the plumber asked us what tool we used to cut such a precise circular hole through the large boulder. My husband exclaimed, "Her praying hands, my friend...her praying hands!"

Each one of us faces some insurmountable boulders in our path that ask us to pause and take the time to reassess the well-defined purpose of our lives. The time that we take to reassess life is precious and of great significance to paving the way for future generations. Coach-Ma'am's assessments of life gave me principles to follow. No matter what family or career direction we pick, the ultimate purpose of life is to have a heart of integrity. In every game, my blood, sweat, and tears were being expended to bring my heart into the right alignment with God-given responsibility towards righteousness and fairness. This God-given responsibility is a double-edged sword calling me to continuously battle and protect my heart from being burdened with guilt, shame, or regret. Now that the 600 square feet salon has multiplied fifteen-fold into a beauty college, I am blessed to be investing my life assessments and principles into a younger generation of women who are challenged by family life, financial responsibilities, and personal endeavors. At my salon, Skin Adore, our motto is to, "Come as a client, leave as a friend." Today at Fremont Beauty College, whenever a student graduates, I think to myself, "She came as a student, but look at her leaving as my sister, my daughter, a confident woman ready to take on the world!" I consider my blood, sweat, and tears well spent into these women, determined to transform their world with hope.

whatever you do,
DON'T CLOSE THE DOOR
on yourself.

—Dede Wills

Be Grounded

Dede Wills

I am 5'9". To most people, I am ethnically ambiguous. When people look at me, they can't immediately pinpoint that I am Filipino and Caucasian. My father is Irish, German, and Spanish and my mother was of Filipino descent. Even though I grew up around a lot of Filipinos, and our family attended a church where we spent a lot of time with our community, I felt like an outcast. I never learned Tagalog, which was commonly spoken at church, so I couldn't engage in conversations. I tried to fit in by growing my hair out long, dressing a certain way, and by having Sanrio stationery (which was the thing back then). Despite feeling like an outsider, I always embraced my roots. I've always been proud of my heritage and the people who made me who I am today. I looked up to my *lola* (grandmother, in Tagalog) and we were very close. While in college, I called her every Tuesday or Thursday just to share about my day and hear her sweet voice. During one of our phone calls, she told me about a Japanese sniper who shot her in the leg during World War II when the Japanese occupied the Philippines. She remembered waking up in a body of water after they tried to drown her. She survived, but the bullet remained in her leg for the rest of her life. She moved to the United States to raise four children to try to find a better life for herself and her kids. My *lola's* strength and courage is something that I've always admired and try to carry with me.

I had a normal childhood. Our house was always filled with love and good people but situations happen that are out of your control and ultimately shape who you are. On August 13, 2001, I was only 17-years-old, and my life changed forever. My family and I took a vacation to Maui. Our plane landed, we picked up our rental car and headed to the beach to have some lunch. Things happened so quickly. We were in a car accident before we could even make it to the hotel. When all the cars involved in the accident stopped, I kicked the door open to get out of the smashed car where my family was trapped. I sat on the side of the highway looking at the wreck my family and I had been in. There were a lot of concerned bystanders who came to help. A lady, also named Dede, came to comfort me. The entire highway was shut down by emergency crews that came out to help us. My dad and brother were severely injured. I heard the Jaws of Life start. I then heard someone say, "It's too late, turn it off." Unfortunately, my mom didn't make it. I saw the medical responders cover my mom with a yellow tarp. On our ride to the hospital, my dad, brother and I were all in the ambulance together. Due to the severity of his injuries, my brother was immediately airlifted to the island of Oahu. My dad had broken ribs so he was admitted into the Intensive Care Unit. I remember walking around the hospital that night by myself after I knew my dad was sleeping; I immediately realized that my world as I knew it had changed and I had to rise to the biggest challenge of my life.

The night of the accident, I was assigned two officers to look after me, and the chaplain frequently checked in on me too. The officers took me to a food court to eat. While in line to order my food, I looked down and saw that I had blood all over my feet and shins from my family members. I had no family with me or near me. I was alone with two strangers on an island. I had to dig deep to find my inner strength because I literally did not have anybody.

You can take each circumstance and use it for bad or for good. I believe everything really starts with you and your inner strength. You should take things as they are and use that for the better. That tragedy really set the perspective and tone for how I look at my life and career. It helps me keep focus on what's important to me: health. I could have taken this life-altering situation and channeled my energy towards a path that didn't include any happiness. In fact, at the time, I couldn't imagine that I had the capability to even smile again. However, I chose to rise above and take the path full of love, compassion, and success. This path is what I had envisioned from a young age and shared with my mom.

In March 2005, I discovered my career calling when my boyfriend (now my husband), and I adopted a dog, Mia. Even though she is no longer with us, Mia's legacy lives on. I wanted to make a difference for voiceless, unwanted, and homeless animals like her. After I graduated from college with a degree in criminal justice, I applied for juvenile probation officer and animal control officer positions. The timing was right and I became an animal control officer. It was the perfect fit for me because it was the combination of being able to serve my community, make a difference in the lives of innocent animals, and apply my studies with law enforcement all at the same time. I started out my career in a uniform and truck, providing field services such as responding to community needs of lost, abandoned, or injured animals, enforcing laws, and rescuing animals. I became a senior officer, and then the supervisor at a veterinary clinic. I moved on to become the outreach coordinator, manager, and then the director of operations. Most recently, I was promoted as the executive director. It has been an extensive, yet gratifying journey! I feel like I still have so much to do for the animals and our community. Among everything, I believe in being consistent and trying to be the best person that I can. I strive to always be hard-working, dedicated, genuine, kind, and honest.

Success is applying yourself, 110%, no matter what aspect of life. The biggest thing for me is to be mentally and physically healthy. This allows me to be grounded and engaged with my career and my family. You can show up to work and occupy a chair but how productive is that when you could be making a difference for your community? My greatest success is my family: my husband, two kids, and our two adopted dogs! I am also so proud of my marriage! I married the man of my dreams. We are in love, enjoy each other's company and crack each other up.

I would advise every woman out there that whatever you do, don't close the door on yourself. Just open the door and walk through it. If you're going to quit anything, quit making excuses and waiting for the right time. Be thankful for every day. Life is too short! It really is. Dig deep and make things happen for yourself!

Try every day
TO BE
better
— THAN —
yesterday
FOR EVERY ASPECT
of your life
EITHER IT'S YOUR
personal life
— OR —
professional

−Uzmee Krakovszki

Be a Dreamer

Uzmee Krakovszki

I grew up in Mongolia, a country sandwiched between Russia
and China. I come from a very strict, yet creative household. Both
my parents were very artistically skilled; they designed and made
beautiful gowns. Despite their talent, both my parents chose not to
pursue art as a profession since it was not approved nor supported
by their parents. Art was not considered to be an honorable
profession in my family and inevitably, and unfortunately, that
belief was passed down to me. My father was very strict, especially
related to my education. I was expected to perform at the highest
level – If I scored anything lower than an A, my father made sure
that I never made the same mistake again, even if it meant having
to sit with me all night long to study. We spent hours reviewing
my assignments and he would quiz me to make sure I understood
everything. Although this was very normal in our household, I
eventually realized that not all families were as regimented as mine.
Though I liked how well I was doing in school, I was too young
to understand or appreciate the time and effort my father spent
to help me become better. He taught me to tackle my problems
head-on; I learned to work hard and to never give up. Looking
back, I will say that it was a well-learned lesson. The discipline my
father instilled in me is something that I've carried on throughout
my life and was even more apparent when I became a mom. I
noticed myself pushing my son in his studies just as my father had

done with me. It's so funny how we fight so hard to break out of our parents' mold, but before we know it, we're doing the same thing our parents did because that's all we know. The older we get, the more we become like them; there's no escaping because our parents will always be a part of us. However, with my son, I've let him choose his own path, which included joining the military.

It was always apparent that education held great importance to my parents. When I was 18-years-old, I had a fantastic opportunity to leave Mongolia, to attend college in Germany, which would allow me to pursue a better life for myself and my family. To my parents, business was a respectable profession with a promising future so that's what I studied. Unfortunately, I often found myself bored in class, which resulted in me doodling and drawing faces on the pages of my textbooks. I was absolutely obsessed with human facial features. I enjoyed sitting on the street and people-watching. It was and still is one of my favorite things to do. While in college, I met my now-husband who was studying engineering. During our frequent walks together, he noticed me doing my thing – observing people's faces. I was pretty sure he thought I was a weirdo! Instead, he mentioned to me, "It's very interesting how you're more into this than your studies. Why don't you go to beauty school, you would be good at it." That was music to my ears and was something that I'd been yearning to hear all my life! Finally, I received reassurance that it was OK to pursue my passion! He really gave me the confidence to go after my dreams. Of course, that could happen only after abiding by my parents' wishes of finishing college. As soon as I obtained my business degree, I ran off to beauty school for a year!

When I started to pursue my passion, it never felt like work! I never studied this hard in my life! I finally understood that quote by Tony Bennett: "If you follow your passion, you'll never work a day in your life." As a result of all my hard work that I enjoyed,

I graduated at the top of my class. Shortly after graduation, my school offered me a makeup instructor position. I always dreamt about makeup, but I was never really encouraged to pursue it as a career. If I hadn't followed my instinct, I probably would have taken a job that I hated and eventually, life would have gotten in the way. I probably would have become even more invested in that choice, to the point that my passion would have just faded away. I hear a lot of older people say, "I should have pursued my passion, but I didn't do it because I had a mortgage to pay and kids to feed." I was so fortunate to finally land my dream job doing what I love! However, when my husband won the United States (U.S.) green card lottery, he uprooted our family from Germany so that we could have more opportunities and a brighter future.

In 2005, I moved to California with my husband and son. When I was starting out my career in Hollywood, I ran into quite a few challenges. To start, I did not know how to speak English nor did I know how to drive! These are critical life skills to survive in Los Angeles. I've always been very ambitious and never received C's or D's in my academic career and I never failed a test in my life until I went to the Department of Motor Vehicles (DMV)! Even though I was a very good student, my driver's education instructors spoke so quickly, I couldn't catch what they were saying. Can you believe I failed the behind-the-wheel driving test, twice? The maximum attempt is three times! Because I didn't want to fail, I was dreading having to take the test once again. Despite my hesitation, my husband encouraged me to keep trying. I was so nervous and I had it in my head that I was going to fail yet again! However, I was determined to pass because I really needed my driver's license. California's public transportation was not as accessible compared to Europe. Everyone drives in California, especially in Los Angeles! Luckily, for my third try, I had an elderly gentleman administering my behind-the-wheel test. He reminded me to take a deep breath to help me calm my nerves. When he asked me

to pull over, I thought, "this is it!" When he asked me to turn off
the engine and take a deep breath again, I thought I failed! To my
surprise, I had passed! I even scored higher than my husband who
had been driving longer than me.

Once I finally obtained my driver's license, I enrolled in the Cinema
Makeup School. It was the most amazing and fun educational
experience I ever had! Even after I graduated, I could still barely
understand English. Despite my language barrier, I searched for
jobs through Craigslist. I got my first gig doing makeup starting at
$25 a day, which wasn't even enough to cover my gas and makeup
kit. In order to make it in the industry, I was told I had to work
for free for at least two years. I was fortunate that my husband
worked to make ends meet so I could focus on my passion. I felt
like we never had enough money, and we certainly did everything
we could to survive in America. We saved whatever we could!
Most of our money went back into building up my business, like
investing in makeup products to build a professional makeup kit,
which can be quite costly.

My ground-breaking moment was when I got hired to assist a
successful makeup artist during a fashion show. I did so well on the
job that she invited me to assist her with other gigs, which gave me
a healthy flow of work! One day, her agent, Crystal Wright, saw
my work and invited me to her office to chat and do her makeup.
Shortly after, I signed with the agency and was able to transition
from assistant makeup artist to a key makeup artist. My daily rate
skyrocketed from $25 up to $1,200! I couldn't believe it! Both my
agent and my husband were my biggest supporters who helped me
get to where I am today! Over the next few years in the makeup
industry, I built up my clientele, portfolio, and confidence.

In 2008, I landed an opportunity to work with Jeannie Mai,
celebrity host of *How Do I Look?* At first, I was so intimidated to

work with her because she is a former MAC makeup artist. Upon meeting, we immediately clicked! I was instantly charmed by her sweet personality. It also helped that she respected and loved my skill. We have been working together for over 12 years now! In my work, I aim to build long-term relationships with people I love. I am very loyal to those I value!

I've always dreamt of becoming a makeup artist, which I was able to achieve and excel in. But once I accomplished that, I wanted to grow and evolve even more! I had a desire to become an entrepreneur. I searched for the next opportunity: MICROBLADING – a semi-permanent eyebrow tattooing technique. Being the master perfectionist that I am, I decided to take classes...at four different schools! I wanted to make sure that I don't mess up anyone's face! I have to say that microblading is, by far, the most difficult skill I have learned. Once I was done studying and practicing, I signed a three-year lease to open the UzBrows Beauty Studio in Beverly Hills, which is my pride and joy. Having my own studio is yet another one of my dreams that have come to fruition! I not only own my own business, but I am able to still pursue my passion for creating art, using the canvas of people's faces. I find so much joy in the impact I make on my clients' lives. They constantly tell me how their new brows have changed their lives, helped them feel beautiful and confident, and how it saves them time with their daily makeup routine. My clients' generous feedback affirms that I am doing the right thing! As I've matured in my career, I realize the importance of doing more meaningful and purposeful things in life.

Throughout my life and career, I've made sacrifices. Although leaving my dream job in Germany to move to the U.S. was a large sacrifice, surprisingly the biggest sacrifice I made during my career was disappointing my mother. Even though I chose to do the total opposite of what my mother wanted for me, I was still afraid that I would disappoint her even more. I'm sure most Asian kids can relate – parents assert a great amount of pressure on their children. Asian families put such an emphasis on family; it's such a strong bond. I often find myself secretly still seeking my parents' approval, even as an adult! When my mother got sick and her health continued to worsen, I was so afraid that she would not see me succeed. Thankfully, she was able to live long enough to see what I was doing before she passed away in 2017. She acknowledged and told me that, "You know what, I could've been a flight attendant if I was as stubborn and brave as you were." Hearing that she supported my choices was such a relief for me!

I know that my mother was very proud of me and extremely happy for all of my accomplishments: I am a two-time Emmy nominated makeup artist, 2019 Guild Award winner for "Best Makeup Artist," and the first Mongolian makeup artist to ever work in Hollywood! My family and I have come a long way from Mongolia to Germany, and finally, to Hollywood! Despite all the accolades, I am most proud of my family. My greatest personal successes are my son and my 20+ years of marriage! I am FOREVER thankful for my husband who I love dearly. He truly supported me and helped me build my dreams into reality!

In all aspects of my life, there are still so many levels to go! Professionally, my next move would be to build my own academy for makeup and microblading so that I can teach and share the knowledge I've accumulated over the last two decades. The best piece of advice I've received throughout my career came from my agent, Crystal Wright. She firmly told me two things that I should never change: my name and my accent. She reassured me that, "Once people know you and they learn how to pronounce your name, you will be the one and only Uzmee! You will stand out because your name and accent make you unique!" I'm so glad I took her advice because she was so right!

If you are considering becoming a makeup artist, you are very lucky to have other Asian makeup artists who came before you. We've been able to build a very good reputation. We are known to be very creative, calm, polite and neat with amazing work ethic. However, being polite and nice can be taken as a weakness, so be careful. You also have to show some firmness. Always practice a great work ethic. You should never neglect it. Always improve on your skills, be better next year, and continue to reinvent yourself. Compete with yourself, never with others! In any industry, there will always be young, hungry creative people. Remember, you can be easily replaced so you have to go beyond measure. Be sure to surround yourself with professional people who are fair to you, who lift you up, and who are trustworthy. When you come across people who are filled with drama or negativity just walk away because it will drag you down!

My advice for a woman beginning the journey into her career is to just take the risk. Your parents may be upset or disagree with you, but your parents will love you anyway. They will eventually accept your choices and will be proud of you no matter what because at the end of the day, parents just want to see their children happy and successful at what they do. So just go for it! Dare to dream! Why not? Just be prepared for every possible scenario, good and bad. Try to see it as a journey of five to twenty years – that's how long it may take to reach your dream! Never take shortcuts! Create momentum and never lose it. If you do, learn to bring it back. Read a book or watch inspiring YouTube videos that motivate and speak to you. These things can really help you bounce back and help you regain your momentum while you work toward your dreams.

just work harder!
Don't wait for things to happen.
Put some sweat into it.

−Joanne Boston

Be Passionate

Joanne Boston

In my last year of high school, I took a class where I learned knife skills and how to bake. I've always had a love for baking and dreamt of becoming a pastry chef. However, my mom urged me to pursue a career in the medical field because she knew there were great opportunities in the industry. I did not like blood or needles, so I compromised with her and went to school for medical administration and business. In the Philippines, my mom was a nurse, but she had to give up her career because her credentials didn't transfer over when she moved to the United States in 1983. Needless to say, I hadn't reached my potential when I worked at Macy's shoe department in Daly City. While working there, I had a regular client who would come in weekly to purchase shoes from me. Over time, we got to know each other and built a relationship. One week, she came in and offered me an externship to do administrative work in an oncology practice that conducted clinical trials. I took on the opportunity because working in the medical world is what I was expected to do and I was excited for the chance to get started. I worked my way up from the front desk, to billing and coding, and eventually became the lead clinical professional in my department. I was responsible for knowing indications and treatments with each of the trials being conducted in my clinic, meeting with biotech and pharmaceutical companies, negotiating contracts, and knowing everything about

159

cancer drugs. During my time there, we received FDA approval on several cancer drugs that helped many of my patients. I found fulfillment through my job because of the work we did; we made a great impact on the lives of our patients. I saw their life expectancy grow and the quality of their experiences improve. I loved my job because it brought hope for everyone. However, a few years into it, I realized I wasn't living in my truth. I knew in my heart that I was meant to do something creative. The medical industry did not have space for me to do that.

We've all heard the saying, "Follow your bliss" and I realized I hadn't done that. About three years into my job, things got really heavy and it started to take a toll on me. I saw the ugly side of the industry and not all of my patients were healing. Even though I saw some of the blessings that this work provides, it just wasn't for me. I was suffering because I knew that wasn't really where I was meant to be. Being able to pay the bills wasn't enough of a reason to stay...looking back, I endured living unauthentically for over ten years!

I started to do some soul-searching in 2007. I thought about all of the things that I loved and what I was passionate about. My mom gave up her dream and started working in the hospitality industry when she arrived here. Since she was in the industry, she was able to introduce me to local chefs and bartenders. I love writing so I started a blog about my experiences. I would eat at local restaurants and write about food, culture, and the environment. Because of my blog, I was invited to cover events. I attended restaurant openings, took pictures, networked, and wrote about my experiences. These opportunities opened more doors, allowing me to eventually host my own events.

Between the years of 2007 and 2019, I was a medical professional working with scientific terms and patients during the day and then

160

an entrepreneur and event planner by night. I worked my 9 to 5 job and would catch a second wind to work on my passion, which is food and events for the community. I started working with nonprofit and community organizations such as the Filipino American Historical Society and kapaMEALya, a Filipino-American social dining group that I had founded with a few friends. I also helped plan the annual Pistahan Parade and Festival in San Francisco, serving as the project manager for the Culinary Pavilion, and later ran social media and the Pistahan Tavern. In 2013, I became part of the Filipino Food Movement's founding board of directors, which is a 501(c)(3), and served as the vice president of marketing. In 2016, I was accepted into the Filipino Young Leaders Program (FYLPRO), which is an organization that was established by a former Philippine Ambassador and supported by the Philippine Embassy. These events and groups helped open doors for me and exposed me to the Filipino culture. That's how I started my company, JBKollaborations, which is all things food, community, and event planning. One of my most successful events to date was a Filipino dinner in New York at the James Beard House, which is run by the same foundation as the "Grammy Awards" for food! For the event titled *Filipino Regional Celebration*, my partner and I brought in chefs and beverage professionals from all over the country to prepare a seven-course meal. It took a lot of work and it sold out quickly!

Part of the inspiration and motivation to start my own company came from the personal reflection I had for this chapter. I knew I eventually wanted to make my passion my full-time work, but I needed to figure out what that work would be and how I could do that in a way that would bring me happiness, allow me to do events for the community, and allow me to make money. After all, I have to pay the bills! Talking with my mentors and visualizing myself living my passion sparked a fire in me. I was excited to make things happen for myself! In April of 2019, I left the medical industry to become the events producer at General Assembly in San Francisco where I get to create events for the community every day! I have also been fortunate enough to host, moderate, and speak on panels about career, pivoting, and passion. Even better, I am able to bring my colleagues and allies in the community into my space so that they can speak out and share their talents as well. I am using my position to empower and encourage anyone who comes into my space. In the winter of 2019, I was appointed to the arts and culture commission for the city of Daly City. Not only do I produce events for a living now, but I also lend my event planning skills to the city that I live in. This is incredible for me because more than 30% of the population of Daly City is of Filipino descent. The programming should reflect the community I serve, and I am driven to do just that as a commissioner.

One of the quotes that speak to me is, "Lift as you climb" – I got where I am today because of other people who have pushed and lifted me here. I also want to bring people along with me. I believe in the Filipino terms *"Kapwa,"* meaning shared identity, and *"Isang bagsak,"* which means if one falls, we all fall. We all need to work together and help each other climb and I'm excited to see more strong *Pinays* (Filipino women) in leadership! This world needs more women who are open to honoring their past and implementing that into their work for their future. I see a lot of millennials who want to climb, but don't honor people who help them get there. I stand on so many shoulders who helped me get to where I am today: my mom, mentors, teachers and advisors in college, Dr. Dawn Mabalon, *Ate* (older sister in Tagalog) Allyson, *Ate* Lily Ann, and many *Pinays* who I talk and work with every day. I want to encourage others to do research and find out who's out there doing what you want to do. Find a mentor and build a support system to help you along the way. Also, make sure to find time for yourself. Glamorizing being busy is not healthy; say yes to yourself and honor yourself!

A lot of choices I made in life are because I didn't want to disappoint my mom. My mom left the Philippines at just 23-years-old. She became a widow when she was only 33-years-old. I was only eight-years-old and I remember her breaking down...but I also saw her rise from the hardship and work so hard. Her drive inspired me. We had to work together as a team; she was a single mom, sacrificing a lot to raise me and my sister. From that point on, we just worked hard and I really was forced to step up! I had to grow up and take care of things at home because my mom was busy working. I had to be a second mom to my sister and I also had to go to school and do well. My mom didn't really know that I had dreams that didn't include medicine. I never really fought for myself because I didn't want to disappoint her. But if I knew then what I know now, I would have been more open and honest with my mom about my dreams and my struggles.

Looking back, I know my mom only wanted the best for me. She steered me in the direction of the medical field because she knew I could handle it. Hospital jobs are not easy! I am thankful she urged me because it taught me how to handle difficult situations and how to juggle several projects. I do not regret working in the medical industry because I gained an amazing skill set and compassion for others. When I quit my job, I was afraid to tell my mom. Though, when I told her about my career change, she was surprisingly supportive. She told me, "As long as you are happy..." That meant so much. My happiness was all that mattered to her. I still get emotional thinking about this moment because, at the end of the day, our parents just want us to be happy. In actuality, it was my mom who introduced me to food and the industry, so no matter how I look at it, she was always there shining that light for me to follow.

For me, success is being at peace, knowing what you're doing is true to you, and knowing that the work you're doing is helping others. I don't need a certain amount of money in the bank to say that I am successful. I believe titles are bullshit. A lot of us enter jobs that suck the life out of us; I was stuck for a while, but I learned that success is being able to exhale at the end of the night and being able to sleep. If it doesn't make you happy or bring you joy then don't do it. When you concentrate on what brings you joy, that's what you emit into the world. You give what you get. You get what you give. Find your why. Your North Star. What gets you up in the morning. Life is too short. Do what makes you happy.

Let your
FAILURES
HELP YOU FIND YOUR
purpose.

—Jennifer Redondo-Marquez

Be Still

Jennifer Redondo-Marquez

I am your textbook Capricorn: ambitious, hardworking, practical, reliable, and disciplined. I am also stubborn, organized, and calculated – which can sometimes drive people crazy, including myself! I've often been referred to as bossy (by my sister), high maintenance (by guys), and strong-willed (by my parents and teachers). But I like to think that I'm a natural-born leader. I have very high standards – in almost every aspect of my life and I am always plotting out my next moves. My mind is always going a thousand miles per hour. It never stops. I never stop.

Entrepreneurship is in my blood – my grandparents were entrepreneurs. My mom's dad started his own meat delivery business in Manila, Philippines and my dad's parents owned a nightclub and hotel in Subic Bay, Philippines. Playing the board game Monopoly as a kid, I got my first taste of owning property and from the first time I played, I became obsessed with business! I was also fascinated with the board game, Operation, which fed my dream of becoming a doctor. A majority of my family is in the medical field, including my mom who is a retired registered nurse. Her work exposed me to hospitals where I often saw doctors giving orders to nurses. Like most Filipino moms, mine stressed the importance of finding a stable, well-paying job. For her, the medical field equated to stability and job security, but

166

she discouraged me from becoming a doctor because she didn't want me to have a hard life. As for my dad, a retired military officer, he didn't think I'd survive in the military because he thought I had a problem with authority. Questioning authority has definitely helped me on occasion, but he was right that the Army wasn't the right place for me. With my desire to be a boss, it looked like being a doctor was just what I was looking for in a career!

At the start of my senior year of high school, when it came time to fill out my college applications, I applied as a biology major, the logical choice for someone wanting to become a doctor. However, after my applications were submitted, I discovered a love for economics. Until then, I had never found school or studying to be fun. Most of the time, I was easily bored and frequently got kicked out of class by my teachers. When I got to college, I decided to change my major and go into business even though it was against my parents' wishes. I tried to gain as much work experience as I could even if it meant taking unpaid internships just so I would be able to add to my resume. Most of my family was either in the medical field or in the military so I didn't have anyone who could help me prepare or give me advice on how to make it in the corporate world. During my first interview for an internship, I did everything you shouldn't do! I didn't wear a suit jacket because it was scorching hot (also because I didn't have a proper suit), I didn't bring a printed copy of my resume, and I had no idea how to answer any of the questions they asked me. It was a massive disaster, and needless to say, I did not get the job. I told myself I would never make those same mistakes the next time I got an opportunity. After that experience, I over-prepared and did as much research as I could. I wrote out my script and memorized my answers to anticipated questions. I practiced speaking out loud, whether it was in the shower or doing mock interviews with my college roommate.

Upon graduating from the University of California, Berkeley, my internships and habits of preparation and research helped me secure a position with Accenture, a global management consulting firm. This position allowed me the opportunity to travel around the world while working on challenging projects for big-name clients. During my time there, I did relatively well and got promoted. I was on the career trajectory to becoming a manager and part of that path included obtaining a Master of Business Administration (MBA) degree. Accenture would pay for my tuition as long as I promised to return for two years upon graduation. While in the process of studying for the GMAT (the entrance exam for business school), I was one month away from finishing up the Riordan Fellows MBA Program at UCLA's Anderson School of Management. I got a call for a work meeting where I ended up getting laid off. For the first time ever, I cried at work. I was supposed to go to grad school and I was banking on Accenture to pay for it. When my plan changed so suddenly and drastically, I felt like my life was turned upside down.

Luckily, I was only out of work for a couple of weeks when Apple invited me to interview with them. This was in 2008, the worst economic disaster since the Great Depression of 1929, and I was fortunate enough to be in the tech bubble while the rest of the economy was crumbling. It was an exciting time for me to join. I had the opportunity to work at Apple while Steve Jobs, one of the world's greatest leaders, was still alive! I had the privilege of working on the most innovative products that changed the world. I was too busy to go back to grad school, but instead, I got real-life experience. I saw the company grow and transform and I am thankful for the time I spent there. After more than a decade, I decided to go outside my comfort zone thanks to the push from John Corpus, former CEO of Photobucket. He told me, "The only way for you to grow is to leave."

In 2019, I was approached by a fast-growing and extremely controversial start-up. I had my reservations about interviewing with them, but my husband, Romeo, encouraged me to be open. He also told me, "You won't know if you don't go." At the time, I was interviewing women for *In Her Purpose* and that inspired me to take the leap into the unknown, giving me the courage to explore new opportunities. I decided to see what this company had to say. After interviewing, I accepted the offer but a couple of months into my new job, I finally understood why people say, "The grass isn't always greener!" I started to question whether I made the right decision. I knew going to a start-up would be challenging, but I didn't anticipate the major growing pains that I would experience. As I moved up the corporate ladder, females and people who look like me were rare. Finally, it was a breath of fresh air to see someone in leadership who looked like me: Marissa Yao, the vice president of sustainability. Little did I know, she would end up mentoring me and giving me the best career advice. There are four key things I learned from her: 1. Think strategically, 2. Stay classy, 3. Keep your integrity and 4. Never go into a meeting without knowing what you want. She also asked me the hard question about what I really want. That's the problem! Growing up in a Filipino household, it's hard for me to think about what I want because I was told to get good grades, go to college and find a stable job. Now that I've checked all of those boxes, I have been struggling to figure out what's next for me.

I've always been a planner. But now, I know not everything turns out as planned. I used to think that things were happening to me, but in reality, things were happening for me. Many times, over and over, I had to be flexible with what life threw at me. I've learned sometimes it takes noise to appreciate silence, and absence to value presence. Most importantly, I've learned that I sometimes need to be still. What exactly does it mean to be still? At first, I thought it meant to stop, as in, "Freeze" Don't move! In elementary school, I hated playing freeze tag because I disliked running and found it difficult to stand, sit, or lay still (some things never change!). Then, I thought perhaps it was a timeout for my mind to relax and meditate. In my attempts to slip into a deep meditative state, I would get bored, my mind would wander, or I ended up falling asleep. When those literal ideas of being still didn't work out, I thought there had to be a deeper meaning to the idea of being still.

I thought back to when I attended a Christian elementary school where we were forced to memorize and interpret Bible verses. I learned theory, but I wanted to be able to put that into practice. When I studied "be still" in the context of the Bible, I discovered that it equates to stop striving, fighting, and living in fear. When applied to my own life, I finally understood that the sheer act of my inability to remain still stems from my unwillingness to let go of control. Being raised by a soldier, I was trained to strategize. So I always had my hands up in defense just like boxers do when they're in the ring. I stayed ready to defend myself from all that life brought my way. For me, being still actually means the opposite of how I had been living my life. Instead, I need to let go, believe, and trust that God has a plan and that everything will fall into place in His perfect timing. I admit that I've not been able to completely surrender to this, but I am a work in progress.

Throughout my life, every time I have had to make a big decision or undergo a huge change, I took a break. There are many instances where I extracted myself from a situation, relationship, and sometimes both. I took time to turn inward and listen to myself. In order to do so, I would travel – most of the time alone so I didn't hear static or the noise of everyone else's opinions. I didn't want to make decisions influenced by what others thought I should do. You'd be surprised how much you learn about yourself when you are alone. The best thing about solitude is leaving everything behind for a moment so that you can hear a true voice, your own! The time away that I took for myself gave me the time to be still.

I often remind myself to look back on my failures and allow them to help me live my purpose. Fear of failing holds me back, which is ironic because I've failed a lot. But, I have my failures to thank because they have led me to where I am today. What I do know for sure is that I want to encourage women who are feeling stuck in their current situation as well as the future generation to find their purpose, pursue their own interests and find their passions. I also want to be able to share my personal experiences along with the experiences of others, and that's where the inspiration for this book came from. Many of us map out our goals and long term plans, which sometimes don't come to fruition. Life brings surprises every day! Don't be afraid of failing; trust your gut and enjoy the magic of new beginnings. Remember to shift your perspective and turn hard times into opportunities. Focus on solutions, always be grateful, and every once in a while take a moment to be still.

find OR *create*
YOUR OWN
TRIBE.
THEY WILL
lift you up
WHEN YOU CAN'T DO SOMETHING.
THEY ARE GOING TO TELL YOU
to go for it
WHEN YOU THINK IT'S
impossible.

— Giselle "G" Tongi-Walters

BE YOU

Giselle "G" Töngi-Walters

I am a global citizen. I was born in Paris, France and I've lived all over the world: Switzerland, Philippines, and the United States (U.S.). I am half Filipino (mom) and half Swiss (dad) and spent the first five years of my life growing up in Switzerland. Unfortunately, my dad passed away when I was just 11-months-old from a scuba diving accident. My mom never remarried so we were left alone. All my life, I saw my mom struggle to support me and my siblings. It was extremely difficult for her, especially being thousands of miles away from her home country. The only option for my mom was to leave Switzerland. She worked as a travel coordinator and tour guide. Her work was based in Italy and all over Europe so she was away from home so much, leaving me with other family members all over the world. When I was five-years-old, my mom sent me on a plane to the Philippines on my own, with my passport around my neck. As I got older, I realized that many Filipinos work out of the country because that's the only option they have. I didn't understand at the time that I have a heart for social justice, but over time, I became more politically inclined, and now I understand why there is forced migration.

I spent a good portion of my teenage years in the Philippines. It's really a grind to survive and make it out there. As such, I started working at a young age, already appearing in commercials at

12-years-old. I gave all my earnings to my mom because I saw that she was really struggling. Throughout my teenage years, I worked full-time as an actor and TV personality even though I had no training. When I was 16-years-old, I was discovered by Eric Quizon, an actor-turned-director and the son of a famous Filipino comedian and actor, Dolphy. I met Eric at a nightclub where he asked me if I would be interested in acting. I figured, why not? I ended up auditioning for his film. I was comfortable being in front of the camera as a former model but truthfully, I didn't have the skills to act. I had no idea what I was doing, but somehow I found relative success. The idea of "fake it until you make it," actually worked. I got to do advertisements as an endorser from cellular phone products and toothpaste to Ajinomoto (Monosodium Glutamate brand). There came a point where I felt burnt out so I decided to leave the motherland, like millions of Filipinos do every day. Similar to my mom, I took the path of leaving to find a better life with more opportunities. Even though I was a working actress and made good money, I knew I had to leave. I felt like if I stayed, I was turning a blind eye to the poverty, landlessness, and injustice of 90% of the people in the Philippines. At 21-years-old, I decided to move to the United States.

In 2000, I went back to school to attend the Lee Strasberg Theatre Institute. I wanted to pursue being an actress because that consumed my life at that time. That's all I really knew. Now that I've been in Los Angeles for over 20 years, I've made a transition into something I didn't expect: producing and arts administration! I decided to transition from an actress to a producer and now to an arts and culture administrator because no one else is going to write or produce our stories or give us opportunities to do so. From 2014 to 2017, I had a daily talk show called *Kababayan Today* that aired locally in Los Angeles on KSCI- LA18 and globally on the TV5 platform. For three years straight, I produced a daily talk of 24 minutes a day, five times a week. I did a lot of research and delved deep into the community to give others a platform to share their stories. I scrambled to create content that wasn't fluff. Along the way, I met some amazing changemakers, most of them being Filipino-Americans (Fil-Ams). I noticed a lot of my younger guests were searching for deeper meaning about their identity. Who the Filipino-American is in the diaspora is so much deeper than *adobo* (a staple Filipino dish marinated in vinegar, soy sauce, garlic, and black peppercorns), festivals, and going to Filipino concerts. How do we connect to our roots in a significant, meaningful way?

Throughout my journey, walking away from the money was probably the biggest sacrifice I had to make. Although I have been presented with opportunities to work a corporate job that could pay me significantly more than the jobs I have taken, the ethics of that job wouldn't allow me to be myself in the long run. I refuse to be a puppet. I had to make decisions that are aligned with my values in order to be true to myself. I have opinions, ideas, and creativity that needs to be expressed. As I got older, I realized what's really important — family, community, and worthwhile causes I believe in, which is the power of arts and culture to represent a diaspora. When I was just a teenager, I had the opportunity to earn a significant salary, buy nice things, and travel, which is what most people desire and what they consider to be a success. I achieved that at an early age and am not burdened with the desire to keep up with the Joneses, so to speak. I can honestly say that I am no longer motivated by money or traditional views of success; I am not tied to things. I live for moments of connection, experiences that capture humanity through the performing arts, and connections of the soul.

I am motivated by my growing family and advocating for my community because if we don't fight for us, who will? Becoming a mother was a defining moment in my life because I had always been driven by my career. That really shifted when I had my first child. I stayed home to raise my child in the first two years of her life. I know now, and it's safe to say, that I am not made to be a stay-at-home mom, at all. And that's OK! I believe I have another purpose in this world besides being a homemaker. Coming to grips that I am OK with that was really a defining moment, and I know I am meant to do other things that fulfill me. I don't feel guilty about it. I'm a better mom because I am able to do these things for myself.

After having my two kids, I went back to school when they were just two and four-years-old. I attended the University of California, Los Angeles (UCLA) and graduated with honors. I majored in communications and double-minored in film, television and digital arts and theater. I am also currently working on my master's degree in nonprofit management at Antioch University to truly give back in a meaningful way. I, like many others, only fully grasped being Fil-Am in college. I craved the Filipino-American experience. I joined Samahang Pilipino (UCLA's Filipino community organization) to network and explore the identity of our people. I saw the struggle of so many Fil-Ams. They were so lost on what to major in or what they wanted to do with their lives. They were conflicted with what they thought they wanted to do versus what their parents wanted them to be. The immigrant elders have big expectations for their children to do well professionally to make their own sacrifices worth it, but they have a hard time understanding that a viable career path includes more than becoming a nurse, lawyer or engineer. That is why I value my work at FilAm Arts because I want to show the next generation that pursuing work in the cultural arts is also a viable and noble way to make a living. It is my hope that there will be more opportunities where Filipino-American artists can have a viable means to support themselves through their art as a sole means of livelihood. That's where the community needs to step in and support our artists by purchasing their merchandise, without asking for discounts!

What I've learned throughout my life and experiences is that WE ARE RESILIENT! I encourage you to be persistent and don't ever let anyone tell you no. When you ask a question and the answer is "no," then you are asking the wrong question. Revise the question until you get the "yes." In terms of your career, if your heart isn't in it, your happiness will fester. You should reach out to people in the field that you want to be in. Humble yourself and seek their advice and reach out for mentorship. You will be surprised at how much people are willing to share! There are many people like us, who have paved the way and who have a strong track record; they will open the way for us to step into their industries. When you see people doing what you want to do, it helps you believe that you can do it too. When I was younger, there were hardly any Fil-Ams creating TV shows, nor were they on TV, yet today is a very different story as representation is now always addressed with the cultural inclusion and equity mandates. Also, the traditional gatekeepers of media no longer exist with the advent of the internet, which gives more room for unheard voices. Now, you can create anything and reach out to anyone. What's stopping you from doing that? Remember to align yourself with people who are doing the same thing and to collaborate. I can't stress the importance of collaboration and mentorship. Find or create your own tribe. They will lift you up when you can't do something and will tell you to go for it when you think that thing is impossible.

I have found that there is a big pocket of Fil-Ams that are searching for meaningful conversations and there is a lack of edutainment of who we are. There is no history being spoken about or stories being told. It's a niche market, but it's important. I want to be able to use my platform and skills to educate others. As a creative,

177

I have lots of ideas but ideas don't mean anything if you don't put that vision into motion. If I have a vision, I make it a reality by working with people who believe in me and my ideas. As a producer, I have to get people to come along for the ride of what I am trying to create. I am also an activist. I want to bring our people together so they know what they can do to give back. I want to create content that's meaningful, either for the Fil-Am community or diverse communities like the city of Los Angeles! I want to create a platform for Fil-Am talent.

I am proud of the reputation I have created in the community. They know my heart, my work, that I am genuine. It has been important to me to keep the best of the Filipino values despite living away from the motherland alive! Many of my friends are now raising their own children – as parents, we need to teach our young ones to understand that there are more important goals than just money. We can be successful in other areas that bring about true happiness and still have a comfortable lifestyle. I am practicing this in my own home by teaching and raising two human beings who I am incredibly proud of. Understanding this new idea of success will inspire a new generation to be genuine to who they are. Don't be afraid to be yourself and go for your heart's desires! Working hard is in our DNA; don't lose your grit or your resilience, and keep working toward your goals! And most importantly, have compassion for yourself. Things may not turn out the way you planned but there is a path for you if you put in the time and the energy.

IF YOU HAVE AN *idea*, IF YOU CAN *picture it*, THEN YOU CAN DEFINITELY GET IT! IF YOU WANT THAT *triple double sundae*, THEN GO GET THAT!

—Charleen Caabay

BE HUNGRY

Charleen Caabay

Success can be so many things. It's not about money. Success is about all the experiences that you go through, your journey, and how you grow as a person because of those experiences. In 2001, I graduated from DeVry with a degree in computer information systems. That was also the year that the tech industry crashed and so many people got laid off, which meant my graduation happened at the worst time possible! I was a fresh graduate trying to find a job, competing with others who had numerous years of experience. Once I finally landed a job as a contractor, I had aspirations to climb the corporate ladder, but I realized it wasn't for me. Being a woman in the male-dominated tech industry, I felt that I had to strive harder. As a contractor, I always got the short end of the stick. I felt that I had to prove myself to the team – not only as a woman but also a woman of color. I tried to work extra hard to obtain acceptance. However, I had a lot of self-doubts and I often felt inadequate even though I was professional, proficient, and had the credentials to be in the information technology field! I knew my true potential, but deep down I also knew that I was only doing just enough to get by. I was doing a half-assed job and barely did enough for above-average work. In my mind, I was a bad employee because I found ways to work the system. I was also frustrated because I didn't like how people were treated in the tech industry. Companies would hire you as a contractor, then lay you

180

off not long after – it felt like a complete waste of time to learn the position and then be let go.

In between jobs, I lived off my unemployment benefits. I also partied often, and several of my friends were club promoters. I used to help them promote by passing out flyers. I thought it would be a great idea to bring food to the scene so I started doing food pop-ups in the club venues (before pop-ups were even a thing). I started at the bar where my friends worked, bringing family-style platters and feeding everyone there. This turned into a more formal pop-up and for years, I provided the food in the back corner of the party. I made Filipino fusion food: tacos, *lumpias* (Filipino eggrolls), and *silogs* (a common Filipino dish that is paired with garlic fried rice and an egg). My food and the pop-ups were a hit! From there, I grew a fan base!

As far back as I can remember, I had a knack for cooking and throwing down in the kitchen. I was always cooking something after school; I would regularly raid my friends' kitchens and cook up a meal for all of us. People used to ask me when I would open a restaurant. It was apparent that my passion was cooking, even from a young age. In 2007, at age 28 I made a contract with myself that I would pursue my dream of opening a restaurant. I busted out this black book where I daydreamed about my restaurant. I drew up the restaurant set up and what equipment I wanted. I didn't know what a vision board was back then, but I was manifesting my vision into existence by drawing in my notebook.

After planning things out in my black book, I took a bet on myself. In 2010, I cashed in my 401k from my previous job to set up a professional establishment. I used the money to buy commercial-grade equipment for my pop-up. While I was working on the plans for opening my restaurant, I did a weekly pop-up in Oakland. I had a full-on menu, just like a restaurant. When that contract ended, my business partner supported me to open up my very own restaurant. I scouted a space and analyzed the costs. I realized that I didn't have the funds but luckily, at that time, crowdsourcing was available, and I decided to create a campaign to fund my restaurant. Thanks to the support of my fan base, friends, and family, in 2013, I was able to open my first restaurant, Kainbigan, in Oakland, California! It was the most challenging venture that I ever jumped into, but I made it happen. I was able to keep the contract that I made to myself! 2013 was a phenomenal year for me! In addition to opening Kainbigan, I ended up on Food Network's reality-based cooking television game show, *Chopped*, on their first New Year's edition. It's definitely one of my proudest moments for so many reasons! I am not a trained chef – I am self-taught and inspired by my family, including my parents, older sister, and my grandma. I learned from their home cooking and I was able to represent the Filipino culture. I wasn't a chef at a Michelin star restaurant – I was a small restaurant located in the cuts of Oakland. When I first opened my restaurant, it was hard to embrace calling myself "chef," until I was on the show. One of the challenges throughout my journey (not just the show) was fully believing in myself. Being on national TV made me vulnerable. It was a surreal experience and exciting. I showcased who I am, and I ended up winning because I was myself! That's when I finally felt assured as a chef.

After the show, I wanted to take a break but I had to continue running Kainbigan. During the slow season, I had to cut costs on payroll so I had a very small staff – I was only able to afford one other person along with myself. Hence, I was pretty much working every position in the business. I had one person working on the floor and register, and I was left to cook, prep, and even dishwash! The restaurant hit a plateau and I was mentally and physically beat. I was successful, but I needed a change. I needed to do what was best for me so unfortunately, after four years, I closed

Kainbigan down. I don't regret closing the restaurant because it brought a ton of other ventures and blessings. Afterward, I took a little break. I went to the Philippines to reset, with no plan after that! I took the time to rest, travel, and experience new things. In the midst of all of it, I had another opportunity for a restaurant space in downtown Oakland. It was a quick turn-key location so I jumped back in the restaurant business, opening up Craft and Spoon. After only a year, when the lease was up, the landlord wanted us to buy them out, but the price was too high. It was ridiculous and beyond my means, so I was on to the next thing.

In 2017, I was unstoppable! I was opening one business after another. It takes a strong team to do these things and thankfully that's what I had. I was running three businesses at the same time with my three business partners: Craft and Spoon (May 2017-May 2018), Town Biz (which opened in 2016), and Benefit Health Collective (as a co-founder). Benefit Health Collective was our first cannabis business, which was a private collective that provided medicinal marijuana to our local members; we mostly focused on marginalized communities. The cannabis business came up because chronic illness was something that my business partners and community were dealing with, along with a lack of access to natural medicine. We wanted to be able to provide that to our people. We then created an equitable cannabis business that supports marginalized communities, black and brown communities that were affected by the "War on Drugs," womxn, LGBTQA, and seniors. Our collective ran underground; we couldn't publicly announce it and all business was through word of mouth. We generated a customer base of 5,000 people and ran it for about two years until the institution of Measure Z: Oakland's Cannabis Regulation and Revenue Ordinance. When Oakland changed the legislation about running private collectives, we were no longer allowed to operate, but we wanted to follow the laws and be taken more seriously in the industry. In December 2018, we obtained a temporary delivery license for cannabis. So we then became a legal cannabis delivery business and changed the name to The People's Dispensary.

I am currently working full-time at The People's Dispensary along with my three business partners. A majority of our co-founders are people of color, LGBT, and we are 75% women-owned. Because the cannabis industry is not equitable, we wanted to create an equitable framework. Folks that are profiting in the industry are mostly white males and we wanted to create generational wealth within our community. Unfortunately, the legislation makes it difficult for us to succeed. However, we continue to move forward: We acquired our first dispensary in Portland and now we deliver in Oakland. Our next steps are to branch out around the nation.

Aside from the restaurants, dispensary, and Town Biz retail shop, I also work on my own projects. The first, Damo, which means "grass" in Tagalog, is an edibles line. Because I still wanted to be in the food business, I also started Baon Deluxe (BDX) in 2018. BDX is packaged frozen Filipino comfort food. All you have to do is boil the bag to get a taste of your favorite Filipino dish. I want to see BDX on the grocery store shelves. Because I have been busy running operations for The People's Dispensary in Portland, it left me little time to grow my other projects. The cannabis industry is complex and changes quickly so I have to do a lot of research and development on how I can make all this happen, legally and the right way. With that, I put Damo and BDX on hold. I wish there was enough time in a day to be able to do ALL of these things. Damo and BDX are definitely still on my bucket list of things I want to achieve.

My journey has had its ups and downs, but I believe what's kept me going is my appetite to bring all of my ideas into fruition. It is important to be hungry! Continue to work hard and push for what you want. Don't hold back, whether it's your career or what you're going to have for lunch. Go for it! If you have an idea, if you can picture it, then you can definitely get it! If you want that triple-double sundae, then go get that! I am rooting for you!

— Carissa Ortega

Be Vulnerable

Carissa Ortega

As a kid, I remember being dragged around everywhere by my parents. Because of this, the entrepreneurial grind did not appeal to me and I was convinced that I didn't want to follow in their footsteps. I wanted a 9 to 5 gig and some stability. But, entrepreneurship is all I've ever known; it runs in my blood. At 19-years-old, I started an event planning business after I fell in love with weddings and brides while working at David's Bridal. In college, I studied graphic design and started my own design agency at the age of 20. I was happy doing graphic design, growing and I had laid out my own career path. I was running my graphic design and event planning businesses at the same time, solidifying that I had followed my parents' entrepreneurial path.

In 2008, when I was 23-years-old, my mom and dad took on yet another business venture with my aunt and uncle. They opened up a restaurant in the valley of Los Angeles called Ninong's Cafe, which serves authentic Filipino comfort food. At the time, both my husband and I were working full-time in the design industry, but every now and then, I would help out at the restaurant on the weekends. I also did graphic design for the cafe, including the logo. Five years after opening the restaurant, my parents didn't want to continue running it. Before design, my husband's dream was to go to culinary school, but his family couldn't afford it, so it felt like destiny when my parents decided to move on from the cafe. But, we had to decide whether or not I would take part in the cafe. I felt I couldn't say no to joining the family business. I knew that I had to put my career on hold to help out. After five years of volunteering my time and services to the cafe, I became the youngest business partner when I decided to officially come on board at Ninong's Cafe in September 2013.

When I began working there, establishing boundaries with my family was a big challenge that I had to overcome. My parents, aunt, and uncle still viewed me as a young, cute kid even though I was 28-years-old. Over time, I realized the importance of creating my own space, even if I wasn't welcomed at the table. I had to take command of my position and let them know that I had something valid and useful to give. I never felt I had to prove anything, but I needed to show them that my ideas could make an impact. Through that experience, I realized how happy I was being around my family all the time. I viewed our business as a family thing, but also as a serious business. When I started helping out more, I found my passion for helping my family and customers. That's where I felt the happiest and most empowered.

A month after I came on board, my mom was diagnosed with breast cancer. Unfortunately, my parents were entrepreneurs and never bothered with health insurance for any of us. Like most Filipinos, my mom was diabetic and my dad has high blood pressure and gout. These pre-existing conditions made them uninsurable. When my mom was diagnosed, I was scared, but my mom remained hopeful. Without knowing the details, I had a sinking feeling. One day, I took my mom aside to have a serious conversation about her situation but she didn't want to talk about it. She was hoping for Obamacare, but instead, she ended up paying $3,000 out of pocket for a biopsy and doctor visit. We didn't have the money to pay upfront, but luckily, the doctor allowed me to pay him in installments. Due to the high costs of medical treatment in the United States (U.S.), my mom resorted to getting a mastectomy in the Philippines. My mom's brother, a doctor in the Philippines, encouraged her to get the surgery done abroad as it was less expensive than the U.S. At the time, my dad was a truck driver, driving from the East Coast to the West Coast. He had to quit his job to accompany my mom to the Philippines. Even though I had no training, I had no choice but to stay behind to run the restaurant.

Despite having the surgery done, my mom's battle with cancer continued. The lack of communication around difficult topics was a huge turning point for me. My mom was not vocal and did not want to communicate with me about the process and her experience. She didn't involve me, and instead, she wanted me to focus on the business. Looking back, I wish I had been pushier. I want to encourage people that have a hard time communicating with their elders, to be brave and just talk about it. Force them! I wish I did! After my mom had been living with cancer for two years, I received a call from my dad. He rarely cries so when I heard him crying, I knew it was serious. My mom had passed away. The moment I received the news, my relationship with my mom flashed before my eyes. The last thing my mom said to me was "drive safely." Before she passed, she was hardly talking anymore. I wish I would have said more when she was able to talk. That's really all we had. During my mom's funeral, there were over 200 people present. How was she able to create that connection with all these people and not me?

Filipino culture is very focused on accomplishments. Because we come from very little, we want our families to be better and have more. My mom was very driven. She was a real estate agent and she quantified success in numbers. As an only child, I grew up with abundance. There was never a shortage of money. She bought me lots of gifts, and that's how she showed her love for me.

We would regularly go to lunch and shopping, and she took me on frequent trips to Las Vegas. That was her way of showing love. When my mom passed away, I realized that wasn't everything. I was yearning for her to tell me that she loved me and that she was proud of me. Unfortunately, that was a lot to ask, considering she had a hard time vocalizing her love for me. I knew she loved me, but it was unspoken. Now that I am a mom myself, I want to show my kids and tell them my emotions. For me, the epitome of success is being able to show my emotions and let people know that I love them. My mom wanted to give me everything so that I had a better life, but I wish I had more intimacy and closeness with her. What you remember the most are memories and what people say to you, not the objects. I've learned that memories are more important than material things.

Before my mom passed, we had a hospice set up in my childhood home. When she was dying, people were afraid to be around her. I didn't want my mom to feel like she was struggling alone so I made sure to show her, and let her know that she was loved. When she finally passed, I cried so hard. I was supposed to be the strong one and the one holding the family business down. The moment I let myself cry, I finally felt that I was able to be myself. I didn't have to hide or pretend to be strong! It helped me make peace with the struggles I faced regarding my relationship with my mom. We shouldn't be afraid to talk to our family about the hard stuff. We have to vocalize these feelings. From my experiences, I've learned that it's never too late and it's OK to be myself. As an only child, I felt so alone and isolated. After my mom passed away, my dad moved to the Philippines. Now, my dad is more vocal. He tells me that he loves me and that he misses me. That's a big deal for him to say and for me to hear. He's not afraid to say it and I will say it back to him all the time. I am so happy and I wish I could have had that sooner. We have to teach our parents to express themselves and to be true to who they are.

Even though I was hesitant at first, I am glad I gave up my career to help my family. The reward of helping them is the pinnacle of my career and the most rewarding thing I've ever done. Being able to help my family and help spread Filipino culture and food to non-Filipinos has been nothing short of amazing. I want everyone to experience Filipino food and culture! Although being an entrepreneur is really scary and extremely hard, if you come from a place of servitude and giving, then you can do it! I encourage you to embrace your ideas and allow them to become something. The worst is the regret of not even trying. I am an advocate of people starting their own businesses as long as they are prepared and know what they are getting into.

We all have dreams – small ones and really big ones! Dreams seem so far away and unattainable, but when you're transparent and have no shame, it's much easier to talk about them. Having a strong support system helps build up your confidence, power, and can serve as a reminder that you're not alone. I have chosen my tribe and the people that I want to surround myself with. Earlier in my career, I found it extremely difficult to connect with others, mainly because I felt stigmatized. I found it very intimidating, especially being a woman and a person of color. One way I was able to overcome the fear and intimidation was through finding my tribe that helped lift me up, mentally and physically.

Knowing what I know now, I would have told my younger self, "Don't be so afraid. Don't feel so intimidated. Don't compare yourself. Fear, intimidation, and comparison are the biggest robbers of joy." Being afraid that I can't keep up or that I'm not doing the best I can are self-inflicted pressures and fears. I need to give myself more credit. You are your own worst critic. You hit a milestone and you are already thinking about what's next. Celebrate each milestone and push for more, but allow yourself to revel in the accomplishment.

Success is not dictated by numbers, whether quantified in dollars or followers. I really struggle with that because I am a planner and a statistics person. I need to see data, but these numbers have been poison for me. No matter how you look at it, Ninong's Cafe has been my biggest success. I've been fulfilled, had a sense of gratitude, and I didn't want to jump ship after just a few months. It's my testimony and a huge part of my story. I am proud of how my family started the business, how it shaped our lives, and how it allowed my husband to pursue his culinary career. I've done a lot of self-reflection and it made me realize that success is happiness. I don't need a certain amount of money to be happy. In some ways, happiness comes with having less. All I want is for my husband, my family, and me to be happy. I want my basic necessities and health!

When my mom passed away, I thought about my own legacy. I want to be remembered as a kind person who was there for people (friends, family, and strangers). The ones that are remembered are those who use their platform for good or philanthropy. I want to create high-quality and meaningful relationships with others. I want to be wholeheartedly invested in people, with no strings attached and to believe there is good in people. I am immensely passionate about encouraging people and letting them know that they can do it so I launched my *Mastermind and Grind* coaching program, which is geared to helping small businesses create success. I am so thankful that I get to help my family with our business, and I am looking forward to helping others grow.

BE KIND TO YOUR
thoughts

YOUR
words

AND YOUR
actions

—Cristina Espiritu

BE REBELLIOUS

Cristina Espíritu

I was born in the Philippines and moved to the United States (U.S.) at 15-years-old. Like typical Filipino immigrant stories, a relative (my grandmother) petitioned my family to come to the U.S. I remember my parents telling me as a young kid that we would be going to America, but that didn't become reality until a decade later when we finally received the approval letter to move.

My immigrant story is just like many others. My parents sold everything we had in the Philippines: my childhood home, cars, other valuables – and we traveled to the U.S. with only a few suitcases and *balikbayan* (a corrugated box containing imported items sent from overseas) boxes. And in spite of the teary farewells with my friends and promises to write letters to each other every week, I was giddy with excitement. For my siblings and me, this was an adventure – we got to ride on a plane for the first time and travel to a place we've only seen in movies. Looking back now, I realize how different it must have been for my parents, with them feeling the anxiety and nervousness of uprooting everything they knew and starting fresh somewhere thousands of miles away.

When we first arrived in the U.S., we lived with an uncle until my parents got settled. My parents worked multiple jobs in order to purchase their first home in Moreno Valley, California which is where I finished high school. I was always a hardworking student, who had been top of my class for as long as I could remember. My first memory of "achievement" was receiving a ribbon for being the #1 student in my first-grade class. Yes, this is a weird concept for American students, but back then, in the Catholic school where I spent most of my education in the Philippines, students got graded and ranked. The desire to excel has always been instilled in me and became even stronger when I moved to the U.S.. Being new to the country and new to the school, I worked hard to catch up on the curriculum. It paid off when I graduated as valedictorian of my class. Upon graduation, I attended the University of California, Los Angeles (UCLA).

I thought I had my life planned out: finish college, go to grad school, work a great job, and then retire. But sometimes, the universe has something else planned for you. At the beginning of my junior year at UCLA, I found out I had cancer. I had just begun my summer abroad program in France when I had a routine medical checkup in a small clinic in Paris. The physician looked at my x-ray and immediately knew something was wrong. He advised me to go home right away to see my doctor. After further tests with my doctor in the U.S., I was diagnosed with Hodgkin's Lymphoma.

Many people who had cancer will tell you that they distinctly remember where they were, what they were doing, and who they were with when they found out the news of their diagnosis. I was the opposite. All I remember was thinking, "I can't go back to Paris!" I was more concerned about missing a year of school than actually thinking about having cancer. The gravity of the situation did not hit me until the chemotherapy treatments started. Everyone who knows about cancer knows of the physical toll that the disease and the treatments can cause on your body. But fewer people are more aware of the psychological, emotional, and mental effects that can result from it. I had cancer before the age of social media which meant that fewer people shared their experiences and it was easy to feel like I was the only one going through something like this. A few friends could not relate at all to what I was experiencing, which resulted in me losing relationships along the way. The feeling that life moves on without you was also challenging and left me feeling isolated at times. However, the support of my family and core group of friends got me through it, along with the determination to achieve the goals I had before I got cancer. After my treatments were over, I went back to college and graduated from UCLA. I am happy to say that I have been cancer-free ever since!

Life after cancer was simply trying to live a normal life again. I did several internships after graduation, trying to figure out how I wanted to shape the rest of my life. That led me down the path to law school. Although I knew I wanted to go into law, I still had this drive to start my own business and I knew I would someday. In 2004, I graduated from Pennsylvania State University with a joint JD/MBA degree. Afterward, I returned to California and landed a job in business valuation, an industry where I had worked for the past 14 years and where I still work today.

Throughout my career, this "itch" to start my own business has always been present in the background, but a voice telling me to take the "stable" path kept on getting in the way. It wasn't until I read about an inspiring woman who was a practicing attorney and also an entrepreneur who ran several businesses that I realized that there could be more than just one path. She inspired me to look beyond the "norm" and create a life that resonated with who I am. Another person who empowered me to fully pursue my passion was my long-term boyfriend (and high school sweetheart). He had quit his 9 to 5 job to pursue his entrepreneurial passions. His resilience and positivity continue to inspire me every day.

My leap into "multi-entrepreneurship" truly honors who I am and my desire to live my authentic self. All of the companies I've started were birthed based on my passions – travel, food, wellness, community, and natural healing. My first venture, World Crave was started in 2014 and honors my passion for travel. We work with nonprofits and artisans to source one of a kind home goods from different countries and bring them to the U.S. so people could discover different cultures.

In 2017, I started my second company called the 420 Foodie Club. I would have never thought in a million years that I would be doing anything related to cannabis! However, my experience as a cancer survivor and a passion for food and natural healing prompted me to start something that could help people who are looking to learn more about the medicinal properties of the cannabis plant. Through 420 Foodie Club, we hold educational events and cooking classes and create menus and unique food ideas for daily lifestyles using cannabis-infused products.

My experiences running 420 Foodie Club emboldened me to branch off and start other ventures in the CBD/cannabis industry. Since then I've started HerCannabiz, a women's cannabis entrepreneur group. My goal through HerCannabiz is to create a supportive and educational community for emerging and established women business owners as they traverse through a male-dominated industry. I also started My Cannawellness, an online platform that connects consumers to CBD brands, activities, and events.

In the past several years, I have reconnected with the Filipino community, especially in Southern California. To honor my roots, I co-founded My Jeepney Stop, a "Filipino Yelp" that connects Filipino businesses, entrepreneurs, and events in one digital platform, and serves as a directory and resource for the Filipino community.

A piece of advice I would give to anyone who wants to take the entrepreneurial path is to get past the fear. We all have fears! It's just a matter of pushing through them that will get you to the next level. The desire to push forward regardless of what people or society think is crucial. There are countless times when someone "advised" me to focus on one thing, or not to do something or another. People will have opinions no matter what action or direction you take. People will always give you advice. However, listen to your gut and honor that voice in your head. It will guide you.

What defines success for me is the freedom to be authentic to who I am. In the final moments of my life, as I'm looking back to what I've done, I want to feel like I have no regrets.

THE BIGGEST RISK I'VE EVER TAKEN IS TO BE *comfortable* IN MY OWN SKIN, AND THAT HAS PAID OFF.

—Jonah Toleno

Be Vocal

Jonah Toleno

In school, I was the quiet kid who would only give answers when called on. I was too nervous to raise my hand to volunteer. When I finally found my voice as an adult, I felt compelled to speak up for others whenever I could. As an attorney who represents individuals and companies in the financial services industry, I use my skills to advocate for others and give a voice to those who cannot speak up or don't have the means to.

When I was in high school, my mother worked as a clerk in the criminal division of the Alameda County Superior Court. I interned there as a teenager, observing trials and working with judges, clerks, and attorneys. After participating in my high school's mock trial team, I knew I wanted to go to law school. I went to the University of California, Berkeley for undergraduate studies. After graduating with a bachelor's degree in legal studies and a minor in music, I spent a year working for an immigration law firm to make sure going into law was the right decision for me. It was a valuable experience, allowing me to learn both about the business of being a lawyer and working with clients. After that, I decided to attend the University of California Hastings College of the Law in San Francisco.

Law school was extremely challenging. At the time, Hastings was one of the top 20 law schools in the country, and the workload was demanding and grueling. But I would do it all over again because Hastings is where I met some of my closest friends, as well as my future husband Doug. I graduated in 2000, and we married in 2001. I graduated a year before him, and I started my career doing defense work in the Bay Area. By the time Doug graduated, we had our first child, our daughter Danielle, who was born in January 2002. Upon graduating, Doug received offers from two large law firms, choosing to join a firm in Phoenix, Arizona.

When we moved to Phoenix, I decided to stay home with our baby daughter. This was a decision I did not make lightly. I knew I would be delaying progress in my new career as an attorney. I decided to take a break from law to devote my full attention to being a mother. We had our second child, our son Christian, in 2003. They are 19 months apart, and my life was consumed at the time with mothering Danielle and Christian full-time. For what felt like an eternity, while my friends were traveling the globe and living it up, or advancing in their careers, I was a stay-at-home mom, taking the babies to playgroups, doing storytime, and changing diapers. To this day, staying home with my kids is the hardest job I ever had and I don't regret one minute of it. This was a special time for our little family, finding ourselves and learning how to stand on our own.

When the kids were a bit older, I took the Arizona bar exam and worked part-time for a sole practitioner with a varied civil practice. He was a Southern gentleman with a booming voice, a commanding presence, and a compassionate heart. He accommodated my desire to spend as much time as I could with my young children while dipping my toes back into the legal world. I still consider him a valuable mentor today.

After nearly five years in the desert, my husband and I made our way to San Diego, California, where we live now and are surrounded by lots of family. I joined the firm, Shustak Reynolds & Partners. We are a small boutique firm that specializes in securities litigation and arbitration, financial services law, and business and corporate litigation. I have been with the firm for 14 years, and I am grateful for the opportunities I've been afforded.

I have been working full-time since joining the firm in 2006, and I can say with all honesty that I am glad I went back to work in an office. I respect every mother's decision to work outside or in the home; I think we all try our best and do what we think is best for our families. I would never judge a fellow mother who does not work outside the home, but I am thankful I get the opportunity to do what I do and show my daughter that we can make opportunities happen for ourselves. It has been challenging, and at times overwhelming, but the rewards have been immeasurable. I get to use my voice to advocate for and to counsel people who are victims of fraud. These are everyday folks who are trying to make an honest living and businesses that are doing their best for their employees. I am proud to use my voice to speak up for others in many different ways.

I'm an active leader in our community, various bar organizations, and nonprofits. I am a past president of the Filipino American Lawyers of San Diego and currently sit on the board. I'm also active with the National Filipino American Lawyers Association. Both of these organizations are near and dear to my heart, as they help me remain connected to my treasured Filipina roots. I also lead committees for the Lawyers Club of San Diego, which is dedicated to the advancement of women in the legal field. It's important to me that I set an example to my children of someone who does not allow cultural or gender barriers to impede success. I am lucky to practice with a firm whose partners support me wholeheartedly as a woman in a male-dominated field, and in a community that is diverse, collaborative, amicable, and supportive.

My children are currently in their last years of high school. I try to keep a small and manageable caseload so I can devote ample time to my clients while prioritizing my family duties. I'm very close to my children, and my husband and I are very proud of who they have become. They are intelligent, warm, humorous, hardworking, athletic, witty, and fun people. My husband is the most amazing teammate and partner I could have ever dreamed of having. He is my rock and my best friend.

As I look back on my nearly 20 years since becoming licensed to practice law, I can recall many hills and valleys on my path. It has not been easy; I am often underestimated by new opponents. But my approach is always to be civil, even friendly where appropriate, and to choose my battles. I go to the mat for my clients and represent them vigorously. But I also recognize that it's not all about the fight. My goal is to bring peace of mind to my clients while preserving my own. I have encountered times where I've stretched myself too thin, and gotten sick in the process. Now, having gone through and overcoming health challenges, I realize that life is precious; we need to take care of ourselves if we expect to take care of others, like our children, spouses, loved ones, and clients. I allow myself to enjoy quality time with my loved ones, spending time with my family, my mother, siblings, in-laws, and dear friends. I love to read, cook, watch the kids' sporting events, try new restaurants with my husband, and snuggle with our dog, Chili.

Over the course of my career, I have tried challenging cases, obtained grand slam wins, gotten knocked down on my rear end, and have been both humbled and devastated. I treasure all of it, even the challenges, because all of it makes me who I am today – a dedicated, passionate, Filipino-American wife, mother, attorney, and friend. I don't back down from a fight, but I also try to counsel and lead from the heart. Before I tried my first case, a mentor told me to just be myself, because only I could do that and that's who people love. I rely on this today when the voice in my head tells me I can't do something because I'm still that shy, quiet girl who was afraid to speak in class. I speak, even if my voice shakes, and I act, even if my hand shakes. This is who I am, who God made in His infinite wisdom, and I am a work in progress. I hope to always be reaching for the next level of excellence, to never stop learning, and to keep loving those around me with a bigger, bolder heart every day.

Some words of advice I would give to other, younger women would be: be mindful, work hard, be kind, be respectful, and be open to opportunities. Don't expect things to fall into your lap. Speak up for yourself – even if your voice quivers and your hand shakes. Put in the time. Guard your reputation with the utmost care. It takes a long time to build it up, and one bad decision can wash it all away. Live in the moment. Put down the phone and reclaim the experience of living in the present. Most of all, don't forget to take care of yourself and your happiness. This is not selfish – this is a necessity. Those around you will be grateful you did.

I FIRMLY BELIEVE THAT
design
CAN CHANGE THE WORLD
AND THAT WE, AS
designers
&
architects,
SHOULD BE RESPONSIBLE
FOR WHAT WE BUILD,
WHAT WE DESIGN,
—— AND ——
THE IMPACT IT HAS.

—Vina Lustado

Be Simple

Vina Lustado

As a young child, I had a calling to be useful and to make a difference in the world. I immigrated to the United States (U.S.) from the Philippines when I was seven-years-old. The only memory I have from my childhood is of the jungle, or the *linang* (Filipino word for land, jungle, farm). When I was a kid, my family would take a donkey and walk barefoot to the *linang*. We cooked over an open flame and my uncle climbed coconut trees to get fresh coconut juice. Everything was simple and primitive, and I loved it. I carry that memory with me. Through and through, I am a nature lover. That love started in childhood and continued through adulthood when I decided to buy a property near Yosemite National Park with a year-round creek that reminded me of the jungle that I remember so fondly. My roots are with the simple lifestyle of the Philippines. My vision has been to create a tiny home community and to become a steward of the land.

I have nine siblings who are all in the medical field and are very accomplished. I opted out of medicine because I am squeamish around blood. I wanted to do something creative so I studied art at the University of California, Los Angeles. That's where I learned that art has no parameters and is very subjective so I changed my major and obtained my architecture degree from the University of Southern California.

For the first 15 years of my career, I worked in corporate architecture firms. I was afforded the experience to work in big cities, doing big projects for well-known offices. Although I enjoyed my experience, it was soul-sucking. I worked 60 hours a week, slept under my desk, and tried to meet deadlines for client presentations. This work really didn't have meaning or purpose for me. I worked directly with corporate clients' CEOs and executives instead of the people who were actually going to use the space, leaving me feeling disconnected from the users. I didn't feel fulfilled because I wasn't making a positive impact that I could see. I wanted to work on a smaller scale and with people who would actually use the spaces I created. That's when I made the decision to leave San Francisco.

For three months, I took some time off to do a fellowship in Germany. The lifestyle there is to live consciously with the environment – using public transportation and conserving energy at home. During my time abroad, I learned that sustainability needs to be a mindset that pervades culture and lifestyle. From my time there, sustainability and affordability became my focus. To be sustainable is to be economically efficient. When I returned to the U.S. I was determined to apply that knowledge to my professional practice. I brought those two things together and started working for a firm in Ventura, California. I gained experience catering to modest families. I did residential projects, but I didn't feel like I was really pushing the envelope.

After seven years at the firm, I went on sabbatical. I took a trip for three months to reassess my values. Upon my return, I got laid off due to the recession, which caused many projects to get canceled. So I decided I needed to take control of my own financial stability rather than being dependent on these firms. I started to strategize. I didn't want my own business, but it was the only way for me to have financial stability. I started to take business classes through

Women's Economic Ventures and was working with a contractor on a residential project at the same time, preparing to start my own business.

In 2009, I started my business from the ground up with no financial resources and no role model. I come from a modest Filipino family where most of my siblings are nurses, not entrepreneurs or architects. The mission of my firm is to cater to modest-income families and clients. By redefining the profession to bring quality housing to modest-income families, I eliminated the competition in my field by specializing in small buildings and tiny houses. However, I faced many challenges like how to grow my business while keeping the integrity of my mission: making beautiful, human-centered design where the quality of living is accessible to all. My goal is to implement environmentally friendly solutions that promote social justice through the built environment. I believe design can be – and should be – a force for good. With tiny houses, spaces are small but efficient, and the building and permitting process is more affordable and not as long of a process.

Through my earlier work, I learned this profession can swallow you up. During university and working for big firms, I found myself living and breathing the profession. I definitely have gone through my fair share of challenges. I struggled with confidence, second-guessing myself, and questioning if I'm good enough. I was, and still am, surrounded by male architects, engineers, and contractors. It has been hard for me to take a stance and be confident in my voice; I wasn't always respected and heard.

I would advise others who want to be an entrepreneur to heed your calling and listen to your heart. There will be many challenges in your career and in owning your own business. There will be ups and downs, and your values will be challenged. Be diligent.

Embrace failures and challenges. Be patient and practice gratitude, especially for simple things.

It's also important to surround yourself with people who support you and believe in what you're doing but are also able to be honest and tell you the truth. Find your tribe and stay connected with your community. It's important to fill ourselves up before we can be of benefit to others.

Lastly, always welcome failure! You may stumble, but get up and try again! That's how you get better and how you learn and grow. Failure is a pathway to success. For me, success is peace of mind and heart. Leading a meaningful life doesn't necessarily equate to financial success. Satisfaction in what you do, being in service to others, and making a difference in others' lives is what equates to success for me.

Staying true to my values in sustainability, I completed the design and construction of my tiny home in 2012-2013 (before tiny homes became a fad). My 140 square foot home is equipped with simple luxuries: a loft skylight and a cozy fireplace. The design of my home is a reflection of my philosophy about simplicity, sustainability, and living within my means.

My dream is to create an intentional community that consists of tiny houses and other alternative building structures. I purchased the property near Yosemite to create this community as a model for sustainable and affordable housing. I'm also developing a prefab modular dwelling that can be re-configured for flexibility. It challenges the traditional stick-built construction and permit process. We are at a critical time in history. Our planet is in crisis, and I am doing what I can to contribute to the solution through sustainable and economically-sound housing options.

There is NOWHERE to go.
CUPPED IN OUR BARE HANDS
IS THIS ONE LIFE WE ARE
empowered
TO
uniquely design,
build AND live.
THERE'S JUST THIS MOMENT

AND SUDDENLY,
the meaning of life
UNLOCKS WITH
astonishing simplicity.
The journey IS THE destination.

—Anne Espiritu

BE.

Anne Espiritu

I am the product of an immigrant upbringing. I was born in the Philippines and at the age of 11, my brave, single mother packed what she could in two large cases and shipped me and my brother off to the United States of America. What I innocently believed was that I was headed to the enchanted kingdom of *Disneyland*; to me, that's what I pictured the United States to be. Upon arriving at the airport, I recall shuffling my feet in eager anticipation to reach the gate, peering through the long line of *lolos* and *lolas* (grandparents in Tagalog), all equally restless to get off the plane. In the subtle corners of my expectations, I was anticipating that Mickey and Minnie Mouse, with their static smiles and flappy, white hands would appear in my line of sight. Suffice to say, they weren't there to greet me, nor did the experience in my new reality accurately match that of a fairy tale journey.

Moving to a new country where I looked, felt, and smelled different was a jarring and confusing experience. Getting replanted at the tender age of 11-years-old – during the most untimely season to be different as our desire to belong heightens – added new layers of complexity to the way I saw myself and the world. I quickly learned to despise every aspect of myself that didn't resemble my peers. My self-worth slowly shattered, as the feeling of unworthiness deepened; this inevitably served as an invisible backdrop throughout my adult life. I learned how to cope with my new reality using a powerful strategy – an unseen language that would inspire and frame the way I saw, behaved, and navigated in the world.

Conformity.

Conformity seemingly melted away the resistance that often colored my reality growing up. The comfort I felt in being just like everyone else was addicting – intoxicating, even. My "representative" felt seen, heard...acknowledged. I talked, moved, and acted like my American peers. Just like them, I would buy into the promises of the American Dream and plotted my life against its playbook. Get into a good college? Check. Find a good career? Check. Make good money? Check. By the age of 35, I was living the ultimate Instagram lifestyle. I had my high profile job as the head of global communications for Yahoo reporting directly under the CEO, a marriage-material, well-to-do romantic partner, brand-name jewelry and trinkets, a splashy luxury sports car, and a million-dollar, Bay Area home. I followed the blueprint of success and on the outside I had all of the markings of a woman who had finally "made it." Yet, in the quiet corners of my consciousness, I was feeling suffocated by the paradoxical life I was living. You see, beneath the facade, I was feeling empty and bankrupt – and I didn't know why.

The Turning Point

I had just arrived back at my lofty, Tribeca apartment and tossed the five bags of my newly acquired wardrobe on the bed – an activity that had become a weekend ritual – an escape of sorts. Several months prior, I made a drastic realization that my job at Yahoo was the root of my unhappiness, so I quit. I moved to

New York City and took on a new sexy job at one of the hottest start-ups in town. I was convinced this was my chance to unleash the "Charlotte" in me, and that I was finally going to live out the *Sex and the City* lifestyle I had grown up admiring. Trying on a new pair of jeans, I twirled from side to side in front of the mirror and caught a glimpse of the woman who had seemingly aged beyond her years. Even with her trendy clothes on, she looked worn out, both from the heavy logs she carried under her eyes and the emptiness that filled her gaze. A surge of debilitating fear ran through my body and the tears began to gush out of my eyes. I dreaded not ever finding an answer to what felt like the ultimate mystery of life – I had all the success in the world, but why wasn't I happy? Was I ever going to experience happiness? Is this life really *it*? A tornado of emotions washed over me – I felt confused and admittedly, guilty for the entitled attitude that I judged was within me.

Suffice to say, I lasted less than one year in my new job, new environment, and new life, until the temptation emerged to undergo another round of changes. Upon introspection, I notice my tendency to fall in and out of two-year cycles where I make a major overhaul in my life. This shift expresses itself in different ways – moving into a new home, ending or starting a romantic relationship, or transitioning into a new job. I was slowly coming to terms with the scary and ugly truth that no matter what I did or how hard I tried, I couldn't find happiness in my current reality. Happiness wasn't buried underneath the status, resources, or even in the extraordinary relationships, I had cultivated through the years. I know because all my life, I searched long, deep, and hard.

In 2017, I finally found the courage to leave corporate America – and along with that decision, I left the comfort that came with the predictability of my future. I had no idea where I was headed, but deep down I knew that living through my misery forever was a

BE.

far greater existential risk than doing what most would not dare to do – tread through uncharted territory. I was fully leaping into the unknown, eyes closed with fears, excitement, and all. I afforded myself six months of space to travel the world and with not much to guide my path beyond unwavering belief that God would lead the way. I set my own voracious curiosity to discover the purpose of life, and a commitment to trust my intuition. A friend, who was known as a psychic of sorts, gave me a profound piece of advice, "The answers to your questions lie in the journey."

Intellectually, the idea that we only truly have the present moment and that the future and past exist purely in the mind made some sense to me. Experientially, it was a much more difficult concept to live by. Still, I decided to commit to the path of consciously living and breathing in real-time, paying close attention to all that surrounds me, and allowing my intuition to guide every inch of my step.

The Unexpected Unfolding

"Excuse me? Would you have an Apple charger I can borrow?" I looked up to see who was tapping my shoulder and there he was, a seemingly luminous being dressed in all white, with his pearly white teeth and effervescent energy. It was my second day in Bali so naturally, I was still orienting myself to my new surroundings – I remember contemplating under my breath, "Is this person in front of me real?"

What started out as casual chit chat turned into a four-hour-long discourse about the nature of self. Little did I know that the person in front of me was Dr. Daniel Cordaro, one of today's leading experts in human emotion and CEO of the Contentment Foundation, a nonprofit organization that is working to bring sustainable well-being tools to schools worldwide. I couldn't deny that the mission – to help teachers and students understand, manage, and process their emotions and life experience – resonated deeply with me. As the former director of well-being at the Yale Center for Emotional Intelligence, Dr. Cordaro, (or Dan, as many of us affectionately call him) dazzled me with evidence-based proof points around "emotions" – something that often felt undeniably real yet intangible, and dare I say, often irrelevant in the fast-paced world I was living in. Who had the time and energy to deal with emotions? Dan gave me a crash course on the role of the ego and put words behind experiences I was secretly having within. All of my life, I learned to see "feeling" as an annoying by-product of being human. It was of course, only appropriate to acknowledge it when the feeling was pleasant. As he described the ways in which he and his team were working to propel humanity forward, I recollected the overwhelm and confusion that I experienced in my childhood years. Despite the fact that I had known this man for only a few hours, I felt seen, heard, and acknowledged – no, not my "representative," but the real me who secretly struggled to find self-acceptance. Free of judgment, Dan helped me fully recognize and embrace the psychological and emotional struggles that I had been experiencing throughout my adult life. At that moment, something inside of me lit up. That day would forever change the way I saw myself, other people, and the world around me.

I felt like I was finally returning back home.

While more would be revealed in time, I was beginning to understand that I may have been searching for happiness in the wrong places. I knew all too well by then it wasn't tucked in between my external success. I was recognizing that all along, my happiness was actually within arms reach – I simply needed to realign my sight *inward*.

Within a short two and a half weeks in Bali, I made yet another drastic and radical decision. I flew back to New York after concluding my world travels, only to put my belongings in storage. Within two months' time, I flew back to Bali, and this time, to stay indefinitely. I didn't know exactly why I had to return – I just knew I was meant to. I made a heart-centered commitment to help Dan, along with the rest of his team, to bring the gift of well-being to all sentient beings worldwide. Most importantly, I vowed to heal whatever wounds were tucked beneath the surface of my skin and once and for all, work to put them in their resting place.

I could not have predicted the way life would unfold following my fateful decision to trade in my comfortable, societally-endorsed life for one that was unconventionally raw, unfiltered, and unscripted. Yet, as time passed, my life was starting to feel more aligned than I had ever experienced.

The answers to my questions lie in the journey...The truth behind this notion was finally crystallizing. I would no longer simply understand it intellectually. I was ready to blindly trust it.

And the Real Work Begins

"I have a solid draft of our communications plan in place," I explained to Dan.

On the surface, I was pretending to have it all together but beneath the walls of my chest, I was crumbling. Dan could sense my energy and tenderly asked, "How are you feeling today, Anne?"

I had just gotten into a disagreement with someone who mattered to me and naturally, it was weighing heavily on me. "Oh, I'm alright. Just feeling a little low in energy," I muttered.

How often do we pretend to be strong...to be OK...while the Earth beneath us seems to be seismically shifting? How often do we feel like crumbling to pieces yet we put on a smiling, happy face?

Before I knew it, my eyes started to well up and just as I was taught both at home and at school, I immediately attempted to shove the sadness back down my throat and fight back the tears.

"Anne, let it out. It's energy that's trying to move through you," Dan suggested.

"No, no, I'm OK. Really," I said.

At that point, Dan repositioned himself and sat behind me. He took both pointy fingers and stuck them on my cheek where he could keep my jaws open. Perhaps, it was the invitation, or maybe it was because my jaws were being pried open, or, because Dan simply has the capacity to hold such a sacred and safe space for people's authentic selves to emerge...I began to sob. This wasn't just a typical weep that you'd see on even the best Korean drama on television. It was the most unfiltered, deepest and perhaps uncontrollable cry I had ever witnessed in any adult, let alone in myself. Despite my best effort to hold it back, the energy flowed through me like a tidal wave. After the sob fest, I felt drained and exhausted yet somehow also felt infinitely lighter.

You see, living under the roof of a single-parent home, my mom seared in me and my siblings the importance of being bold and brave. I grew up believing that in order to thrive in life, we can't buckle under the pressures of emotional breakdowns. To put it simply, in our household, there was no room for such nonsense, like feelings.

BE.

Like many others, I afforded myself opportunities to travel across many ends of Planet Earth to explore breathtaking views and awe-inspiring sites. Yet I rarely gifted myself enough space to navigate and explore the uncharted crevices of my inner world. I had a single strategy to deal with pain-stricken moments – to dust them under the rug, steady my chin high, and put on a steadfast face. This virtue was rooted in both my Filipino and American upbringing. I had no idea that by not fully processing, acknowledging and allowing my experiences to come and go, I'd be signing up to unconsciously relive past moments over and over again.

My New Horizon

Since then, I have been working tirelessly to peel back the layers of social conditioning and flip every stone within my subconscious mind for programs that no longer serve. I poured over and studied concepts related to quantum energy, neuroscience and different facets of spirituality in an attempt to learn about the nature of self – to fully understand myself. I gave myself permission to color outside of societal lines and explore the intangible world fully and unapologetically. I knew the path I chose (and the one I'm still on today) wouldn't always feel easy – heck, at times it all still feels unbearable. Yet, I was ready to hang up the victim cape, own up to my self-destructive patterns and finally claim my birthright as the creator, designer, and architect of my life.

Today, I continue to work hard in deepening my relationship with the most important, yet neglected person in my life – myself. This means relearning – or perhaps, even learning for the first time – how to acknowledge, accept and love myself, *unflinchingly*. I'm learning to honor and trust myself more – and listen to the invisible voice inside of me that all my life, has guided me in the direction of my alignment. I'm learning to fully immerse myself

218

in and celebrate all of my emotional experiences, no matter how tempting it is for me to judge them as good, bad, right or wrong. I'm also learning to sit in absolute stillness within each moment – to be lovingly detached from all that surrounds me knowing that the world will shift and evolve without ever, asking for my permission. It's entirely up to me to experience suffering by resisting the ways in which life is unfolding in front of me or tune into and move with the vibration of love and light, an energy that is constantly and eternally within my reach.

I'm learning to finally...*be*.

As I conclude this short chronicle of my journey, I leave you with these final words...

There is a sea full of wondrous unknowns waiting for you to explore. Paddle towards it – with fears, doubts and all. If you must, start with a series of tiny tippy toes forward. Each one you take is an act of bravery. Celebrate each movement and watch as your curiosity expands your view. Our rational minds are designed to build walls around us – "What if?" Acknowledge it and gently flip the question on its head, "Indeed, what if? But what if there is more that exists beyond what the borders of my current sight? What could possibly exist beyond these walls?"

Observe the tension between your heart and mind with tenderness and acceptance. The discomfort is a necessary part of the process. Find comfort in that knowing. It simply means you are expanding.

One fateful day, you will awaken and realize just how far you've traveled. And upon such discovery, every fiber of your being will illuminate. You will look back and all will finally make sense. And as you look ahead, you will realize that the fiery need to make sense of what could lie ahead has vanished. There is nowhere to go. Cupped in our bare hands is this one life we are empowered to uniquely design, build, and live. There is just this moment.

And suddenly, the meaning of life unlocks with astonishing simplicity.

The journey is the destination.

PART OF
Cultivating
A GOOD LIFE
—— IS TO ——
HONOR WHAT
excites YOUR *heart*
—— AND ——
TO LET YOURSELF
gravitate
TOWARDS
EACH INTEREST
THAT *calls* YOU.

—Onelia Miller

BE INTERESTED

Onelia E. Miller

Jack of all trades, master of none.
As a child, these words were seared into my heart and my brain.

The full saying was originally, "A jack of all trades is a master of none, but oftentimes better than a master of one." According to a deeper search on its origins, it was formerly intended as a compliment, the phrase means that a person is a generalist rather than a specialist, versatile and passably adept at many things but not an expert at one[3]. Over the generations, being a "jack of all trades" has become quite a negative notion. But I've never seen it that way.

Growing up, I was interested in learning and excelling at anything and everything; I still am that way. Over the years, my area of interest would change by the week but they rotated around a few major buckets of interest: service, design, art, and civic duty. One week I wanted to be an actress, the next week a veterinarian, the next week a reporter, and another week a handbag designer. And then start from the top again. This started as early as five-years-old and to this day, I still have "when I grow up, I want to be…"

---

[3] https://www.quora.com/What-is-the-origin-of-the-phrase-Jack-of-All-Trades-Master-of-None-and-what-does-it-mean

moments. As I write this, I am 39 and now planning the next chapter of my life.

In her book, *Becoming*, Michelle Obama talks about the question of "What do you want to be when you grow up?" She laments, "As if growing up is finite. As if at some point you become something and that's the end." She makes a great point – because deciding on and taking one path in life is, as we all will come to know, not the end. We are all constantly evolving. And becoming. And more often than not, one path leads to another...and another... despite our best intentions. The more troublesome association with this type of thinking is that this bouncing around gives you less of an identity than picking one thing to be. As if spending time in multiple areas of interest, detracts you from some falsely dubbed "main" area of interest. This couldn't be farther from the truth. Identity doesn't have to rest on one skill that you do, one area you work in, or the one thing that you're good at. You can have many interests and skills and still have a strong identity. However, as many children in my era were taught, if you do one thing great, you will be successful. Growing up and throughout my college years, I felt this type of thinking was unfair, but didn't quite understand it yet nor could I label it.

Looking back, I realize that while my parents didn't necessarily agree with the things I wanted to do, more often than not, they supported all my interests (though they were very vocal about their disagreement). They let me play hockey. They let me write for a kids' newspaper at age 11 that required a long commute to West Hollywood from West Covina every week to get mentored. On top of my tennis lessons, on top of my piano lessons, on top of my swimming lessons, on top of my baking contests, on top of letting me rescue every animal I could off the streets (at one point, we had six dogs, one cat, 24 parakeets, two hamsters, and two mice). They let me indulge every passion, of course with lots of convincing on my part. Eventually, they realized discouraging me from my wide range of interests wasn't going to stop me from pursuing them. By the time I got to college, they didn't protest when I finished my double major in political science and communications at the University of California, San Diego (UCSD) in three years and wanted to spend a year doing theatre before I graduated. They also didn't express too much concern with my over-programming of collegiate extracurricular activities: sorority social chair for four years, student government, newspaper op-ed writer, chancellor's office event planner, and big brother/big sister volunteer. Each and every one of these things completed me and they knew it.

After graduating from UCSD, my plan had been to go to law school. Soon after getting accepted, I began to develop anxiety as the time approached to start the program. Many classmates talked about the type of law they wanted to practice, who they clerked for last summer, who they had connections to, and other humble-brags and lofty goals they would pursue once finished. I had zero interest in any of these potential directions. And while law is pretty open-ended when it comes to possibilities, I wasn't interested in finding out where my path could lead in the legal realm. I realized I loved being a student of the law: I liked the idea of learning about history, civil rights, and civic duty. But becoming a practicing lawyer was not for me. Frankly, nothing gave me more anxiety than the thought of actually practicing any law.

So I quit. But what to do next?

I knew I was an entrepreneur and a creator at heart. No traditional form of "making a living" appealed to me, and I was interested in so many professions. While I was still at a loss at 22, I also knew I couldn't just sit around. So I applied to and started business school. I figured this would be a better use of post-grad time given my many interests. I realized everything I might pursue eventually had to be a business for me to make a living, and every potential job's goal was to increase that business' revenue and brand value, so business school was definitely the next step. Even if I didn't know exactly what the next step was after that.

Shortly after graduating from business school, I worked various jobs over the course of two years, "sampling" work in my areas of interest – I had short stints at a home-health company, a nonprofit cancer foundation, a handbag company, and even acted on a few soap operas. Looking back, I realize how these varied interests did not fall too far from my original apple tree of ideal professions as a child. The world was my smorgasbord, why limit my appetite?

Tim Harford, an English economist and journalist has written and discussed a lot about what he likes to call "slow-motion multitasking." It means working on multiple, seemingly different projects at the same time – and moving back and forth as the spirit moves you. While this may seem counterintuitive to some, due to the possibility of not being able to be a finisher of tasks, it is actually a powerful way to unleash your natural creativity and can allow you to unblock some blockage you are feeling in other parts of your life. At one of his TED Talks, Harford shared how Albert Einstein, Charles Darwin, and Michael Crichton found their inspiration and productivity through cross-training their minds. Whenever they found themselves at a mental roadblock, they would turn to another project that would help them unconsciously solve the original problem they had been struggling with. The idea that different ideas from different topics would allow you to "cross-fertilize" and gain new perspectives in your passions is what led me to where I am today.

After pursuing many passions and professional interests early in my career, I found myself at an Oscar party at the famed restaurant, Spago in Beverly Hills. As luck would have it, I engaged in a long and animated conversation with a classy, funny, and stylish British woman. She asked me what I did, and I told her that I was looking to start a marketing/ideation company that encompassed branding, events, and giving back. I told her about my MBA background and my forays into many different fields and what I loved about each of them. To my surprise, before the end of the night, she found me and gave me her business card. She was the Chief Marketing Officer of Mulberry (a luxury British handbag and leather goods company popular with celebrities and royals) and she was in town from London working on a new campaign launch for their store. She wanted to meet me the next day to discuss a potential project (which I eventually got).

From that chance meeting, my business was born.

In 2006, I founded an events production and branding company, Conspiracy LA, and went on to be a special projects and brand partnerships consultant for global brands such as Diane von Furstenburg, the Susan G. Komen Foundation, BMW, Rock and Republic, Smashbox, and many more. From producing runway shows to galas, to charity races and working with publications from *Vogue* and *Marie Claire* to *Forbes* and *The Wall Street Journal*, I found my ability to wear different hats successfully very empowering and very needed in a time where most consultants were one-dimensional.

To this day, my team and I work with celebrities, influencers, and other global brands in developing digital strategy, public relations strategies, events, ad campaigns, branding, and social media content. Every day is something new and different. Each day poses new challenges but also new perspectives. And I couldn't be happier with how my career continues to be one big multi-faceted endeavor. And what's even more exciting? The rest is still unwritten (cue Natasha Beddingfield and the *Laguna Beach* theme song).

So if I can impart one piece of advice from my "jack of all trades" life: Be Interested.

Be interested in all that catches your attention. If you truly pursue the things that you gravitate towards, that your heart directs you to, it will lead you to a life big enough to embrace ALL your dreams and not just one, leading you to ultimately and wholeheartedly pursuing the fullness of who you are – your true legacy.

Don't let the burden of specializing keep you from living the truest version of you – may answering every opportunity and interest lead you to a lifelong determination to embrace EVERY part of your story. Doing this allows you to marry the old and the new, who you are and who you are becoming.

This allows you to never stop learning, evolving and being interested in the ever-changing world around you. And if by chance you DO find the ONE thing you want to stick to forever, well that's just great too.

WORK HARD
to the fullest,
so you could
PLAY HARD
to the fullest.

—Cecilia Gutierrez

BE DARING

Cecilia Gutierrez

"She believed she could, so she did."
- R.S. Grey

Despite all the naysayers, I started my business in 2005, during the height of the recession. I believed I could do it. I had to ignore the haters. I had to be daring! My parents encouraged me to work hard and they really helped me get through school and supported me as I started my career and business. They've definitely contributed to helping me get where I am today, but I am proud to say that when I started my business, I had no investors, nor did I have a business loan. I was able to achieve success all on my own!

Filipino culture raises women to take care of their families. Family is of the utmost importance. It's rare to see a Filipina housewife since most of them work and raise kids at the same time. We are so hardworking, driven and reliable, and our culture takes pride in education, especially nursing! Once you get your degree, you are expected to get married, have kids, and take care of your family.

I started undergrad at Marymount University College in Palos Verdes, California at 18, but life took a turn when I became pregnant with my son at the age of 20. Even though I got pregnant during my last year of college, I did not quit. I continued to study and gave birth immediately after my last final exam. I was still able to obtain my associate's degree in nursing. Then five years later, after attending the LAC+USC Medical School of Nursing, I graduated with my second college degree. Once I became a registered nurse (RN), I was hired to work in the operating room (OR) of a level one trauma county hospital. Being a mom, working, and being a full-time student was no joke!

The mom guilt would settle in when I had my son (part-time due to joint custody) because I was unable to focus solely on him if I had to study for school. I worked in the OR full-time on the graveyard shift from 11 p.m. to 7 a.m., and simultaneously I went back to school at night from 6 p.m. to 10 p.m. to obtain my bachelor's degree in nursing. After my shift, I would take my son to school at 8:15 a.m. then I would try to sleep while he was in school from 9 a.m. to 2 p.m. Helping my son with his homework was also challenging after he got off school because I also had my own homework to do. At the time, my parents also had full-time careers. But they helped me when I really needed them to watch or pick up my son. There were times I needed their help just so I could study. They supported me and encouraged me to keep going no matter how tired I was or how discouraged I would get.

One morning, on my drive home from my graveyard shift, I saw a sign above a laser clinic for a job opportunity. Back in 1999, the word "Medical Spa" (MedSpa) didn't exist. It was often referred to as a laser center where RNs were able to operate lasers to treat scars, acne, brown spots, and perform hair removal. I decided to pull up to the clinic's parking lot even though they didn't open until 9 a.m. I stayed in my car and took a nap until they opened. When I inquired about what the job entailed, I met a very nice RN who worked part-time at the clinic and also the hospital. She explained to me that the center performed cosmetic procedures such as laser, microdermabrasion, Botox, and dermal fillers. All the laser procedures and microdermabrasion were performed by RNs and the injectables were performed by physician assistants and doctors. I instantly became curious and wanted to get into this specific field. This ignited my passion which stemmed from an accident that took place when I was less than a year old when I fell out of my walker, landing cheek down on a heater vent on the floor. The vent in our home had a flower printed metal cover. When I fell, my face sizzled over the heater vent and I had flower print marks over the right side of my face. Since I did not make a sound or cry, my parents didn't even notice that I had fallen over and burned my face. When they realized I had burned my face, they quickly rushed me to the emergency room. There are no baby pictures of me because my parents felt so bad about what happened and the scars that stayed with me. Growing up, I remember my dad constantly ensuring me that we would get my face fixed through plastic surgery. Not only did I have scars on my face, but I was teased because of them. Because of the impact that this had on me, I knew that I wanted to be in an occupation that helped people feel and look good. It's no surprise that I was drawn to the MedSpa field! I was simultaneously working full-time in the OR, pursuing my bachelor's degree in nursing, and training for my certification from an accredited training program in laser application, chemical peels, microdermabrasion, Botox, and filler injectables!

Upon leaving the hospital, I assisted with opening surgery centers to help them get accredited and worked part-time for multiple laser clinics. At this time, the word "MedSpa" had become more prominent and started to include services such as facials and massage treatments so as to not have that "feel" of a medical clinic. MedSpas were becoming more of a plush and comfortable setting where you could also get aesthetic and cosmetic procedures performed. Though we didn't know which direction the industry was going, it turned out to work in my favor because registered nurses were able to run and co-own MedSpas alongside a doctor to perform treatments like lasers, Botox, and dermal fillers under the direction of a physician. After a few years working in the OR and opening MedSpas for others, I realized that I was doing everything: opening the doors, answering phones, selling, doing the treatments, ordering supplies, and locking the door at the end of the day. I was making a ton of money for these companies, with no commission – just my hourly wage as an RN! After years of doing this, I wanted to open my own place except I didn't have the capital. I also didn't quite have a solid business plan, but I was able to craft something based on my experience. In 2009, I made a drastic move by opening up the Rejuvenation Center, which was my own MedSpa business. Meanwhile, I continued to work full-time at Dr. Harrison Lee's medical center in Beverly Hills.

When I decided to leave the hospital to build my MedSpa, people questioned my motives. Was it for money? Yes and no! I wanted something lucrative so I could give me and my son a better life, but I also wanted to help others in a different way than I had been doing, one that made people feel better about themselves. Working in a trauma hospital was a great experience and I always went home feeling like I really accomplished something with patient care, but it was sometimes tough physically and emotionally. I loved helping others and the fact that I could save lives was very rewarding, but I was ready to become an entrepreneur and be my own boss! Because most people don't leave a full-time job at a hospital, I realized how brave I really was.

Starting my business, I put in so much time and energy and I neglected myself. I am typically very active, but I didn't even have time to exercise or for my hobbies. I am a classically trained pianist (since the age of five) and a former Polynesian and hip hop dance choreographer. I also enjoy doing Muay Thai and yoga. When I failed to make myself and my health a priority, I gained a lot of weight and I didn't feel good about myself. Because I have always been in the fitness industry, I knew that I had to make some changes in my life for my health. Opening a business and being a mom made it so difficult for me to get back into shape. However, once my business was up and running, I decided to just focus on myself. If I was not at work or with my son, I would work out. Sometimes, I would go twice a day to kill time during rush hour traffic. Because I spent so much time at the gym, I started to catch the eye of a certain gym member. His name was "Myron" – at least, that's what I thought his name was. My friend corrected me and told me that his name was "Byron, not Myron!" I had no idea he was Byron Scott, the former NBA player of the Lakers, even though I've lived in Los Angeles (LA) my whole life! He didn't strike me as extremely tall and he didn't look like the same person as he did when he played, with a flat top and mustache.

In early 2014, Byron had moved back to LA after leaving the head coaching job for the Cleveland Cavaliers. He was working as a commentator for the Time Warner channel in the evenings, and he would work out every morning, whereas I worked out during the evenings. In February 2014, I decided to shift my workouts to the morning. Soon after I made that switch, Byron said hello and officially introduced himself to me. He stated that he had recently seen me and wanted to comment on my beauty and dancing skills. After that, every now and then we would wave to each other or make small talk upon passing one another at the gym. Every time I saw him, he was always working out with his business partner, Charlie Norris. Three months later, Byron invited me to hike Temescal Canyon with them. Our first "hang out" outside of the gym was with Charlie, which we still find very humorous. Four days later, the three of us went hiking *again,* followed by a nice breakfast in Malibu. When Charlie stepped away to use the restroom, Byron asked me out on an actual dinner date that evening, but I had to politely turn him down because I already had plans for my best friend's birthday. He persisted and asked me if I would like to join him for dinner the following night. He said, "This time ALONE, and not with Charlie." At the end of June 2014, we had our first official date. He took me to Houston's for a romantic dinner. Since then, we have been inseparable.

After dating for a few months, I learned that Byron was up for the LA Lakers head coaching position. When he became the Lakers' head coach, we both celebrated with a nice dinner at The Strand House, which ended with a small surprise party with some friends, cake, and dancing! We were still getting to know each other; it was a bit stressful and quite overwhelming for me because I was running my business and getting used to balancing a relationship after not being in one for so long. Shortly after we started dating, I was asked to be on the reality TV show, *Basketball Wives* but I brushed off the request. Two years later, when the producers realized that I lived in LA, they asked me again. In 2017, I signed up for the show as an opportunity to promote my business. I had no idea what I was getting myself into. I was exposing myself, my business, and my relationship! I was very vulnerable during that really crazy time in my life – I was dating a public figure and my company was going through a merger. It was extremely difficult to juggle a full-time job, run a business, and film for *Basketball Wives*. As a business owner, I found it hard to detach from work. Even when I wasn't present, I was thinking about my business. Being a nurse and providing quality care is something that I highly value and take pride in. Because of the great work that we were doing, my MedSpa grew really fast and we hired six RNs to work under me to help with the workload. I am proud that we are currently recognized as the #1 MedSpa in the LA South Bay area.

As I get closer to retirement, it has become even more important for me to invest in a good opportunity. When I was approached by OrangeTwist, they only had four locations and I opened the fifth (the first LA location). OrangeTwist locates existing MedSpas and acquires them while branding their name on the existing locations. After 11 years of running the Rejuvenation Center, it was bittersweet to let go of my standalone location that I was running on my own. Even though I no longer have to run the business, as one of the investment partners, I've stayed on board as one of the main nurses so that we can provide the same continuity of care during the transition process. Now that I am a partner in one location of this larger corporation, I don't have the day-to-day stress of running my own business. Finally, I can work hard and play hard! Since partnering with the business, this is the first time that I've really come up for air.

I am happy that my business is thriving and I am in a loving relationship with my fiancé, Byron. I am extremely proud of my son, Gerod, who has grown up to be a fine gentleman. He graduated from the Los Angeles Film School with an associate's degree in recording arts and a bachelor's degree in business entertainment. I am also really proud to be a part of *In Her Purpose* because there really isn't anything out there to motivate Asian women who don't know where they want to be or go in life. A lot of women hit me up on social media and ask me for guidance and career advice. We need more Asian women mentors who can provide direction for younger women. Being on *Basketball Wives* provided me with a powerful platform. On the show, I am one of the only Asian girls featured. They portrayed me to be the stereotypical Asian girl: quiet and not one to speak up for herself but that's not the case in real life! I wouldn't have thought about this if I wasn't pushed or picked on while I was on the show. They couldn't really find anything to pick on me about – except where I got my nursing degree from! What I learned from being on the show is that different cultures have different lifestyles: we may not think or speak the same because we were raised differently. Despite how

I was portrayed on the show, I have been able to inspire a lot of women to start or change their careers along with juggling their love lives. I was able to meet the man of my dreams after the age of 40 and I am ready to start my new life with him as his wife, at the age of 48! I am a testament that you can find love at an older age after working full-time and being a mom!

No matter what the situation, I advise other women to not give up. It will be hard but if you don't put your goals first, then you will not succeed. I am also a huge proponent of education. Get your degree! Obtaining your degree proves that you can accomplish something. It's important! You just have to start somewhere! If you don't know what you want, start with a degree. It can help you get where you want to be.

I cannot believe that I am nearing 50-years-old! I try to eat healthy, exercise and live a less stressful life as I age. I am constantly drinking tons of water, I stay out of the sun, and I have a skin regimen that I do in the morning and night. I am my walking business card so I have to show women that I can take care of myself. I only use medical grade products and I maintain anti-aging by doing hydrafacials, chemical peels, and laser face treatments once a month. If you feel that you look good on the outside, you will feel much better on the inside too.

What's next for me? I am looking forward to marrying the love of my life. I am also looking forward to spending more time traveling with Byron and my family. I am not sure I will return to reality TV, but if I were to, I would consider a talk show or reality show that showcases Asian women doing amazing things! I want viewers to have access to strong Asian women. It would be great to see more Asians present in the mainstream.

THERE'S
—A—
lesson
WE LEARN
IN
EVERY
situation,
good AND *bad.*

—Sumita Batra

Be Different

Sumita Batra

You really don't know what "different" means until you start meeting others and learning from people who are not like you. Until then, your life is your reality! I grew up thinking everyone was like me and today I realize that is not the case. My journey helped to shape the individual I am today. I was born in England and raised in Iran, India, and London. I really didn't know what "normal" was because I moved around and lived all over the world! When I was six-years-old, my family and I traveled to London. During our trip, I contracted chickenpox so I was quarantined at my uncle's house to avoid spreading it to my siblings. While we were in London, my mom learned that she had to quickly return to Iran to relocate our family to India because trouble had started brewing. She knew we couldn't continue living our life as we had been, under the new regime. I was young, and I loved the attention I got from my aunt and uncle in London so much that when she had to leave, I told my mom that I wanted to stay! So in 1975, she left me in London and my family transitioned from Iran to India when the Khomeini Regime took over Iran. I later regretted this decision because I really missed my family, especially my parents.

One year later, I reunited with my brother and sister in India, where they were attending boarding school. At 12-years-old, I asked my mom to enroll me in boarding school too because when

I heard my siblings talk about their stay in boarding school, I felt like I had missed out on an important experience. The boarding school I chose had different rules for girls and boys. Girls were day-boarders, while the boys were full-time boarders and stayed overnight. I didn't quite feel like that would give me the full boarding school experience I wanted, so I convinced the principal, a retired Lieutenant Colonel of the Indian Army, to let me stay with his wife and daughter on campus. I was already pushing against the grain at an early age. Three years after I left school, they changed the rules to allow girls to become full-time boarders. There were over 250 girls boarders when I left. I didn't know it back then, but looking back, I definitely had a different perspective!

In 1988, my family migrated to the United States. My mom obtained her esthetician license and later that year, she opened up Ziba, a beauty salon in Artesia, California (which is also referred to as "Little India"). It all started in a 400 square foot studio and never in a thousand years would I have thought that it would grow into what it is now! Ziba is our family business that she started with no help and very little money. We needed help, but that was hard to come by when we had no money! To solve this, we had to get creative! When I got into the family business and the beauty industry, I was just 18-years-old. I am a self-made makeup artist and self-taught marketer. I ran all of the marketing promotions and did a lot of bridal makeup up myself. I created events like pageants, bridal shows and dance competitions that would eventually pay for themselves and allow us to sponsor advertisements in newspapers and radio stations in the Southeast Asian community. Through these events, we obtained a lot of publicity. I had no idea what I was doing at the time, but what I was really doing was building up our brand!

Eventually, I started my own family. I got married and helped my husband run Subway sandwich franchises. While helping him,

I was still helping my mom with the salon on the weekends. I was a year away from achieving a bachelor's degree, and I was immersed in the businesses which came easier to me than school, so I continued to focus on the businesses and never finished my degree. My growth has come from being a natural entrepreneur. I was also very good at product development and ideation; marketing came easy to me. So that's what I've been doing! I've been building and growing our family businesses! At the time of publishing, we now have 14 Ziba Beauty studios, a cosmetic line, and a beauty academy. I have made two documentaries, authored a book called *The Art of Mehndi*, and am very involved with community organizations like Sikhlens and The Indus Entrepreneurs (TiE).

Being a Southeast Asian-American, female CEO, and business owner, I've faced quite a few challenges. Mainly because there aren't many other women in my position; there are probably four other women that I know, mostly older than me, who are in similar positions. Growing up, I didn't really have any role models who I could look to, other than my mom. I cannot tell you how many environments and situations I found myself in where I was the only woman in the room. I belonged to the Orange County Young Presidents' Organization (YPO), which is very difficult to get into; I was the first and only woman, ever in that chapter! It's a man's world out there, but women are rising up and things are changing. I feel that it will flip where there will be more women leading the path! Until then, men will hold positions of control and power. Luckily, we are starting to see a shift.

Another challenge that I still go through is building the right team of hardworking and loyal people. Being in the service/beauty industry, I've found that if personnel make mistakes and don't deliver quality workmanship, business owners are the ones who suffer. It's a challenge to manage people and hire the right staff.

Good people are very hard to find and even harder to keep. We have created a category in our industry that is now responsible for thousands of, mostly women, threaders around the globe. It's a great feeling and a great responsibility. We are on a constant quest to elevate our brand and the category.

Through my experiences over the years, I've learned organically and on the fly. In 2009, I finally learned what human resources (HR) really was. It was through a class-action lawsuit that went on for almost six years. At that moment, I understood the importance of HR and how critical it is to the success and failure of a retail brand. While this was happening, I felt like it was the end of the world for my business. However, I had to find the lesson! There's a lesson we learn in every situation, good or bad. Though I can't share details, this experience, really taught me about perseverance and it helped shape our business into what it is today. My biggest takeaway was that when a thing like a huge lawsuit hits you, it is not necessarily the end. It takes time for things like this to resolve and if you have the right team, it is imperative that you let them do their job and you go back to focusing on your brand. Let the experts handle their part.

I can't believe how fast time flies. All of a sudden, I look up and I am 51-years-old! Today, I am so grateful to have a lot of flexibility and freedom to explore. Ziba Beauty and all my ventures along the way have taught me so much! It has been years and years of really hard work and sacrifices. Even with all the work, there was no guarantee. There was a lot of pain; we've been knocked out like nobody's business! There are times where we came up with an idea, only to have it stolen by someone else. But we keep going; we believe that there really is enough for everyone to go around! Since I never finished school or was never formally trained, I was always sort of self-conscious that I didn't know what I was doing. Throughout my journey, the best advice I received was from consultants and advisors who told me, "You know what you don't know, so you allow other people to help." I lacked confidence so I surrounded myself with consultants who were educated and more experienced than me. Working with them, we were able to learn from each other. I was able to teach them what it was like to live the crazy life of an entrepreneur, and from them, I learned the importance of collaboration. I allowed whoever the expert was in the room to share information to help me make a decision. I hired them so I could learn! I learned and I listened.

Now that I am wiser and in a position to give advice, I would encourage others to make choices you won't regret. Along your journey you will be faced with different forks in the road. Choose a path that you know you won't be sorry for in the future. No one can have it all. You will have to give up something, especially as a woman. Before you decide on having children, take some parenting classes. Really know if you want to be a parent! Entrepreneurial women are a different breed. I didn't know what I was getting into with three kids! My career pulled me in different directions. When you have children, they need you and they are your responsibility! Tread very carefully into the realm of parenthood because that responsibility is your choice. If you do decide on kids, make sure you have the right people to help you raise them. From the outside looking in, I have it all: married with three children, a nice car, and nice things. Women often ask me, "How do you do it all?" My answer to that is, "I don't!" I was really fortunate to have my mom, sister, aunt, sister-in-law, and mother-in-law to help me! My strong support group enabled me to grow our businesses. The path I chose was growth. I had to be OK with my family helping me raise my kids. I understood that I could not be both: an entrepreneur and a full-time mom. I had to make our businesses work so I could give my children the life I wanted them to have.

With that, my greatest success is my children. Even though I wasn't the "typical mom," I was around my children a lot. I had the help of others and I did my best, juggling between being a women business owner and a mother. All three of my children are talented, creative, and smart. I did what I needed to do to survive. My children now have choices to do what they want and be whoever they want to be in this world. They have the freedom and the ability to blow with the wind.

Aside from taking Ziba on to the global stage, my next venture is to focus on my youngest daughter, Hansa. In this chapter of my life, I plan to enjoy and spend time with my children. I want to make sure they are all healthy and happy. I want to be there to help them along their paths to achieving their goals. I enjoy mentoring young kids through a program called The Young Entrepreneurs (TYE). I give myself time daily to connect spiritually with the divine. I try to be a good friend and a giving human being. I continue my journey toward growth and purpose. Always have, always will.

GSD:
get shit done!

WHEN ALL ELSE FAILS,

just get it done

EVEN IF IT'S NOT PART OF YOUR

— job! —

IF YOU HELP OTHERS

connect the dots

THEY WILL DO THE SAME FOR YOU

Without questions asked.

—Roslynn Alba Cobarrubias

Be a Connector

Roslynn Alba Cobarrubias

I am a triple minority: a woman, Filipina, and, at 4'11", vertically challenged. In the entertainment world, Asian women are portrayed to be hard workers and very passive. Though we are known to work hard, we don't always take ownership of our work, don't document it to share with others, and we tend not to promote our successes. Over time, I realized this must change. We need to share our experiences and be examples for our future generations.

My mom comes from a family of seven siblings who lived in a three-bedroom home in the Philippines. At the age of 22, my mom came to the United States. She worked as a dietician and started her own insurance business. She raised four girls as a single mom. Because of her experiences, she wanted us to be able to support our own families, so there was no flexibility on what she wanted us to do for our careers. Our mom encouraged us to become either a doctor or a lawyer. When I enrolled in college, I wanted to do something in music, but I didn't want to disappoint my mom so I enrolled at the University of California, Irvine (UCI) as a political science major. After just a year, I hated it! I felt like I was memorizing books and I was always looking forward to my weekends so that I could go to hip-hop clubs or play vinyl music all night long.

245

As a music lover, I spent a lot of time watching music videos on TV. I distinctly remember seeing an advertisement for MTV's contest for the next video jockey (VJ), which is similar to a disc jockey (DJ) but for music videos. I thought it was my calling so I drove to the audition. After competing with hundreds of people, I made it to the top ten! When the casting agent asked me how tall I was, and I responded "4'11" on a good day," and she told me, "I'm sorry you'll never be on television. You should try radio!" That felt like the end of one dream but it sparked something else in me. On my drive back, I kept repeating what she said. After that, over my summer break, I started to research local radio stations where I could volunteer and learn. I found a radio station at the local community college, Mt. San Antonio College, in my hometown of Walnut, California. I wanted to have a radio show that promoted hip hop and positivity, but to have a show, you had to be registered for classes in broadcasting. So, I signed up for Broadcasting 101 where I learned how to get a radio show, market myself, and how to get a job in the music industry. I couldn't believe college could be this fun! I went to class early and stayed late, and ultimately I got the radio show I dreamed of. As part of my job, I attended concerts and interviewed artists. I would travel wherever I needed to and even made the drive up to the Bay Area to see the Invisibl Skratch Picklz! I featured artists such as The Beat Junkies and Nas when they came to town. It was also important to me that we featured local artists too so I interviewed The Black Eyed Peas, Jurassic 5, and The Pharcyde who were all popular local hip hop groups at the time.

During that summer, I found myself happily lost in music and artistry. Eventually, I dropped out of UCI and broke the bad news to my mom that I no longer wanted to pursue law. She was really disappointed because in her eyes, pursuing a career in the arts was seen as a failure and a stupid dream. I didn't understand the root of her belief. For my mom, there was definitely a disconnect between living a dream and living with stability, but I felt like I could do both. I transferred to California State University, Fullerton and switched my major to radio television. Outside of going to class weekly, I spent a lot of time volunteering and interning at radio production companies like Radio Express. I also brought over my radio show from the community college station called "Third Floor Radio." I started to produce concerts and I threw parties with DJ Vice at The Dugout. I remember making $100 after one of our parties and we thought we were killing it! We were finally in the music industry!

While in college, I landed a job at Radio Disney as a member of their street team. I then transitioned into being a programming DJ at the first online radio station, Onair.com where I created an online database and started helping artists with bookings and marketing. When I became the director of marketing at the National Association of Record Industry Professionals (NARIP), my life changed. I was marketing a conference where I met the creators of MySpace.com. It was quite exciting, given it was the very start of creative social networking with the purpose of advancing one's career. It had been important for me to respect my mom's aspirations for me, but I knew I had to go after my purpose. Everything came full circle in 2006 when my mom finally understood what I did. That year, Lionel Richie came out with a new album and I produced a concert for him while I was at MySpace. I invited my mom to come and she got to meet Lionel Richie. When she met him, she told him that she sang all of his karaoke songs and always obtained the highest score. She was so proud! I ended up working at MySpace for over nine years!

Looking back, I should have started volunteering and interning earlier on so that I could have figured it out sooner. I learned more from real-life experiences rather than being in class. I loved my professors at school, but they were book smart, which is very important, but being involved within the industry gave me real-life exposure.

My advice to anyone looking to level up would be to network and make sure you provide value to anyone you approach. I learned this the hard way! When I was promoting my radio show, I asked my friend who owned a gym if I could print out some flyers to pass out there. He told me, "You don't know what networking means. Networking is a two-way street, it is social currency. Come back when you have something of value to me." From then on, I learned to provide value before asking for anything. One of the traits I've developed since then was the ability to connect the dots. As soon as I meet someone, I am immediately able to identify three other people that he or she should meet. I want to help people get to their next level. This lesson was further solidified when I worked at NARIP. My former boss taught me how to connect the dots for artists and people I worked with, without necessarily asking for anything in return. This focus on helping others and providing value created the social currency my friend had talked about. By doing this, I was not only able to help others, but I was also able to ask them for help in the future if I needed it.

Despite what I've accomplished, I have always been challenged by my own limiting beliefs. When I started at MySpace, I was only 24-years-old and I thought I was just lucky to be in the room. When I walked into the office, I looked like an intern! Even though I was a leader of the organization, I was sitting on the outskirts of the table instead of leaning in within the leadership position I had. I went to a Cal State, not an Ivy League school, so I felt intimidated by the guys who had MBAs. I didn't know anything about equity or start-ups; I had to learn how to ask for what I deserve and believe that I deserved it. For example, even though I wasn't on the sales team, I brought in over $50 million in programming from talent and shows. I was continually generating sales but didn't receive a commission until I asked. You have to be confident: Know your worth and speak up! I had to rethink my value proposition to this world. I had to know what my purpose was, and that's when everything else came easily. Your purpose will always guide you!

A defining moment for me was at the age of 36 when I took my first trip to the Philippines. Apl.de.ap. of the Black Eyed Peas invited a group of us to travel around the country to help promote tourism and to show the world that #itsmorefuninthephilippines. He invited over 20 celebrities and influencers including Jo Koy, Liane V, and Cassie. We were also joined by entertainment executives from companies such as Netflix and YouTube. During this trip, I was also able to meet my family for the first time but I was not expecting what I saw and experienced. I wasn't ready to witness the poverty even though I'd seen it all over the world. To see people that looked exactly like me on the street really hit me! The children were helpless, just skin and bones. I asked myself: "What am I doing for my own community; what am I doing for them?" I do a lot for the hip hop and music communities, but I wasn't doing anything for the Filipino community except for those closest to me: my 12 Filipino best friends I've had since junior high and my amazing Filipino family.

As soon as I got back from my trip, I volunteered to help produce the Los Angeles Festival of Philippine Arts and Culture and the Filipino Heritage Night at the Clippers game, and I have made it a conscious effort to regularly be involved in the Filipino community. I want to bring people together and help others. I want to continue to build upon that, bring different industries together to collectively uplift and put Filipinos on the world stage. We have been doing this for others for years so it's time that we do it for ourselves! I want to create memorable experiences that make people feel valued and acknowledged so they have the strength and confidence to pay it forward to serve and help others.

Fast forward to where I am today, in my current role as the ABS-CBN Global Head of Music and Talent. In this position, I help market Filipino music, talent, and events across the world. We have a dream to bring our talent to the world stage and create new opportunities and paths for others to follow. We have big goals of bringing Tagalog to the Grammys, which I know is all part of God's plan to come.

IF YOU DON'T KNOW
who you are
&
IF YOU DON'T KNOW
what your purpose is,
NOTHING YOU DO WILL BE
effective.
LOOK BACK, BE PROUD OF
who you are
& SEE HOW FAR YOU'VE COME.

— Freska Griarte

Be a Survivor

Freska Griarte

At eight-years-old, I would pretend to host my own radio show. I recorded my voice on cassette tapes using my parents' karaoke machine. I started playing piano when I was four-years-old and continued to play throughout grade school, high school and even after college I played professionally and toured Japan as a jazz trombone player. Eventually, I became a singer in my own band and I studied music in college. Oddly enough, I didn't want to live and breathe music, but I still wanted to foster my passion for music. Growing up, I really enjoyed music, but my parents never encouraged my interest because they didn't think I could make a career out of it. To be honest, I didn't either, because it was drilled in my head that I couldn't make a viable career making money in music. It's fascinating because when I look back, what I was pretending to do as a kid is exactly what I am doing now 20+ years later – but I am finally on the air, doing the afternoon drive in the Bay Area on 96.5 KOIT radio. It's amazing to think that I have been in the entertainment industry since I was 19-years-old.

In 1993, I attended a music conference at the Dunfey Hotel in San Mateo where I met many professionals in the industry. They opened my eyes to other opportunities and helped me focus on radio, which is what I wanted to pursue. However, my parents wanted me to be an accountant! Like many teenagers, I was very confused about what to do after high school. My passions were not supported by my parents so I decided the best decision would be for me to enlist in the Air Force because I thought that would make them proud. A week before I was set to leave for boot camp, I ended up landing a job in radio.

My career started out at a radio station in San Francisco in 1993. I was determined to work my way up. I started out in the research department. My main responsibility was to cold call listeners. I did that for four hours every day until 9:00 p.m. While working in that department, I managed to intern in every other department I could. The moment I set foot into the studio, I loved it. I knew that I wanted to do this! The journey I'd take to get on the air was unclear, but it was clear that I had a strong desire to do radio. It got to the point where I cut school just to work at the station. Once I had my foot in the door, I asked a lot of questions, did everything I could to learn about different departments and people, and I took lots of notes. I wanted to make myself indispensable, but unfortunately, it was at the expense of my education. Not to mention, I racked up tons of parking tickets that I had no money to pay for. I had to do community service to pay them off.

My parents were embarrassed to tell people I was in music. I was the child that my parents looked at as a disappointment. My dad worked for the National Aeronautics and Space Administration (NASA) and my mom was a social worker who spoke three languages. They made me feel like I was the "stupid sister." My older sister and I are complete opposites. She graduated from the University of California, Berkeley and worked at Lockheed – my parents were very proud. Even though we are very different, my sister supported me and my dreams. She helped convince my parents to let me move to Hawaii to pursue my passion and continue my radio career in 1995.

253

I followed some of the folks that I interned for in San Francisco to Hawaii. I started out as the programming assistant making $7 an hour. Eventually, I made my way to becoming the assistant music director, mix show coordinator, and then the night show host. I was also doing mixes and rocking clubs. But because I was broke I had to rummage for change just to eat. I didn't have a car so, after hours, I would walk through Taco Bell's drive-thru to order a taco and a cup of water (which was free). I only ate half of my taco for dinner and I would eat the other half for breakfast, but I didn't have a microwave to heat it up so I ate it cold. I had no cups or plates where I lived, just the cups from Taco Bell. That's all I could afford after rent. I was so embarrassed – I would never invite anyone over to my studio apartment. It was unbelievably small that you had to sit sideways in the bathroom so your knees wouldn't hit the wall. There were also lots of bugs! That's how horrible my living conditions were, but I was doing what I loved, so I put up with it. I was learning how to make it in the industry, but I was also learning how to make it living on my own for the first time.

After working in Hawaii for three years, I moved back to San Francisco to finish college while working at the station where it all began for me. In 1999, I was working on the air, going to school, interning at a TV station, and also hosted my own show, *Stateside*, which aired on The Filipino Channel (TFC). My success there helped my parents' pride to grow. My parents finally felt proud of me. But only because I was on TV! It wasn't an easy journey to get where I am today as it definitely came with struggles.

I moved to Sacramento to do morning radio and would head back to the Bay several times a week to shoot my TV show. I was in Sacramento for less than a year because it wasn't a good fit for me. I decided to pursue my other passion: acting and stunt work. I took acting classes and commuted back and forth to Los Angeles several times a month. I was auditioning for jobs and looking for an agent. I was also looking for another radio job on the weekends. I was tapping into all of my interests and trying to make a living but I also had to keep in mind that I had a biological clock! Back then, many women in the business felt that they shouldn't get pregnant in order to stay on the radio. I saw older women in the business hold off and then have difficulty starting a family. I sacrificed my career to start a family in my hometown, the Bay Area because family was more important than a career. Being a mom in this industry is tough. After I broke up with my kids' father, it became even more difficult. The San Francisco market is very expensive. Becoming a single mom of two kids and not having financial support from their father was tough. I had to pick up multiple jobs to support my radio "habit."

I ended up quitting radio for four years because it wasn't paying the bills or putting food on the table for my daughters. I was over 30-years-old and I was only getting paid $10 an hour working at Wild 94.9! I had to figure out how I was going to support a family and have a career. That's when I decided to get a corporate, 9 to 5 job working at Playstation. But I enjoyed radio so much that I just couldn't be away from it for too long. Plus, when you're out of sight, you're out of mind so I eventually got myself back on the radio again and worked part-time.

The path I've chosen for my life has been difficult, even more so because throughout all of this, I was taking care of my mom who has Alzheimer's. I ended up being a part of the sandwich generation as the caregiver for both my aging parents and my children. For five years while at 99.7 NOW, sometimes I would have my kids and my INCONTINENT mother at work with me. Between sets, I would have to take her to the bathroom and wipe her down or feed my kids. It felt like I had no other option than to do it myself, and I rarely accepted help from others even when they were offering. What other option do you have other than to do it?

On top of everything else I was going through, I was diagnosed with stage one breast cancer at the age of 39. I went through chemotherapy, radiation, and surgery. That's when I decided that the things I've been focusing on prior to my diagnosis weren't actually serious! Financial stress, personal drama, career obstacles – none of these are serious compared to living or dying. When you actually break it down to if you are going to live or die, nothing else matters. I told myself that I had to relax! The situation I was going through was not a big deal – I am alive! There are challenges that we will all go through while on our journeys, but we often stress out about things that are pretty trivial. Would you rather be dealing with not having enough money to pay a bill or be dealing with your own mortality? Learn from what I went through and focus on what is truly important.

When my first program director gave me my own show in Hawaii, he told me that I should be imagining myself doing radio mid-days. This has helped guide me throughout my career. You have to imagine your goal and think about it often so you can automatically transition into it when the opportunity finally comes. You have to manifest your dreams and already be doing what you want in your mind. There will be some tough times. You have to be resourceful. Don't be upset when things don't go your way. Find another way. You may have to work harder or be more creative, but if you really want something, you will find a way to get there.

If you don't know who you are and if you don't know what your purpose is, nothing you do will be effective. No matter where you are in life, look back, be proud of who you are and see how far you've come. I survived a lot and I am still killing it! I've done a lot of things in my career, which may not be part of the standard

256

way of life, but what matters is – I am doing it! Be positive during the hard times. Know that you will always get through them! Don't ever doubt that!

I would advise young folks to get real-life experience, no matter where it is! It shouldn't matter where you're working, you should take the opportunity. Get an internship, network and figure out how you can get connected to wherever you're going next. Learn as much as you can! Don't pass up these opportunities. Also, don't let people or situations stop you from pursuing your dream. Keep going! If it's not working out for you, leave. You will find something! Regardless, be grateful and work from the heart. Believe in your dreams and just do it!

OUR OPPRESSORS SPEAK
ONE LANGUAGE:
money.
WHEN WE TEACH YOUNG PEOPLE
THAT OUR *dollar* IS NOT JUST
A TOOL,
BUT A *weapon* WITH WHICH
TO VOTE,
ORGANIZE *and* RESIST,
WE *level* OURSELVES WITH THOSE
WHO HAVE BEEN IN *power*
FOR FAR TOO LONG.

— Berna Anat

BE INTENTIONAL

Berna Anat

"You have to learn the rules of the game. And then you have to play better than anyone else."
-Albert Einstein

Hi! I'm Berna. I was born and raised in South San Francisco by Filipino immigrant parents. I have always been a teacher's pet; I never rebelled. I got straight A's, I strived for the gold stars, and I was always jealous of those people who didn't feel the need to follow the rules. I was never a bad-ass – I like to learn the rules and abide by them. But over time, I also learned that if you understand how people succeed and fail, you can then decide what rules you want to follow and which to throw out. It took me time, but I learned you first have to understand the rules – then, you play the game according to your goals.

I was always a good student, and like so many Asian-American families, my parents pushed for me to become a doctor. When I was 12-years-old, I remember having a panic attack in a Chevy's restaurant when I told my parents that I wanted to be a writer. They weren't too shocked considering that, for years, I told them that I wanted to be a performer, comedian, actress, or on Broadway.

Even though I've been mentioning my love of writing for years, I was finally adamant about it – I finally said, "No, for real, I choose this life." I wanted to run and hide but I was so happy that I spoke up and really shared my dreams. Growing up, I was fascinated with variety shows like *In Living Color* and *All That*. I was excited to see people of color on TV, but rarely did I see a woman who looked like me. The only Filipina on any main stage was Lea Salonga. When I closed my eyes and only listened to her, I couldn't tell she was Filipina. She didn't sound like the Filipinos I knew. And when I opened my eyes, she didn't look like the Filipinas around me, either – she had light skin and straight hair, which is very different from the way I look. I sacrificed my dream of being a performer because I didn't feel like it was accessible. I didn't realize I was experiencing a simple principle of the world: If you can't see it, you think you can't be it. So, I had to pivot.

I stuck to my dream of becoming a writer. When I was in high school, I wanted to be the editor-in-chief for a teen magazine. I started as a freelance writer for *Seventeen* magazine when I was chosen to document my "Freshman 15" experience at the University of Southern California (USC). After graduating in 2011 with a B.A. in Public Relations, I moved to New York City (NYC) to work as the executive assistant to the editor-in-chief of *Seventeen*. I quickly learned that there is a *big* difference between what it *sounds* like what your job is compared to what you *actually* do day-to-day. I thought I was going to help 13 million teen subscribers improve their lives, discover themselves, ask important questions, and build their self-esteem. In reality, I was helping predominantly white, mostly Jewish, women passive-aggressively fight with each other in a sleek office setting. I thought I would be living my purpose of helping teenage girls, but instead, I was learning how to run a magazine – especially one that serves mainly as a business. That's not the impact I was looking to have on the world.

However, while I was at *Seventeen*, I organized a volunteer event at a summer camp. The magazine's employees shared what it was like to be an editor and work at a magazine of that kind. I was only there for four hours, but I didn't want to go home. I felt all the lightbulbs light up inside me. I fell in love with the feeling of directly impacting those teen girls who were in such disbelief that they were talking to editors of their favorite magazine; I fell in love with the knowledge that, that day, we tangibly changed a few girls' lives. I didn't know that my brain or heart was capable of this kind of joy. I went home that night and I thought about what role would make me happy. I realized that I didn't want to be an editor-in-chief anymore; I wouldn't have cared if they handed me the job that night. I suddenly had a different measurement for what happiness meant. I put in two more years at the magazine, knowing that although I didn't want to be an editor anymore, I did want to create the high-level connections that might help me pivot towards a career in helping teen girls more directly. Even though I was repeatedly told that girls would kill for my job at such a popular magazine, I decided to leave the industry. As I left *Seventeen*, I clung onto this Stephen King quote, which I once saw on a Post-It: "Go then, there are other worlds than these." It gave me the hope I needed when I was letting go of what I thought was my dream; that was just one world. There are so many other worlds that you can go into. All the fears you have about leaving this world are justified, but it's never the end of the world when there are so many others waiting for you.

Even though it was a major career pivot (and pay cut), I took a summer job as a teen program director for the YMCA of NYC in 2013. It was the most engrossing, most fun job I've had, and it was bliss for three years. But because of the cost of living, I needed several jobs to make it in the Big Apple. In the non-summer months, I also did freelance writing and produced videos. I was always banging my internet drum about teens and teen empowerment – whether it was through posting blogs, videos, or ranting on Twitter.

I always tell young folks to be as loud as you can about the weird thing that you like. The biggest and best steps that I took in my career were offered to me because I was intentional and loud about my passion for teens. You will be offered things that feel right to you when you constantly let the world know what you're about. In the summer of 2015, my former colleague and mentor, Liz, called me about a new team she was building at Instagram. She asked me if I wanted to come work for her as the very first teen community lead.

I decided to take the job at Instagram because, after four years in New York City, I really wanted to be home near my family in the Bay Area. After freelancing for so long, I was also hyped to have a stable paycheck every other Friday. The moment I realized I'd be getting a regular paycheck was the moment I realized I finally had a chance to get my money in order. I had about $50K in debt: $38K in school loans plus $12K in credit card debt that I racked up while I was living in NYC. So, with a stable job and regular cash flow, I taught myself about personal finance.

Just like any millennial, I relied on Google: I crawled through blogs, articles, books, and listened to podcasts. I would talk about my discoveries with my colleagues at work. During our conversations, they gave me recommendations for books and podcasts, which were almost all old white dudes like Warren Buffet or Dave Ramsey. When I did come across a woman, most of them were older white women who came from the finance world and spoke that specific finance language. I couldn't relate to any of those people. Despite feeling detached from who I was learning from, I got sound advice.

During this discovery period, I learned how to tee up different personal goals one at a time: how to pay off a credit card and student loan debt, build an emergency fund and then build up my travel savings. While I was at Instagram, I was earning a stable paycheck. Thank goodness for the spoils of tech company culture: free food and company shuttles! I'm grateful that my Filipino family embraced me living back at home, and that, combined with bi-weekly paychecks, allowed me to work towards achieving my financial goals. My partner, Peter, and I did it together. We crafted a plan to each pay off our debt and, together, save enough to travel for a year.

My unofficial job at Instagram was to be the teen trends translator for the company. I was 25-years-old when I started, so I wasn't too far removed from youth culture. My day-to-day job consisted of staying on top of what teens in the United States were doing on Instagram, like creating memes, political movements, and incredible art, keeping up with who are the big influencers that have rocketed to stardom, and soliciting feedback on how we could improve the product. The problem was, older folks at Instagram didn't always take the power of young people seriously. It was thrilling to see teens make their own money from the platform while creating value for the company itself by attracting advertisers on the backend. It really changed the way every other generation thought about marketing; they had to increase the speed of innovation because young people were beating them out! Teens instinctively know how to think fast and they have a natural barometer for building culture.

Being an Asian-American woman in a leadership position at a big company was challenging for me, especially due to tokenism. I felt excited and honored to be there, and electrified by all the brilliant people I worked with, but I was often the only woman or person of color (POC) in the room. Several times, POC like me were asked to move to the front of group pictures to showcase "diversity" for marketing materials – a story I hear over and over from so many other POC to this day. Sometimes, it was demoralizing to think that my brown skin was used as proof that a company is "checking off boxes," even though I, and every other POC, were more than qualified to be there.

When I reached my goal of paying off my $50,000 debt after two years, I quit my job at the end of 2017. I booked a one-way ticket and boarded a plane to New Zealand in January 2018. Peter and I spent the year traveling, while I produced free financial literacy content online. I never dreamt that I would have a career even remotely related to finance. Before all of my research, I had no idea what that even meant, and I was always bad with money and numbers! Neither of my parents came from a finance background; we never really spoke about money as it was considered a taboo. But despite all that today, I'm a producer, speaker, entrepreneur, and *fin-fluencer* (is that a thing?) dedicated to making financial literacy more fun and more accessible to teach young people the absolute basics of money. I obnoxiously call myself a financial hype woman. That's my made-up way of saying that I write articles, create videos, and other ridiculous internet things – in a way that is not boring, dry, and frankly, not hella male or hella pale. I became passionate about personal finance from my journey to take control of my own financial situation. Along the way, I saw the need for melanin, women, and cultural context. I've been yelling in all corners of the internet, trying to make money fun for young people ever since. My inner child definitely loves that I am now a public figure and entertainer. I always knew I would be on some kind of stage!

There are no set career paths to follow in the personal finance world. I am one of the trailblazers, especially amongst women; we're figuring it out as we go along. To be honest, we don't totally know what we are doing, but we're competent and confident about the urgency of our message. It is exciting, but I constantly cope with identity crisis because I don't have a blueprint. There are so many possibilities and I am only one person. But I am most proud of my career now because I am, somehow, still here as an entrepreneur.

I used to tell myself for years that I could never be an entrepreneur because I really like structure, being managed, and I am a really good worker bee. Every day that I am still in the game is an accomplishment. Every day is an effort to throw away my self-doubts, which sometimes cut deeper than what others think of me. I have my mom to thank for drilling into my mind, "If that person can do it, why can't I?" This mindset allowed her to jump into many different careers without a college degree and no experience, and I have carried this lesson throughout my own life. We all have to put building blocks together in our own way, and we have to start somewhere. There's one good thing about growing up as an obnoxiously polished student: I am super teachable. I get excited to be the dumbest person in the room and I am never afraid to start at level one. When I learn new things, I do it with enthusiasm instead of insecurity or pride.

Success to me is being able to pull up people behind me and sharing my success with others. I always strive to be the role model I wish I had in the past. I want to encourage others to remember to take breaks. During my breaks, it's always a dance party – I turn on some music and dance around my room. It's a good release and when I get moving, that unlocks the rest of my brain. I also love taking kindergarten-style day naps to recharge and I'm always encouraging others to not be afraid of therapy. Glory be to therapy! I have been in therapy since August 2019 and it has helped me realize that I don't have to model my life around accomplishment. I am worthy, awesome, and a full contributing human being, whether or not I'm being "productive." I don't need gold stars. I don't have to get straight A's or follow all the rules. I've always rooted myself in accomplishments and achievement, and a lot of first-generation Asian daughters feel this way. As long as you are being intentional with what you want, you're taking care of your own needs, and you're directing your energy towards lifting others up the ladder behind you, I think that in itself is success.

Keep
IT
Simple.

-Kathleen Engel

Be Creative

Kathleen Engel

I have a passion for bringing people together and for all things fashion or vintage!! In my teens, I would go "thrifting" (finding things at a thrift store) for unique gems. My passion for vintage fashion was borderline an obsession. I could never get enough of the thrill I felt during my hunt for interesting finds that made others feel beautiful and inspired before they were discarded.

"Viva la Vintage" was born from my thrifting hobby. As a way to make extra cash as college students, my sister, Desiree, and I would scour local thrift shops and sell the pieces we didn't keep for ourselves to resale shops like Wasteland and Buffalo Exchange. We had so much fun searching for all things unique from the 1940s-1980s. We had an eye for silhouettes and pieces that were stylish and could be paired with new clothing we had in our closets.

In the early 2000s, I saw a rise of independent designers in Los Angeles (LA) who hosted private sales, ranging in size from "invite-only" backyard events to events welcoming anyone, hosted in large venues. My sisters, Desiree, Scarlet, and I loved attending these events and they inspired me to host a private event selling vintage. In 2002, Viva la Vintage's first pop-up took place in our parents' backyard in Chino Hills, followed by additional pop-ups at my condo in Covina. After outgrowing our personal spaces, we rented out larger venues in Brea and Silverlake. I continued curating vintage for the mini retail shopping experience for customers to purchase my one of a kind finds. From 2002-2012, I did pop-ups throughout LA and Orange County. Little did I know my hobby was just the beginning of a journey that would lead to opening the doors to my very own brick-and-mortar store, MAKE Collectives in 2012.

At the beginning of the journey, while selling to Wasteland, the clothing buyer asked me if I was a seller at the Rose Bowl flea market in Pasadena. "Me...a vintage buyer!?!?" It was a boost of confidence! At that moment, a lightbulb lit up inside me that really made a huge impact on my career. The Rose Bowl flea market is famous for attracting buyers and fashion designers from all over the world. I checked out the next flea market and low and behold, I loved all the eclectic vibes and wanted in! I found a place that sold clothing racks, punched handmade price tags in the shape of a heart to attach to all the clothes, thrifted my ass off, and even got my sisters and parents involved. We loaded all our finds into our family van and had our first Rose Bowl flea market experience in 2002. We set up shop in space #3270, Lot K for ten years before opening our permanent space. I enjoyed selling at the Rose Bowl because I was able to get face-to-face with an emerging market of vintage lovers. We sold pieces to fashion-forward locals who loved to incorporate unique vintage clothing into their modern closets, and even sold to celebrities like Zoë Kravitz, Lisa Bonet, Christina Ricci, and Rumer Willis. We had regular customers who were costume designers, stylists, and buyers from boutiques all over the world who came to find the best vintage. We even sold to designers looking for inspiration for their designs from high-end companies like Chloe to surf and skate companies like Roxy. Month after month the same faces always returned. My customers always left me hungry to find the best vintage. When I was able to find pieces my customers would love, I felt like I had a personal connection to them.

When I started Viva la Vintage in 2002, I was a college student at California State University, Fullerton (CSUF). At the age of 26, I graduated with a Bachelor of Arts in Criminal Justice with dreams of working with at-risk youth. Unfortunately, within a couple of years of graduating from college, finding my ideal job felt impossible even though I was in the hiring process and on the waiting list for LA County's Juvenile Probation Department. Impatient, unfulfilled, and frustrated, I took a leap of faith and went back to school. I decided to follow my passion and purpose so that I could get paid to do what I love. There was no turning back because I enrolled in the Fashion Institute of Design and Merchandising (FIDM) in downtown Los Angeles to obtain my second college degree in merchandise marketing. After graduating from FIDM in 2005 and working as an assistant for an independent designer in Beverly Hills for a couple of years, I landed my dream entry-level corporate job at AG Jeans. I worked my way up to become a men's retail buyer. I helped open multiple AG Jeans stores and outlets. This experience planted the very first seed and the vision that someday I would open my very own storefront.

Throughout school and starting my first job in fashion, I always had my vintage side hustle. The rise of Viva la Vintage happened at the same time as the rise of social media, particularly Friendster and MySpace. MySpace was my jam! I loved being able to reach out to and connect with other fashion-obsessed women. The platform allowed me to invite them to shop at my events or visit my booth at the Rose Bowl. It was then that I realized the power of word-of-mouth. Having a booth every month helped me to organically grow my customer base, face-to-face. Email marketing also became a means to reach a large number of people, so I collected information from every single customer I had in order to build my database.

In addition to the pop-ups, Desiree and I opened an Etsy eCommerce shop in 2011 called La Femme Vintage. We changed from Viva la Vintage because there was another existing website with the same name. To this day, I regret changing the name because that's how we were known. We used my garage as a makeshift photography studio with a white backdrop and basic lighting and we hired models and collaborated with makeup artists. I taught myself how to take photos of our products on my DSLR camera and I edited and uploaded our photos onto our Etsy store. From there, our eCommerce store was up and running!

While things were taking off professionally, my personal life was going well too. After marrying my long-distance boyfriend Matt Engel in 2010, we purchased our first home together in Long Beach, California. We were on a mission to fill our new home with mid-century modern pieces, many of which Matt restored himself. My vintage obsession expanded to home goods and furniture. Our new home was filled with one of a kind pieces, which we used as display tables during the La Femme Vintage pop-ups. We received so much love and inquiry about them that we started selling the furniture. As I continued to do the pop-ups, we needed a name for our new hobby of curating vintage home goods. We decided on M.A.K.E. Collectives, which was inspired by both mine and my husband's initials: Matt and Kat Engel. Using our initials felt meaningful, and we loved to find and re-MAKE things together. Finding vintage home goods was our thing that we did together. And that is how MAKE was born!

We continued to have our monthly booth at the Rose Bowl, as well as other pop-ups. Matt and I rented space inside a couple of local antique stores in Long Beach; we sold vintage clothing and home goods inside Orange Avenue Estate, Salvage and Garden, and Magnolia and Willow Antiques. By late 2011, packing and unpacking a mobile shop was depleting. I felt it in my core — the time had come and I was ready for a storefront.

In December 2011, I reconnected with an old friend, Patrick Santa Ana, owner of ELEV 8, a small boutique in the East Village Arts District of downtown Long Beach. I went to drop off a holiday card and he encouraged me to open up my own shop. The first retail space we visited wasn't the right fit, but the property manager showed me another space on 1st Street. I instantly fell in love with the space's history. Back in the day, the space was once an old trophy shop, then the old ticketing location for the Long Beach Grand Prix, then a denim shop, and later a nonprofit shop. The minute I stepped into the space, filled with natural light from the big windows, I knew I had found the perfect space, full of positive energy. We loved the idea of the space being one big collection of all things we were obsessed with: vintage clothing and accessories, homewares, and vinyl records.

MAKE Collectives opened its doors in April 2012. A week after we signed the lease, Matt and I found out we were also expecting our first child who was born six months later. At 36-years-old, there I was: new business, new store, and newly married with a beautiful baby boy. So many life lessons and balls to juggle all at once. Our shop was more than just a storefront filled with beautiful things. It had become a place for the community to connect and feel inspired, to find something unique and interesting for themselves or for a gift, or to take a workshop and learn something new. My greatest achievement is the space we created. The store also taught me my greatest lessons about business, but most importantly, about myself.

Events, another one of my passions, became an extension of the business. After hosting creative community workshops, collaborations, and pop-up art galleries over the years, I organized my first community event in 2013. Maker's Mart was born, an annual event on Small Business Saturday that takes place right outside MAKE's storefront. The closed streets are filled with over 50 local artisans and small businesses who showcase their work in celebration of American Express' national campaign to promote local shopping. During the second American Express Small Business Saturday campaign, we were selected to be featured in their national commercial. Maker's Mart just celebrated its 7th annual event in November 2019, which was the biggest and most successful to date.

Throughout my journey, the best piece of advice I've ever been given was to know my numbers and set sales targets. A simple Excel spreadsheet with a few columns is enough, or write it in a notebook if that is what it takes. Carve out one hour a week to track where you are. It is so easy to get stuck in a perfectionist mindset that everything has to be done professionally or in a fancy spreadsheet. Believe me when I say, do not wait to have the perfect strategy to track your progress. Do not get stuck in overthinking and overanalyzing because that is when you will find yourself behind and feeling like you can never catch up. Make the journey fun and celebrate your WINS. And lastly, make time to review and reflect on what worked and what didn't. When your business grows, allocate a monthly budget to hire a bookkeeper or service to do this for you. Until then, if you don't know your numbers every day, your business is just a hobby.

Owning a small business, being an entrepreneur and working mom, experiencing trial and errors, and having many wins but more failures have taught me so many lessons. I don't have a degree in entrepreneurship or management. When I fall, I have to get back up, figure things out, and not give up. I really wish my entrepreneur class at FIDM had a dedicated lesson on the importance of taking care of yourself when you own a business. Over the last seven years, I put my personal health on the back burner and it isn't until now, at 44-years-old, that I am feeling that regret. It wasn't until I moved to Maine in 2016 and I hired a life coach to help me during the struggle of my transition that I finally learned that "self-care" is a thing. These days, we often hear about the importance of self-love and self-care; it's a movement that people are becoming aware of because it is one of the secrets to achieving your dreams.

Not prioritizing your self-care does no good for anyone, and most importantly, it is a disservice to yourself. How are we supposed to be the bosses that we can be if we don't fill our own cup and nourish our souls every day? Let me be clear, we all know how important it is to nourish ourselves with healthy food, but it is just as critical to feed your soul in a way that is on purpose and intentional. I put myself last while I built my business. I was so unaware and was on auto-pilot. My life coach used to ask what I've done to "fill my cup." It's something that I am trying to be better about, starting with my morning routine. After I had my son, I started waking up at 5 a.m. to carve out time for myself. Each day, I start my day with coffee and I practice Hal Elrod's "Miracle Morning" SAVERS routine: Silence (S), Affirmations (A), Visualization (V), Exercise (E), Reading (R), Scribing (S). You can spend as little as one minute on each letter. This is game-changing. It's one of the best gifts I've ever given to myself! Also, I give thanks in the morning and at night. Finding gratitude in our surroundings is especially helpful when times are tough. Journaling is an amazing avenue for me to express my gratitude on paper. I honestly believe the world would be a better place if everyone journaled!

While you're on your journey, have patience and take the time to get things in order. Avoid instant gratification. The continuous need to hustle and the "go go go" mindset can be very deceiving.

It's a trap that often leads to burnout. Instead, do the research, allow space for trial and error, do-overs, and new beginnings. Keep going. Show up daily and you'll find yourself becoming a little more effective each day. Make big moves but strategically line up your ducks and plant seeds. Keep learning and studying the right role models. Patiently waiting is great self-love. Trust that the process is preparing you for what you really want and is on it's way to you.

Lastly, BE CREATIVE! Creativity is everywhere – find inspiration in nature, go outside, and take more walks! Nothing feeds my purpose more than unleashing the creativity I have in me. But be creative, on purpose. Unleash creativity by surrounding yourself with other creatives or like-minded women. Learn something new and do what interests you. Energy goes where attention flows and magic is all around us! Believe in the magic you create for yourself. I'm lucky to have found an avenue to express my creativity. It's even better when I can share it with my husband and community!

Centering humanity AT THE CORE OF **OUR BUSINESS** IS THE MOST *important lesson* I'VE LEARNED THROUGHOUT — MY — *entrepreneurship journey.* OUR BUSINESS MODEL IS NOT ABOUT MAKING THE BEST *Cheesecake* BUT RATHER UTILIZING FOOD & BEVERAGE AS A VEHICLE TO CREATE *meaningful human connections.*

—Chera Amlag

Be Human

Chera Amlag

In second grade, a year after immigrating to the United States (U.S.), I picked up my mom's *Betty Crocker* cookbook and started making desserts. Our house was never filled with many sweets, so I remember taking it upon myself to satisfy my sweet tooth by baking. I loved seeing my family's excitement when I would bake something new from the cookbook. I still remember the smile on my mom's face when I baked her first-ever lemon bar.

Growing up in Olongapo, Philippines, my mom and I would make *ube halaya* together (a Philippine dessert made from boiled and mashed purple yam). She would pull up a chair next to the stove, hand me a wooden spoon, and tell me to stir until the *ube* jam no longer fell off the spoon. This purple dessert soon became one of my favorites too. We left the Philippines at the tail end of Martial Law in 1986 via the U.S. Navy and moved to the Pacific Northwest in a military town called Bremerton, an hour away from Seattle.

When I started school, I was enrolled in English as a Second Language (ESL) classes. I would later learn from my parents that my teachers told them to stop talking to me in Tagalog because they thought it would stunt my development in English. Now that

I have my own children, I often think about what it would be like to move them from their birth country, ask them not to speak their native language, and start a new life. I admire my parents' grace and fortitude raising four children in the U.S.

Unlike most military families, we didn't move around much. My parents decided to stay in Bremerton, even when my dad was stationed elsewhere so that my mom could finish nursing school. When my dad was stationed in San Francisco, he would drive almost every weekend to Bremerton on a Friday afternoon and turn around and drive back to the Bay on Sunday. I'm glad we stayed in one place. I ended up meeting my now-husband and business partner in Bremerton.

After high school, I moved to Seattle to attend the University of Washington (U of W). I was a very indecisive student, changing my major from business to pre-med, to nursing, to education, and finally to psychology. I remember taking macroeconomics as a prerequisite for business school and struggling; one hard class discouraged me and I felt like business school was not for me. I think it's funny that I now run my own business; being an entrepreneur was never part of my plans.

My experience working with young people in high school helped shape what I wanted to do with my life. During my sophomore year at U of W, I started an internship at a nonprofit domestic violence agency where I supported youth groups. Working with the youth and community made me feel alive! I became a community organizer and helped build grassroots community organizations fighting globally for human rights for Filipinos. My first job after graduating from college was as a drug and alcohol prevention specialist, where I ran youth programs in Seattle's Chinatown-International District. I got married shortly after college and had my first kid a year later at 24-years-old.

278

Navigating being a new professional, wife, and mother in my early twenties was both exciting and challenging. I was often the only one amongst friends with a child, and I struggled with balancing career, commitments with community work, and family. These often competing priorities helped shape me into the woman I am today. They required me to realize and commit to what is most important to me, lean on community and family, and understand what "it takes a village" truly means.

I spent over a decade of my career in the education sector before entering the hospitality industry. My last job prior to opening our business was working with first-generation college students as a director for the MESA (Math, Engineering, and Science Achievement) program. Our students in the program were often children of immigrants or immigrants themselves; students just like me. I really loved my job, but I was also really passionate about food.

My husband, Geo, and I always enjoyed gathering people together and hosting dinners. As parents, it was a perfect way to still see our friends! A group of families began rotating potluck dinners. We looked forward to these potlucks because everyone brought their best dishes. We loved it for the community we were building with other parents and the opportunity it created for our children to grow up together.

In 2013, Geo and I were preparing to take our two young boys to the Philippines for the first time. We wanted to show them both the beauty and struggles of our homeland. As community organizers, alongside two other families, we planned a multi-family "exposure trip" to the Philippines. This led to discussions about fundraising and we eventually birthed the idea of *Adobofest* – an *adobo* cook-off. We raised some money for our trips by organizing a block party in our neighborhood (Beacon Hill) where 20 contestants brought an *adobo* dish and the 200+ attendees decided whose dish was the best.

A month later, Geo and I continued our own fundraising efforts by throwing a pop-up dinner to celebrate our ten year wedding anniversary at Inay's, a beloved Filipino restaurant in our neighborhood. I had heard about pop-ups in other cities and thought it would be a unique way to celebrate our anniversary. We had no idea what we were doing, but we were having fun!

Our first pop-up, called *Gumbo & Sh*t*, was supposed to be a one-time event. Both Geo and I had never worked in the food industry, so this was a new experience, and boy was it hard! We were so tired at the end of the night and excited to never do it again. Our families were the first ones in the kitchen helping prep, cook, serve, and wash dishes; they supported us wholeheartedly and truly wanted to see us succeed. It was their encouragement and support from other friends that motivated us to try a pop-up a second time, and then a third, and eventually it turned into *Food & Sh*t* – a monthly Filipino pop-up dinner series, which we ran for almost three years.

Our side hustle was fun and exciting. But what I realize now, that I didn't know back then, was that I was not entering the food business, but rather the hospitality business. What I enjoyed most about our pop-ups was being able to bring the community together, share our food and culture with others, grow pride in our cuisine, and eat some good ass food in the process. We were cool if we broke even, and any profit made was reinvested back into the pop-ups.

Early on, we learned on the job. We reached out to friends in the food industry, fellow community organizers, and chefs for support. Many of them became part of a rotating crew of back of house and front of house pop-up staff. We received a crash course on sourcing ingredients, scaling recipes, cost of goods, kitchen lingo, how to run service, and more. I read a lot of books and liked sifting through online blogs and articles to help me learn anything and everything that interested me in this industry. Meanwhile, I was still working full-time.

Every month at our *Food & Sh*t* pop-ups, we would curate a menu specifically and only for that month. I decided to make an *ube* cheesecake in October 2013 for our second pop-up. Like all our other menu items, it was supposed to be a one-time offering. However, guests were coming to the pop-ups just for the cheesecake! It was the one thing that guests were talking about, regardless of what else we were making. This purple dessert was being shared on Instagram, and even friends from outside Seattle were starting to ask us about it. In November 2014, after a year of pop-ups, we received the opportunity to wholesale our *ube* cheesecake in Uwajimaya, the largest Asian grocery store in the state.

Starting our wholesale business, Hood Famous Bakeshop, alongside our pop-ups, changed our business and lives. What was once a monthly event turned into a daily business. First, I had to figure out how to scale the *ube* cheesecake recipe. Baking a handful of cheesecakes for a pop-up was very different from scaling a recipe to meet the demands of wholesale. It took me forever to get the recipe down! When I did, we started out in three grocery stores and sold out in two hours on our first day. I remember receiving a call that day from one of the store managers asking if I could bring more cheesecakes the following day. Unfortunately, I didn't have any in stock in our commissary kitchen and I still had to go to work so we couldn't supply more cheesecakes that week.

I had naively thought wholesaling the *ube* cheesecake to a local grocery store would also be a side hustle – I would bake on the weekends and deliver once a week. The reality was quite different:

I would go to my day job, have dinner with my family, go to the commissary kitchen to bake throughout the night, get a few hours of sleep, and then head back into work. I did that for several months. I was so appreciative of my closest friends who would come whenever they could to help me in the kitchen. However, this schedule really took a toll on my physical and mental health. I didn't realize how bad it was until I rear-ended a car on my way home from the kitchen one morning because I was so tired. I knew something needed to change; I just didn't know if and how I could continue this business.

I had two young children and my husband was a self-employed performing artist. Since the beginning of our marriage, I was the parent with the salaried job and benefits. I wasn't ready to throw financial stability, my retirement fund, and health benefits out the window. I turned to my mom for advice about how I should move forward. Out of all the trusted people in my life, my mom said to me, "Why not? You only live once. You have enough experience in your career that you can go back if it doesn't work out." My mom was battling cancer at this time. Our entire family was feeling the impact of understanding how short life truly is.

My mom's encouraging words and seal of approval helped me make my decision to quit my job and pursue this business full-time. I needed her reassurance that I was not crazy or irresponsible! Even though I quit my day job, I was able to transfer my love for education in a different way by educating our guests and the Seattle community about Filipino flavors, culture, workers and land rights, and other issues I have always been passionate about. I knew our business had to be more than just about cheesecake or food to be a fulfilling job for me.

In 2016, Hood Famous Bakeshop opened its first brick-and-mortar location in Ballard, a tiny little production kitchen and retail counter offering an expanded line of cheesecakes with more Filipino flavors including *ube, buko pandan,* and mango *calamansi.* We also added a line of goods featuring specialty food and drink items from fellow Filipino-run businesses like Kalsada coffee and Kasama Chocolates.

When I first got into the hospitality industry, I did a lot of research to see who was already doing what I wanted to do with Filipino flavors and desserts. It felt really lonely and isolating seven years ago but since then, I've met many amazing people on my journey as an entrepreneur. Pursuing a business is a different kind of path, which doesn't look the same for everyone. The best piece of advice I was given while I was building the business was to, "Go slow! Take it step-by-step and build it the right way."

It's easy to start something new, but even harder to sustain it. If you take your time to build a good foundation, the sustainability piece will be easier in the long run. I didn't have a lot of experience, training, or education in the food and hospitality industry. There were times I felt like I was making mistakes every day, and I actually still do. As an educator for 12 years, knee-deep and in my groove, I used to wake up and go to work feeling good that I knew how to do my job and I understood what to expect. When I switched careers and became an entrepreneur, waking up was a jarring feeling because I knew that my core job was to solve problems I may or may not know the answer to. With a little more experience, waking up is not so jarring anymore. The expectation for daily change, challenge, and choices await me, and I try to wake up every day thinking about why I do what I do, not what I will be doing that day.

As a business owner, my biggest fear is letting our team down – whether that means making a small or large mistake that impacts our team negatively or not being able to make payroll. In 2019, we opened up our second location in Seattle's historic Chinatown-International District. Hood Famous Cafe + Bar is a small 20 seat coffee to cocktails brick-and-mortar, which highlights our cheesecakes and offers an expanded menu of cafe and bar fare. In the year we expanded to our second location, our company grew 400%. This growth came with its fair share of growing pains. What has helped me mitigate my fear is remembering what we are doing well, humanizing this process and giving myself the same grace that I give our employees, learning from mistakes by understanding why I made them in the first place, and lastly, apologizing when needed. I would advise aspiring business owners to be bold and daring. Do it in your own way that's your differentiator. Be brave enough to step outside of your comfort zone and be comfortable with the unknown. It's OK – most people are also trying to figure it out.

Filipinas are often caretakers of others, but it's important to also take care of yourself in order to take care of your team. Success for myself is built around our staff and having a strong company culture. Our company will only be successful if we have the right team with us. My ultimate success, however, is making sure that each team member truly enjoys what they do. I am also really proud of our business because of the impact that I've seen it make in the community. We often hear from our guests that they feel seen and heard in a city that increasingly does not reflect them, that we have helped increase pride in our culture, and even inspired others to start their own business. I love that we can make a positive impact. I like to say that if it were just about cheesecake, I wouldn't be doing this. Anyone can make cheesecake, but why do I want to make a living off of cheesecake? Being a female and a person of color (POC), I often think about how I can help other women and POC business owners as well. While we planned and built out our second location, we were intentional with who we decided to partner with. We wanted to make sure we were giving business to women, POC, and queer designers, architects, vendors, and contractors.

My journey into entrepreneurship and the hospitality industry allowed me to meet a wide range of people and has taught me many lessons. The most important being: center humanity at the core of our business. Our business model is not about making the best cheesecake, but rather utilizing food and beverage as a vehicle to create meaningful human connections. I hope I leave a legacy that extends beyond *ube* cheesecake – a legacy of bringing Filipino-American culture, cuisine, and community to the forefront. For people who are close to me, I want to be remembered as a courageous optimist who encouraged my family and friends to live their best lives and fight for others to be able to do the same.

BE confident who you are. KNOWING WHO YOU ARE IS WHAT MAKES you Successful.

—Elizabeth Pura

BE ASSERTIVE

Elizabeth Pura

**Disclaimer: The views expressed in this segment are those of the author and do not reflect the official policy or position of the Department of the Army, DOD, or the U.S. Government.

Can you recall where you were and what you were doing on the morning of Tuesday, September 11, 2001? On 9/11, I had just left Virginia to go to Bahrain. I was in the middle of the Indian Ocean when I heard rumors of terrorist attacks by the Islamic terrorist group Al-Qaeda against the United States (U.S.). That moment reminded me of why I serve. Even now, these threats are real and run deep within me.

I never imagined being in the military service for over 23 years and counting, nor did I imagine making it to Lieutenant Colonel! Growing up, I didn't even know what that meant. I am the first generation to be born in America, the first college graduate in my family, and the first child in my family to serve in the military. Even though my dad served in the U.S. Navy for 22 years, I always thought that I would be in the medical field. At least, that's what my parents dreamt of for me.

I come from a middle-class family of four kids. My parents didn't have the money to send all of us to college which meant we'd have to support ourselves. When it came time for me to go to school, I studied nursing at an all-girls private institution called Mount Saint Mary's College. In addition to going to school full-time, I also worked full-time to pay for my tuition and books. Instead of the standard four-year plan, I was on the five and a half year plan. After a year and a half of nursing school, I had to figure out what I was going to do and how I was going to fund the rest of my education. Even though I was working full-time, I was searching for other options to pay for school. One of my dorm mates was a military medic, which is how I initially found out about the Reserve Officers' Training Corps (ROTC). The military gives out scholarships for students that join ROTC. Initially, I wanted to join the Navy or Air Force, but they told me I had to cut my hair, which I didn't like. They also wanted me to go active duty immediately, but I was a freshman in college and I wasn't ready to leave just yet.

I wanted to live out my own dreams so I switched my major to community health education and ended up changing schools. I hurt my parents' dreams when I chose a different route, but I knew I needed to make the change. My younger sister, Debbie, was starting college so we decided to become roommates at California State University, Long Beach (CSULB). It was quite a transition for me. I went from a campus with a population of 300 to over 30,000 students and I finally felt like I was at a real university. I also joined the Army Reserves to obtain scholarships to fund the rest of my education. Because I was already in school, I had to choose the shortest amount of training. That's how I ended up starting my career as a motor transport operator. When I first joined the military, I remember crying in the corner of the shower asking, "What did I sign myself up for?" The Army requires us to stay physically fit, and we are tested every year. The first time I had to do a 12 mile ruck march, I had to trust in myself and believe that I could do it. When I was stationed in the 10th Mountain Division, all soldiers had to run ten miles. I never ran ten miles before in my military career, but after I finished I couldn't feel my body. I never understood why runners got chafing, but now I definitely understand! Even when I struggled, I was committed to doing the best that I could, and that's something I've carried with me throughout my career.

After graduating from CSULB, I was commissioned as an officer and was stationed in Fort Eustis, Virginia. I had no idea where that was, but I packed everything up and moved across the country. In the Army, we are in the profession of arms. The Army challenges soldiers physically, mentally, emotionally, and spiritually. There are competence and characteristics that armed forces leaders need to have; our leaders must show intellect and sound judgment. The Army develops and pushes people to grow. We learn values such as loyalty, duty, respect, integrity, and personal courage. The most difficult challenge for me has been learning how to balance everything. Throughout my 18-year career, I've moved 14 times! If I found balance earlier on, maybe I would be married by now. My parents still give me a hard time about not being married. Instead, I got my master's degree and moved up in rank.

I am part of the top 20% of the Army; it's hard to get this high in the ranks. The military doesn't have many females – it is still a male-dominated industry. To be honest, there are not a lot of Asians in the Army either. We go to ground combat and the thought of going to war scares many Asian parents so this is a career path that is not encouraged in our culture. But I never let my ethnicity or my gender affect the decisions I make as a leader. I just do my job and try my best. I treat people with dignity and respect, no matter what race or gender they are.

In combat, I learned to never let people disrespect me. I once had a superior leave a voicemail where he undermined my team, and then he let my subordinates hear the message. I approached him for disregarding my position and authority. I had to be assertive and had to stand up for myself and my team. I was confident in my work and I didn't let him run over me. Don't ever let people interpret your kindness as weakness. I've also learned to trust my intuition, to know the difference between what's right and wrong, and to speak up when it's needed. But, I didn't know that when I was a young Second Lieutenant. At the time, I experienced seeing a young E4 (Specialist) sitting on my boss' lap in the orderly room. I froze because I didn't know what to do. I should have said, "Hey Soldier, get off the Commander's lap." I was in shock! I didn't say anything to my boss. Instead, I did an about-face and turned around as if I saw nothing. I headed towards my battalion headquarters to explain to my Battalion XO what I saw and let him know that was completely inappropriate. Over time, I have gained patience, trust, and confidence in myself, and I have learned to lead by example.

In my current position, I have the authority to make decisions that impact people's lives, in very serious ways. I am faced with a lot of decision-making challenges and every day I hope and pray that I am making the right decisions for the Army. After all, these are the sons and daughters of our citizens. The decisions I make have an impact on our soldiers on and off the battlefield. When I was a Senior Captain deployed in Afghanistan, I yelled at a Captain. She was doing homework and studying for her nursing classes while bullets were flying in the air. We were stationed on Forward Operating Base Salerno, 12 miles from the Pakistan border. We were in charge of supporting an entire brigade combat team. When we are deployed, we need to be focused on our combat mission to defeat the enemy. Her college courses took her focus away from providing logistics support to ground combat troops who were in constant contact with the enemy daily. In addition to these types of situations, I am faced with many legal and ethical decisions regarding young soldiers, non-commissioned officers, and officers that range from finance issues, spousal support, family advocacy, physical fitness standards, and applying non-judicial punishment for violations of the Uniform Code of Military Justice. Punishment can include such things as reduction in rank, forfeiture of pay, restriction to post, or extra duty.

In addition to these challenges, I also miss out on spending time with my loved ones. I cannot count the number of birthdays, graduations, weddings, and anniversaries that I have missed. I wasn't able to attend my best friend's wedding because I was in Afghanistan. I had to tell her not to stop her life for me due to the job that I have. I couldn't even make a quick video for my Maid of Honor speech. I was working 16-hour days and it was tough being out on the battlefield. There are good days and bad days, with some days being worse than others. I've seen a lot in the military. Some days, I want to quit. In my first week in Afghanistan, we lost ten soldiers. It was tough to see a new soldier get killed and leave behind a one-year-old daughter, but you have to move on and see what the day brings us. You also have to learn how to manage your time and emotions. The work will always be there tomorrow. Despite these challenges, I am happy! I cannot do my job if I do not love what I do. The day that I don't like being a soldier is the day I need to get out.

My advice to others would be to set personal goals for yourself. Find your purpose in life and create your own definition of success. Success is defined by the individual, regardless if you choose the public or private sector. If you're not happy, then you need to find a new goal for yourself. There's always something new to learn.

I started out as a Second Lieutenant and now I am the Battalion Commander in charge of the young soldiers and officers at the Army Logistics University Support Battalion. I am back where

I started out over 15 years ago. I am in charge of six companies and the administrative and logistical support of the students of the Army Logistics University. We train soldiers before they get deployed. At this time, I am also the only Asian-American officer in command at Fort Lee. I didn't imagine that I would make it this far, but my dad has encouraged me to stay until I become a General, which typically requires over 30 years of service! As I've said before, tomorrow is a new day, let's just see where the day takes us.

chase your dream!
CHASE IT WITH SO MUCH
dedication
THAT OTHERS WILL BE
inspired
BY YOUR EFFORTS.

—Katrina Cruz

The Illustrator

Katrina Isabel Cruz

Hi! I'm Katrina Isabel Cruz. I go by Katrina or Kat. I am a self-taught artist born and raised in Manila, Philippines. As a child, my main hobby was drawing. I spent my free time practicing how to draw characters from my favorite movies and TV shows. Growing up, my family and I didn't have a lot of extra money so I wasn't able to afford art supplies. My parents focused more on our necessities and my school-related expenses. I didn't imagine myself pursuing art as a career so I didn't invest money into the craft. Because of that, I thought it would just be a waste of money. Unlike most Filipino families, my parents were very supportive and encouraged me and my older brother to pursue whatever profession we wanted, as long as we do our best at it. I'm very lucky to have a strong support system. I wouldn't be pursuing my dream if it weren't for them.

I moved to the United States (U.S.) at the age of 14, just in time for me to start high school. In comparison, the American school system is very different from how I was raised in the Philippines. America really is the land of opportunity – students have more options and the freedom to choose what they want to do. When I turned 16, I got a part-time job to help out my family. I was able to save up some money for college and, of course, for myself. I finally had some money to buy things I couldn't afford before, such as art supplies.

I recall taking a trip to my local art store. I was blown away! That's when I decided to research the different types of art mediums: watercolor, acrylic and oil paints. I experimented to see if I would be inspired to make more art. Each medium was different and required patience and different techniques. I had the most fun with watercolor because I was mesmerized by how the water would make the paint move around as if it were dancing on its own. It was therapeutic.

As I continued to do traditional art, the more expensive it became. I didn't have the money to keep up with my hobby and passion. That's when my brother suggested that I shift to making digital art. It would be an investment but he assured me that it'll be better in the long run. He does photography on the side so he understands what it means to have a passion for art. He wanted to support my creative side and has provided the resources I need in order to continue learning. For my 18th birthday, he gifted me with an iPad Pro, which allowed me to experiment with digital art. Once I got my iPad, I became obsessed with drawing faces. I mostly enjoyed drawing girls' faces because I loved studying their faces. I am intrigued by what makes us different from one another. This includes unique features that we may hate or love. I wanted to learn how to recreate emotions and be able to let others see and feel that as well.

I am currently a student at Skyline College pursuing my degree in digital illustration and animation. I was surprised to find a Filipino Learning Community on campus where I met teachers and mentors who looked like me. That's where I met my counselor, Kimberly Davalos, who published *Delilah's Daughter*, a poetry book about the Filipino experience. I connected with her poems because they tugged at my emotions. I realized the shame that I felt. How could I, a native-born Filipina, have less pride than Filipino-Americans who had only dreamed about visiting the Philippines? When I arrived in the U.S., I tried erasing the Filipino part of me outside my home. I wanted to feel like I belonged in America. Seeing students and mentors that looked exactly like me, assured me that I was not alone! I no longer felt ashamed.

I was so moved by Kim's poetry – I created a design using one of her poems that resonated with me during the time. During my counseling session, I showed her my artwork that was inspired by her. This led to a project of six posters that I designed with Kim's poetry. These posters were sold at the Cipher Holiday Bling Vendor's Fair as well as the UNDISCOVERED SF night market (which is where Jennifer Redondo-Marquez discovered my art).

I am beyond excited and honored to be a part of *In Her Purpose*. As I started to draw the illustrations, I got to learn more about each woman. Through them, it reinforced that I am not alone! I hope that the readers, especially those who are my age, will find *ikigai* (your purpose, in Japanese). Your reason for being. It may be hard, but know that it'll come and you will just have to trust the process. Being a part of this project is so special to me because it proves to me and others that I am able to succeed in this field. I want to express my gratitude and appreciation for Jennifer and Rose. Thank you both for believing in me and pushing me to strive hard. Thank you for allowing me to touch the hearts of others through my work. This project means so much to me and it has given me empowerment, inspiration, and motivation. *Maraming salamat po* (thank you, in Tagalog).

To reach me or for more information, please visit www. katrinaisabel.com and follow me on Instagram @kicruzart.

We aren't
here on
EARTH
to find ourselves,
WE ARE HERE
to create ourselves.

—Dee Jae Pa'este

The Starving Artist

Dee Jae Pa'este

Art has been my life since before I can remember, and I don't think I've ever thought of being anything but an artist. It's everything I hoped and dreamed it would be. I wake up and get to do what I love and what I am passionate about. I get to share my art with the world! The best part of every morning and beginning a new day is knowing I will make the best of it.

I didn't always have this sunny outlook in life. There was a time when I nearly lost everything: a business that I once loved, a home that became plagued with bad energy, and projects that just didn't seem to fit! Looking back, it was a blessing in disguise. Things that weren't meant for me were being taken out of my life. The timing was just right! It was the reset that I needed but didn't know at that time. Life has gotten better ever since!

Though, my life isn't a beautifully painted picture. On the real, being an artist is difficult. The "Starving Artist" is my personal brand. That's what I label my food and art tours (food is another passion of mine). I enjoy taking people around the streets of Poblacion, the red-light district of Manila, Philippines, which I now call home. It's very different from growing up in Silicon Valley! The "Starving Artist" was born out of the struggle I had with people not knowing or offering me what I'm worth. Some people think that it's easy to do what I do. I am always down to help and share my art, but some people take advantage of that. Even though Filipinos do not have a dominant presence in the art world, I believe that we offer a different perspective. It fuels me to do more and it motivates me to create with more of a purpose.

Pursuing your passion can sometimes be challenging, but I would encourage you to never give up. Always believe in what you do and know why you do it. I would tell my younger self to stay excited about art, and explore more instead of wasting time on things, people and projects that don't help you grow or don't serve you in a positive way. The world needs less negativity and more positivity, fewer advertisements and billboards and more art and creative spaces! I've been lucky to be able to cover cities around the world with my art and energy. I am happy, creative and full of love and light. Those are things that are lost in this time and age.

When I was approached about *In Her Purpose*, I was really honored and excited to take part in this and bring some of my art to the project because I have the highest respect and admiration for women, especially my mother, grandmother, and my partner (who is also my muse). You'll find a lot of color, feminine faces and bodies in my artwork, which are all inspired by the strong women in my life.

The best advice I was given came from a woman I met on my first trip to Asia, who told me that we are not here on this Earth to find ourselves, but rather we are here to create ourselves and to create opportunities for us to grow and shine. That's my mantra and it stays with me every day. When I leave this Earth, I would like to be remembered for my art, my good energy, community building and connecting.

I tend to leave murals in the places I love so my energy and creativity resonate long past my presence there. You can find me on Facebook and Instagram @deejae408.

TRUST
yourself
— & —
YOUR
instincts,
BUT ALSO KNOW THAT
you can change
YOUR mind,
YOUR plans,
— & —
YOUR path.

–Sara Robinson

The Editor

Sara Robinson

Hi there, I'm Sara Robinson! I'm honored to be involved with the *In Her Purpose* project and am so happy that I was welcomed to help, despite not being of Asian heritage. I came to this project through co-author Jennifer's husband, Romeo. He and I went to high school together. Many years ago, as a theater student at New York University, I admired Romeo for getting leads in college plays and then getting accepted to what had been my dream school, UCLA. I love how we both ended up in the right place for each of us, and am amazed at where our paths have taken us.

Nearly 20 years later, we've stayed connected (mostly on social!) and we now live in the same town in the Bay Area. In early 2019, Romeo invited me to be a guest on his *Soul Greatness* podcast, where I talked about *Choose You*, a self-care journal that I had written. It was in his home that I met his wonderful wife, Jenn, who told me a bit about this project. I let her know I'd be happy to talk more when she was ready. I was familiar with the writing and editing process, having done both professionally, and loved that I could possibly help support my friend's wife in this very cool endeavor.

Fast-forward and I have had such a great experience working on this project. I have learned about so many amazing women

301

and am inspired by their stories. Through the editing, I aimed to help their stories shine while remaining true and authentic to each woman's voice.

Twenty years ago I wouldn't have guessed this experience would be a part of my personal or professional story, so the advice I give to younger women is to be open. Have goals and plans, but be open to what else comes your way. You never know where those choices will take you, and they might even be more amazing than the goals you had originally set.

In addition to freelance editing projects like this one, I am a project manager for a content development company and do freelance writing when I can. I also work as a mental skills coach and am the author of the book, *Self-Care for Moms*. The majority of my work is done from home, which means I am able to hang with my two sons a lot and drive them to all of the places they need to go. We aim to have fun as a family, we laugh a lot, and we support each other as we grow.

Lastly, a big thanks to Jennifer and Rose for trusting me to assist with this project. You can find me at www.getmombalanced.com.

THE WOMEN: IN HER PURPOSE

Jhoanna Alba
Chief Visionaire
ALBA and Mi Armore
alba-la.com
☉ @albalegacy @miarmore @_v.i.e.w
Page 77

Chera Amlag
Co-Owner and Baker
Hood Famous Bakeshop
hoodfamousbakeshop.com
☉ @hoodfamousbakeshop
Page 277

Berna Anat
Producer and Speaker
Hey Berna
heyberna.com
☉ @heyberna
Page 259

Isis Arias-Clermont
Marketing and Branding Executive
linkedin.com/in/isisarias/
☉ @isarias
Page 31

Sumita Batra
CEO
Ziba Beauty
zibabeauty.com
☉ @thezibabeauty @sumitabatra
Page 238

Joanne Boston
Founder of JBKollaborations
Events Producer at General Assembly
jbkollaborations.com
☉ @jbkollaborations
Page 159

Rose Buado
Entrepreneur and Business Coach
Co-Founder and Co-Author of IHP
Manager of The Filharmonic
Co-Owner of Cassidy's Corner Cafe
rosebuado.com
baebusiness.com
☉ @rose_buado
Page 61

Charleen Caabay
Chef and Entrepreneur
Co-Founder of The People's Dispensary
☉ @chefcharleen
Page 180

Alexandra Carson
Professional Dancer
Bloc Talent Agency
☉ @alexandra11
Page 14

Nancy Choi
Co-Founder
House of Carbonadi
☉ @nchoi0201 @houseofcarbonadi
Page 114

Roslynn Alba Cobarrubias
Global Head of Music and Talent
ABS-CBN
roslynnc.com
☉ @roslynnc
Page 245

Raquel Cutchon-Quinet
CEO and Founder
The Results Group
☉ @itsraquelq @superwomantribe
Page 101

Ami Desai
Beauty and Lifestyle Expert
amidesai.com
🅾 @amidesai
Page 88

Jennifer Boyd Desai
CEO and Founder
Prosperity MD, LLC
prosperitymd.com
🅾 @jennclarindesai
Page 47

Anh Duong
Senior Director
Quay
linkedin.com/in/aduong810/
Page 22

Joanne Encarnacion
Health and Wellness Blogger/Life Coach
GoFitJo
gofitjo.com
🅾 @gofitjo
Page 69

Kathleen Engel
Co-Founder and Owner
MAKE Collectives
makecollectives.com
🅾 @makecollectives @kat_engel
Page 268

Anne Espiritu
Chief Outreach Officer
The Contentment Foundation
🅾 @anne_espiritu
Page 211

Cristina Espíritu
Valuation Expert and Entrepreneur
🅾 @mespirit @420foodieclub
@hercannabiz
Page 194

Christine Gambito
Comedian
HappySlip
happyslip.com
🅾 @happyslip
Page 95

Freska Griarte
On-Air Personality
KOIT Radio Station
🅾 @freskaontheair
Page 252

Cecilia Gutierrez
Registered Nurse and Entrepreneur
🅾 @cecegutierrez4
Page 229

Jackie James
Entrepreneur
Jackie James, LLC
jackiejames.com
🅾 @jackiejames
Page 40

Uzmee Krakovszki
CEO of Uzbrows Beauty Studio
Makeup Artist at Uzmee Beauty
uzmeekrakovszki.com
uzbrows.com
🅾 @uzmeebeauty @uzbrows
Page 151

Ginger Lim-Dimapasok
Co-Founder
Café 86
cafe-86.com
🅾 @cafe_86 @gingaroo
Page 82

Vina Lustado
Founder and Principal
Sol Haus Design
solhausdesign.com
🅾 @solhausdesign @vinalustado
Page 206

Jennifer O. Manilay
Professor
University of California, Merced
linkedin.com/in/jennifer-o-manilay
Page 133

Onelia E. Miller
Founder and Creative Director
Conspiracy LA PR
@ @oneliamiller
Page 222

Evelyn Obamos
International Program Manager
Pinterest
evelynobamos.com
@ @evelynsees
Page 108

Carissa Ortega
Co-Owner and General Manager
Ninong's Cafe
justkissa.com
@ @justkissa @ninongscafe
Page 187

Lyn Pacificar
Artist. Healer. Entrepreneur
Herbalaria
herbalaria.com
lynpacificar.com
@ @iamherbalaria @lynpacificar_art
Page 119

Elizabeth Pura
Military Officer
linkedin.com/in/elizabeth-pura
Page 287

Jennifer Redondo-Marquez
Co-Founder and Co-Author
In Her Purpose
linkedin.com/in/jennredondo/
@ @jennred24 @inherpurpose
Page 166

Gina Mariko Rosales
Founder and CEO of Make it Mariko
Co-Founder of UNDISCOVERED SF
makeitmariko.com
@ @ginamariko @makeitmariko @pinayista
Page 53

Sunita Sharma
Founder and Owner
Skin Adore and Fremont Beauty College
fremontbeautycollege.com
@ @browsbysunita
Page 139

Jonah Toleno
Partner
Shustak Reynolds & Partners
linkedin.com/in/jonah-toleno
Page 200

Giselle Töngi-Walters
Cultural Media Practitioner
7101 Communications
gtongi.com
@ @gtongi
Page 173

Angelia Trinidad
CEO and Founder
Passion Planner
angeliatrinidad.com
@ @angeliatrinidad @passionplanner
Page 7

Danette Vives
Licensed Esthetician and Business Owner
Skincare by Danette
vivesexperience.com
@ @vivesexperience
Page 126

Dede Wills
Executive Director
Municipal Animal Control Agency
Page 146

305